LEADING
ON THE
EDGE

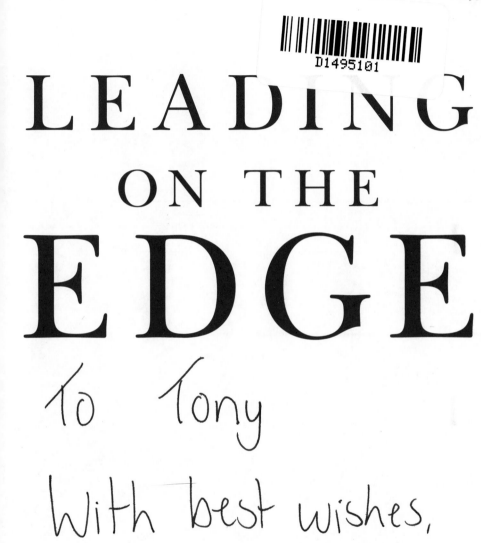

To Tony

With best wishes,

Rachael

2018

LEADING
ON THE
EDGE

Extraordinary stories and leadership
insights from the world's most
extreme workplace

RACHAEL ROBERTSON

WILEY

First published in 2014 by John Wiley & Sons Australia, Ltd
42 McDougall St, Milton Qld 4064

Office also in Melbourne

Typeset in 11/13.5 pt ITC Berkeley Oldstyle Std

National Library of Australia Cataloguing-in-Publication data:

Author:	Robertson, Rachael
Title:	Leading on the edge: Extraordinary stories and leadership insights from the world's most extreme workplace / Rachael Robertson.
ISBN:	9780730305491 (pbk)
	9780730305521 (ebook)
Notes:	Includes index.
Subjects:	Robertson, Rachael — Travel — Antarctica.
	Australian National Antarctic Research Expeditions.
	Leadership — Australia — Biography.
	Leadership — Antarctica — Biography.
	Teams in the workplace — Antarctica.
	Antarctica — Biography.
Dewey Number:	998.0092

Cover design by Paul Dinovo

Cover photo © Michael Hicks, www.wildaustraliaphotography.com

Author Photograph: © Rachael Robertson

Printed in Singapore by C.O.S Printers Pte Ltd

10 9 8 7 6 5 4 3 2 1

Disclaimer

Contents

A note from the author

Firstly, a big thank you for buying this book. I really hope you enjoy reading it as much as I enjoyed writing it and reliving one of the most incredible times of my life.

I spent an amazing 16 months with 17 wonderful people. We had our ups and downs and highs and lows, but each one of my Antarctic expeditioners is special to me and unique in their own way. Living in such close proximity for so long meant we got to know each other intimately. We saw each other at our best and at our worst.

Now, our worst is something that usually goes unseen, because in normal environments we're just not put under so much pressure that we reveal it. So to protect the privacy and reputation of my fellow expeditioners I have been a little creative with names and genders in some of the stories. I hope, reader, you don't mind too much. But if you put yourself in their shoes, it would be unfair to be written about in a way that doesn't reflect who you are in a normal environment or under normal circumstances.

We took *so many* photographs down there! I wanted to include them all, but to keep the size and cost of the book manageable I've introduced just a few in the book. But don't despair! Visit my website, www.leadingontheedge.com, where I have uploaded lots more photographs depicting what was going on at each stage of the story. You'll also find a short epilogue, just in case you were wondering what happened in my life after I got back.

Lastly, I'd love to hear about your own leadership journey and your reflections on the book. So please make a comment on the website. I'll endeavour to respond to each one.

Enjoy the book and remember, *it's always better to regret the things you did, than regret the things you didn't do.*

Regards,

Rachael

Acknowledgements

Several important people have made this book possible and I would like to thank them publicly.

Firstly, to my gorgeous husband Ric. You have given me the confidence to go out and do something I love and supported me all along the way. Thank you for your wisdom, insight and guidance as you read, and re-read the draft chapters and prepared the book for publishing. You inspire me! My life changed irrevocably the day you walked in and I have loved you, and been in awe of you, every moment since.

Secondly, I want to thank my four beautiful stepchildren, Doug, Julian, Anthony and Georgina, and my wonderful son Louie. You make me smile and balance my life. You teach me new things every day and I watch all of you in wonder. I'm so proud of you all.

To the 17 men and women of the 58th Australian National Antarctic Research Expedition—my heartfelt thanks and gratitude. While we all had our moments, myself included, I remain so proud of every one of you. They way you pulled together as a team, the way you delivered on every project and, most importantly, the way you cared for each other, truly inspired me. I hope whenever you hear the Pina Colada song you think back and smile.

To my fellow expeditioners and station photographers Peter Nink and Ian Phillips—thank you for generously and willingly supplying many of the amazing photos contained in this book and uploaded on the website. You both captured this wonderful place in all its vivid glory.

Thank you, Mrs Purcell, for opening my eyes to English literature at the age of 15 and setting me on a course of adventure and excitement.

Thank you, Mark Stone, Brett Cheatley, Annie Volkering, John Goodman and David Young at Parks Victoria, for your support, trust, guidance and patience.

To my former colleagues at Parks Victoria—thanks for a fantastic 18 years. I have so many wonderful memories of my time at PV. I know the critical role you play in protecting and enhancing our precious natural assets is often unacknowledged, so from me to you— a bloody huge well done!

To the wonderful team at Wiley—thank you, especially Lucy Raymond and our awesome editor Jem Bates. Your patience, insights and advice were much appreciated. This publishing game is a tricky business and your support and belief in the book made all the difference.

I also want to thank the audiences who continue to invite me to present to them. I have spoken at more than 350 events over the past six years. I am continually amazed at the questions from the floor. You have given me many insights into my own life that I would not have had otherwise. Seeing your faces and interacting with you is one of my greatest joys. Thanks too, to my fabulous management team at Ode Management for supporting and inspiring me and for keeping my professional life in order, especially Julie Winterbottom, Leanne Christie and Heidi Gregory.

To the best friend a girl could ever have—Michelle Arthur. You have been my buddy for over 30 years now and I look forward to sharing the next 30 years with you. You are simply wonderful.

Thank you to my wonderful family, Shaz, Loz, Aunty Pammy, Ben, Jane, Sam and Tim. The only reason I could take up the challenge of leading an Antarctic expedition was because I knew I would be coming home to the most amazing, supportive family in the world. It made the decision that much easier.

Finally, especially, to my beautiful, wise and extraordinary Mum. I love and adore you. Your strength got me through the dark times down south. You were, and you remain, my aurora in the dark sky. Shine on!

Preface

I don't know exactly what it was that woke me up that time. It could have been the crash of my laptop as it slid off the table onto the floor; it might have been the crunch of my neck as I yet again slid up the bunk and whacked my head on the bulkhead. Perhaps it was the series of ship's noises as the icebreaker crested the 11-metre swells, the mighty rush of water and the 120-kilometre-per-hour winds ripping through the superstructure, the feeling of weightlessness as the ship first hung in the air then plunged downward to hit the surface again with an almighty boom, jarring every rivet, every tooth and every frayed nerve … Yes, maybe a combination of these things woke me.

It wasn't the first time I had been woken that night. By this stage I hadn't slept through the night in over a week. What sleep I did get was 30 minutes snatched here and there when my body simply shut down. It was cold, uncomfortable, wet and terrifying.

I rearranged my pillows for the twentieth time, searching for some combination of cushioning that would protect the top of my head, my neck and my ankles from the fore and aft sliding along the bunk. But then I would have no protection from the side-to-side rolling of the ship and my sides would be battered!

They say people who have never been seasick can't appreciate the depths of despair it brings. It's not just an upset tummy. Everyone's heard the term 'green around the gills' … it just doesn't capture the sallow, pasty sheen you turn when you're seasick. Plus you feel a million times worse than you look. There are stories of cruising sailors locking up their sick crew (difficult in a small sailing craft!) for fear they will throw themselves overboard. Death really does feel like a viable option.

As I lay there, willing myself into a coma, I thought back to our training—three months in Hobart accruing all types of skills, cramming checklists into our already overburdened brains and 'weather-testing' our bodies. Our seasickness checklist came to mind:

- *Ginger*: Check. Glazed ginger between tongue and cheek now for two weeks—no effect.

- *Water and dry food.* Yep, drinking lots of water and eating dry biscuits, which usually take about four minutes to reappear from the same place they went down.

- *Stay above deck in fresh air.* Ahhh...no. Can't do that, I'd be blown back to Hobart.

- *Avoid anything that requires small motor skills.* Does this include buttons and zippers? I can barely manage to speak, so anything as complex as buttons and zippers is out of the question.

- *Lie down on your back, near the centre of the boat.* Check. That's not working either, for obvious reasons.

- *Avoid strong fumes.* This would include diesel, yes? A thin film of the oily stuff covers the cabin floor and my clothes and has leeched into my hair. I can't avoid this. Showers aren't an option, even if I wanted to relax standing under the hot water I couldn't. It takes two hands just to hang on and stay upright. Level of difficulty: 4.5.

- *Steer the boat*: Hmm...I'm not sure P&O Maritime Services, the owners of our expedition ship, would consider this appropriate!

- *Swallow your pride.* Thanks for that. Whoever wrote the handbook obviously had never been seasick! After half an hour, any pride I had is emptied into my bucket—which, by the way, is currently strapped to my wrist.

So as I lay there thinking, 'This did not end well for the *Titanic*...but you know what? I don't care', I worried how my team would perceive my 'weakness'. On board were 24 full-time ship's crew and 120 passengers. Well, as far as the crew were concerned we were passengers, but we considered ourselves expeditioners. We were professionals. We were trained. We had been chosen. We were going to live in Antarctica. For a year. And I was their leader. And I was very, very sick.

My close friend Graham Cook, the incoming Station Leader at Mawson Station, stuck his head in at some stage. 'Can I get you anything, mate?' In my head I replied, *Yes. You can take your happy bloody sea-dog face out of my cabin doorway*, but in reality I mumbled, 'All good Cookie, thanks'.

Still no closer to my hoped-for coma, and with several new bruises and half a kilo lighter, another knock on my cabin door. The captain, bless him, resplendent in his P&O finery, poked his cheery head in. 'Morning! Oh...no better I see. Still, don't worry, you're not the only one.'

I tried to respond, opened my mouth and just...squeaked. I had no voice, no energy and barely the will to respond. I opened and closed my mouth like a mute and flapped one hand feebly. I managed to get out one question. I'm not sure how it sounded but the captain understood. 'The other passengers? Oh...pretty much the same as you. In fact, if it's any consolation, over 100 of you are laid up. Several are even on an IV drip for fluids.'

It alarmed me to learn that out of 144 people, only some of the crew and 16 expeditioners were still functioning. They were probably slogging it out in four-hour shifts trying to keep the ship running. For some reason, this made me feel a bit better. Not physically, of course. But knowing that not only the passengers but even some of the crew were suffering made me feel a little less hopeless.

It's one thing to be an expedition leader. It's another thing to be a *woman* expedition leader. And it's yet another to be a *young* woman expedition leader. At 35, I was one of the youngest expedition leaders ever and only the second female leader at Davis Station. And the last time I had even seen snow was on a Grade 6 school excursion to Mount Donna Buang. And seriously, I hate the cold....

Feeling a bit better about myself, I spent the next three hours reconstructing how on earth I had been selected to lead the 58th Australian National Antarctic Research Expedition to Davis Station. Then I panicked!

Part I

How I got there

Be restless. Create a life that seeks challenges, root out opportunities and jump in the deep end.

You don't have to be the smartest in the class. You don't have to be super-driven. But you do need to have an eye open at all times for interesting things that might come your way. When they come along, take a leap and back your judgement. If it doesn't work out you will have learned something about yourself. And seriously, what's the worst that can happen?

Chapter 1

Leadership can be learned, and taught, early

My first memory of leadership is from Grade 1. I was an early reader; my parents had encouraged me to read the newspaper over their shoulder at breakfast on Saturday mornings. I was also the youngest in school—I started at the tender age of four so from the outset I felt 'behind'. This was one reason Mum pushed me hard to learn how to read before I got there. She knew that I would be less developed physically and socially when I got to school and wanted to make sure I wouldn't be behind intellectually. I quickly got the hang of it and by the time I reached Grade 1 I was topping the class.

Leader without a title

My teacher was the most beautiful woman, Miss Barton—who became Mrs Williamson later in the year, dashing the hopes and hearts of many young boys in my class. She quickly recognised that I was not only a great reader but also very encouraging with those around me. Rather than have me sitting bored at the back of the class and destined to distract others (a trait that came to the fore in secondary school), Miss Barton gave me a special job. I would no longer have 'reading time'—instead, I would be a reading coach. She gave me a small group of classmates to sit with, listen to and help with words they were stuck on as they developed their own reading skills. Through one small intervention, this very wise woman managed to keep me interested in school and improve the learning outcomes for the other kids, while allowing her to spend time with the kids who were a bit behind. Importantly, I think this was the first time I had been given a leadership role. I didn't recognise it at the time, of course, but on reflection that year changed me. It let me see that you can lead people with, or without, a special title or a shiny badge.

Loz, my father, was a sales representative working the stores and supermarkets on behalf of big manufacturers. He was a pretty good one too, so I thought! Every week or so he'd come home with extra treats from work and delight us with a box of Wagon Wheels, Mint Patties or Golden Roughs (my favourite). Which, in hindsight, seems odd as he worked mostly in pharmaceuticals! But whenever he went on a country trip he always returned with some little treasure. He still knows where every factory outlet is located and to this day will say to me, 'If you're heading to Bendigo don't forget to drop in to the Ardmona factory for some cheap canned food'. Sure Dad, will do.

His own father died when Dad was only four years old and he grew up in a household of women. All of his parenting skills were home grown and intuitive—fatherhood books didn't exist then, and I doubt he would have read them anyway. The idea of being the 'stern patriarch', which was still popular at the time, would have never entered his mind. We didn't even call him Dad—he was just 'Loz', short for Lawrie, which we were astounded to find out later was short for Lawrence!

He was, and still is, a gorgeous, fun-loving father, now grandfather to six grandchildren. We went where Loz worked, and during the mid seventies Loz tried out a few jobs in different locations. What this meant for me was that I attended three different primary schools in the three years from Year 4 to Year 6. Thankfully, he was able to time his moves so they occurred over the long summer holidays.

Starting a new school is tough. And starting a new school every year, at the stage in your life when you are just starting to understand your world and that you are an individual, distinct from those around you, was particularly hard. I don't remember being coached but I found a method of assimilation that worked for me—a method I had to quickly unlearn when I entered the workforce. I would survive by being a chameleon. I would blend in, try not to attract the spotlight, keep a reserved distance and hope that somehow I would make a friend. It was pure self-preservation.

To a large extent this worked and by the time I entered Grade 5 at Waverley Park Primary School I had it down to a fine art. Such a fine art that by week four of the first term I had been voted Red house captain. Taking on this leadership role a good year or so younger than my peers didn't faze me. I was a big sister to two siblings, I had survived two changes of school and the kids had voted for me!

It was at this time that my gorgeous mum, Sharon, went back to work full-time. My little brother Ben (later an AFL player for Carlton) was in Year 4 and my sister Jane (who we called and still call Sparky for her extremely energetic mind, crazy curly hair and unshakeable optimism) was just starting school. Straight away I was shouldering a great responsibility. From 3.30 pm, when we walked home from school together, to around 5 pm, when Mum would arrive home, I was in charge. Sounds awesome, doesn't it? And at first I was very excited. I enjoyed the responsibility and the chance to boss my younger brother and sister around without the watchful eye of Mum and Dad. Quickly, though, I started to learn what it was really like to be a 'mum'. Making afternoon tea, constantly bugging Ben to 'stop kicking that football on the road and come inside now', playing with Jane for an hour.

I'm sure Shaz and Loz wouldn't have organised it this way if they'd had a choice. We had just moved into a new house in a new suburb and like most Australian families we needed the second income to support our simple suburban lifestyle. If Shaz hadn't had to go back to work, would I be a different person? Sure. I'm convinced I would be less resilient and resourceful. I learned a lot during that time about responsibility, remaining calm in tricky situations and settling disputes. All skills I would need in Antarctica, more than two decades later.

A code to live by

By the time I hit Year 9 at school I had a reputation, and not a great one. I was, or was always close to, achieving straight A's, but not through application or hard work. I think early on I learned how to work the system. My report cards were unanimous: 'Can do better. More focus and effort required.' I was fast and accurate when I wanted to be, and would often finish my work before my classmates. At which time I would whip out a Rubik's cube (my record was 1 minute 46 seconds for the complete cube; I even used silicon lubricant to speed up my spins), pull out a copy of *Dolly* magazine or do something generally annoying and disruptive, just to signal that I had finished. I wouldn't explicitly interrupt or disrupt the kids around me, but just the fact that I was amusing myself while they were still plugging away at their work was enough for the teachers to take note.

And take note they did. At the end of Year 10 I was called into the deputy principal's office. 'Do you *really* want to go on to years 11 and 12?' she asked me. 'Wouldn't you prefer to go and get a job? You would love the freedom to be able to do what you want, when you want and the way you want. Your teachers all say you are bored with school.' I looked at Sister Mary in silent disbelief. *Are you throwing me out?*

Two of my best friends had left school after Year 10. Both were a month into their 'retail careers', working at Woolworths full-time, with all the money they could spend. I was seriously thinking about joining them, mainly for the lucrative income. Oh the glamour! What I could do with the princely wage of $150 a week! I went home and told Shaz. Now, Shaz was totally gorgeous and glamorous. Think about the late '80s—Oscar de la Renta perfume, red lippy and permed blond hair. She was stunning. But she was also very wise. She said, 'Darling, why don't you just finish Year 10, then try out working at Woolworths over the summer? You'll earn lots of money and you'll get to see what it's like working on the checkout all day, every day. If you still love it after two months, chances are it will make you happy. But if you don't like it, then you can go back to school and do your Higher School Certificate'.

What a great response. She affirmed my concerns, outlined the options and, importantly, gave me an 'out' if my chosen course didn't work out. Giving people an 'out' is a key leadership skill, and like many parents, Shaz intuitively knew that if she laid down the law either way I would have rebelled. Better to give me some options and let me choose; after all, I was 16 years old and like most teenagers there wasn't much I didn't know.

Mrs Purcell, my English teacher, steered me through years 11 and 12. She consistently reminded me that raw intelligence alone is not enough for success. It needed to be married with dedication and application. Intelligence alone would make for a waste of school, and the choices I made now would affect me for life. While she adhered to the curriculum and taught us the usual classics, one particular project stayed with me all my life and really set the scene for my home life, career and relationships.

After closing Steinbeck's *Of Mice and Men*, Mrs Purcell turned to the class and said, 'I want you to choose a popular song. A song that you love, a song with strong lyrics. Then we're going to deconstruct it and find out what is at the heart of it. We're going to explore what drove the lyricist to create this song, the message the writer was trying to get across'. It was an English Literature class in sentence structure, prose and rhythm dressed up as something quite exciting and even a bit daring! Perfect for bored teenagers like me.

This was 1986, and I had one particular song constantly running through my head. The writer, Peter Garrett, was at that time particularly critical of US military activity in Australia. He was passionate about the environment and social justice. Over the course of a month I pulled apart the incredible Midnight Oil song 'Power and the Passion', a classic rock anthem from 1982 (I'm sure many 40+ readers will now have the chorus resonating in their heads!). One particular line hit me and hit me hard: 'It's better to die on your feet than to live on your knees.'

Truly.

As I thought about this I realised I had two choices: I could continue to meander through life, putting in minimum effort, taking no chances and accepting whatever was dished out to me as if it was my preordained destiny; or I could live by a new code, one that could take me well out of my comfort zone, make life much more risky — but also open the world up to me. As I shaped and then wrote out my new code, I made the personal commitment to live by it as much as I could. My new motto as a 16-year-old high-school student, which changed my life forever and set me on a course of adventure, excitement and challenge was: 'I would rather regret the things I did than regret the things I didn't do.'

Rather than saying, 'Oh, Mark Twain and Emiliano Zapata — not very original . . .', Mrs Purcell offered me affirmation and the licence to make this pledge my own. The first true test of this personal commitment came at the end of Year 12.

By now, thanks to my teacher's wonderful guidance, I was passionate about words and people. Writing was easy and I was good at it. Maths was a whole other story. I loved to understand what made people tick and put this into words, so I chose to study either public relations or journalism. I thought these occupations might enable me to exercise my love of writing but in such a way as to create broad influence for the people I worked with. My Higher School Certificate score (the primary assessment criterion for entry to university) was good enough to afford me the choice of enrolling at Melbourne University (arguably the best in Australia), or at one or two other universities in Melbourne, or taking a leap into the unknown by moving 300 kilometres out into the bush and enrolling in a new degree that combined journalism and public relations.

Melbourne University had lots going for it. Several friends were going, transport was easy, and there were many, many excellent cafés, student digs, parties and extracurricular activities in and around the Carlton campus. I was tempted, but as I weighed up the options I thought, I can go to Melbourne, get a great degree, stay in my comfort zone and end up with a good job; or ... I could go right out on a limb, leave all my friends and family, and study for an untested degree but one that was a better fit for what I wanted to do. I would live in the 'bush' and learn a whole lot more about myself while building critical life skills.

To the dismay of those closest to me, I changed my university admission preferences at the last possible moment and chose to attend Deakin University, Warrnambool campus. I vividly remember the day Shaz and Loz drove away from my student accommodation. I felt a mixture of dread and excitement for what lay ahead! I knew nobody in Warrnambool, not a soul. I had no way of getting to university from my rented student accommodation (a 10-kilometre round trip), no job, and even coming home for the weekend would involve nearly five hours' travel on public transport.

I started university at age 17. No driver's licence, unable to legally drink, many miles from home. It was a very difficult introduction to university life. But two part-time jobs, one as a waitress and the other working in a supermarket, a gaggle of new, similarly displaced friends, and the charms of a blue-eyed blond local surfer called

Chris who became my first real boyfriend, made university fun and interesting. My part-time work was predominantly on the weekends, which meant that I stayed and played in and around Warrnambool and really got to know and love this little city on the big coast.

Of my six best friends at university, two of us made it into the final year and I was the only one who graduated. Some found the work too hard or uninteresting; others simply missed their family and friends too much. Two things helped me persevere through the loneliness and complete my degree without dropping a subject and with reasonable grades. The first was my motto. The second was a conversation with a stranger on the long, boring train ride home one day. Her pivotal advice was that a future employer wouldn't look so much at grades, prescribed learning and tuition. A future employer would look for the ability to finish something you started. Stickability, resilience and perseverance against the odds would be accounted more highly than the academic transcript and conferral of the degree. So I stuck it out, made my sister spend her sixteenth birthday driving down to Warrnambool and back with Mum and Dad for my graduation ceremony (she still reminds me of this quite often), moved back to Melbourne and went looking for work.

What I learned

- *It's never too early to learn the basics of leadership.* Start small and safe. Do it in an 'unofficial' way. Focus on just the next step and see your new recruit or pupil step up and flourish.

- *Step out from safety — it's a sure-fire way to make something happen.* You may fail, you may succeed, but along the way you will grow.

- *Stick it out.* Never underestimate the importance of perseverance. Tough times don't last but tough people do. It builds resilience and shows strength of character.

Chapter 2

Very few decisions in life are irreversible, so make some!

It was only upon graduating and getting my first job in PR that I realised I really didn't like PR at all! My first job out of university was with a government agency. I quickly found the work to be deeply annoying! Looking back, I realise PR itself wasn't the problem; I simply didn't have the maturity to work in that field.

Convinced by an act of grace

In any government agency, much revolves around your minister. It's your job to keep them interested in your portfolio, up-to-date with the latest goings-on, and to give them opportunities to shine in front of their staff, the media and the community. A big part of our role was to create events for the minister. We would work for weeks and weeks, often very long hours, to schedule, plan and conduct fantastic events for our minister. More often than not, and primarily because we were a reasonably low-profile and small agency, the minister wouldn't attend. We would get a call from his office the night before the event to say that 'something has come up' and he had to reprioritise to attend to more urgent matters on the day, which meant all our preparation and planning was wasted. At the time I found this deeply demoralising, but later (after working in and with government for 15 years) I realised it's often not appropriate for politicians to attend a launch or a breakfast, particularly when bigger issues and higher priorities exist. As a 21 year old, though, I found this frustrating and disrespectful and started looking around for different things to do.

One of my roles in PR was to lead bus tours. On these tours we would take lovely retired people on outings into our metropolitan parks. My favourite at the time was Jells Park, in Glen Waverley. Smack in the geographical centre of Melbourne, Jells Park contains waterways, bush trails, barbecues and a visitor centre. The thing I loved about Jells Park is that I always felt good when I was there. I loved how the park rangers obviously loved their job and took great pride in explaining the fine details of the flora and fauna to visitors. One visit I witnessed a remarkable example of customer service that inspired me to pursue a career as a ranger.

A young boy, no more than eight, came to the rangers office cradling a very sick starling in his jumper. He was quite upset, on the verge of tears, when he knocked on the rangers office door. The ranger looked at the starling, looked at the boy, then carefully took the injured bird from the boy and promised to 'fix it up'.

Now, anyone will tell you that starlings are not high on the list of birds that rangers want to see flourish, or even survive! As an introduced pest, they crowd out native birds, destroy habitat and breed like crazy. So the ranger had a dilemma that he solved in a beautiful way. Once the boy had left he quickly euthanised the bird—I know some people won't like this idea, but (a) the bird was nearly dead and (b) that was the ranger's job. Then he wrapped the bird up and disposed of it in a way that wouldn't spread any disease, feed the rats or risk it being found by park visitors. Job done.

Two hours later the boy, with his father, came back to see how 'his bird' was getting on. The ranger took them outside and, with the boy holding both the ranger's hand and his father's, walked them deep into the surrounding bushland. Pointing up at a totally healthy starling, the ranger said, 'There she is. She's all better. We fixed her right up'.

It wasn't the time to be gruff and practical. It wasn't the time or place for this boy to be given the story about introduced pests and our absolute requirement to manage their numbers in order to protect our native species. It was the time to show grace and compassion. To give a worried boy a song in his heart and a story to tell at school.

The next day I applied to be a park ranger.

Since I had started, my agency had been renamed and merged with two other agencies. It was now virtually unrecognisable from the small operation I had joined just two short years earlier. Parks Victoria, as we were now referred to, managed both national and metropolitan parks. It had a specific responsibility to improve the biodiversity of plant and animal life in *all* state-owned crown land. To meet this challenge, Parks Victoria was recruiting Park Rangers—Customer Service. These rangers would work primarily with visitors, lead possum prowls, manage events and be 'the face of the Park'.

I didn't like my chances. I had no background in sustainability or the environment. Apart from the bus tours and work at the supermarket I had no background in customer service. But I wanted to be happy in my job and all the rangers I knew loved their work. I didn't want to wake up anymore thinking, 'Can I take a sick day today?' So, motto in mind, I applied, winged my way through the interview process… and got the job!

Me…a park ranger?

I really landed on my feet in the role of park ranger. I loved the interaction, the planning, working with the environmental specialists who knew every tree, every shrub and every animal track in their park. But it wasn't long before I realised that my ignorance of the technical aspects of the environment was holding me back. I needed to be able to talk to visitors with more knowledge and authority. I needed the environmental understanding to write the park notes, media releases and newsletters. I needed the confidence that comes with fully comprehending what it was we were actually doing at Jells Park. Importantly, I understood that in this male-dominated environment, where I was one of only two women in a team of 18, I had to be technically competent to be taken seriously.

With this in mind, I enrolled in the Associate Diploma in Applied Science—Environmental Management at Frankston TAFE. The travel drove me nuts. Three nights a week I would drive for over an hour in peak-hour traffic to Frankston, engage with the lessons and then drive an hour home. After a year I reflected on the value of the course and came to realise that there was a better way to build my technical understanding of environmental management: through a mentor.

I attached myself to John Goodman, who at the time was the Operations Ranger at Jells Park. John was a long-time ranger, highly trained with deep expertise in both the operations and environmental aspects of the park. He was very highly regarded by everyone on the team and was well respected by all our stakeholders. He was a sound, down-to-earth father of seven who absolutely lived for his family. An all-round good bloke.

I didn't approach John and say, 'Will you be my mentor?' Unassuming and humble people like John often feel uncomfortable in 'official' roles like that. Rather, I just joined him in the park and peppered him with questions, asking 'why' a lot. John taught me obvious things like identification of flora and fauna but also the more esoteric skills that rangers often require, such as how to estimate the tonnage of crushed rock needed to create a walkway of a certain depth, width and length; how to touch up park signage with enamel paint—and clean up the brushes and tins afterwards! He even taught me how to drive a manual car, with much mirth and merriment—well, at least from his side of the vehicle.

I'm sure I drove John crazy at first, but after a while it started working both ways. John had seen me excel at dealing with difficult people at the park, both visitors and staff. He started to seek my ideas about what he should do in particular situations. I had such an immense respect for the man that when he was promoted to Ranger-in-Charge at a new park I followed him there as his Customer Service Ranger. We worked very well together and often shared a laugh over the absurdities of life and people. And after nearly 20 years we still have this relationship!

Mentoring was a fantastic way to accelerate my learning. It had two great advantages over the formal qualification. Firstly, the advice was practical, grounded in real-life experience and knowledge of the local environment. Secondly, the mentoring relationship enabled me to develop a deep and highly visible relationship with someone who was trusted throughout the organisation.

I quickly became head of the customer service team in the park and at the grand old age of 22 I managed four rangers. In private industry it's normal for quick learners to be rapidly promoted. In government, particularly back in those days, it was unheard of. Promotion was usually based on years of service. People, particularly park rangers, could typically work at the same park for 10 to 15 years at a time. There was talk: 'It's because she's a girl' was one of the rumours I heard around the traps. From time to time it became more overt, and one of those times stands out in my memory.

The day in question started with a light summer fog over the park, giving everything a warm orange glow as the rangers unlocked the gates. By 10 am the park was full of parents and young children taking full advantage of the bike tracks, playgrounds and visitor centre. By lunchtime most families had gone home and were replaced with several large groups of young adults, mostly men, with eskies full of beer and sausages. Most were in board shorts and singlets. As they arranged themselves around the park I made a mental note. By 1 pm it was already hot, about 32 °C, and it would soon be hotter still as the northerly pushed through the city, bringing with it parched dry air from the centre of Australia. As it heated up, my visitors would drink faster, and it was also unlikely to cool down quickly, as the northerly was predicted to stay for at least three days. Tomorrow and the next day were forecasting 40 °C plus. This is not unusual in Melbourne, and I had an inkling of how this would end for the groups enjoying their barbecue in my park.

By about 8.30 pm I was concerned. The noise levels had continued to creep up, voices becoming raucous—they were all good natured and enjoying themselves at this point, but I understood alcohol, and I knew it could turn in an instant.

At 9.00 pm, the last of Melbourne's wonderful twilight was falling and I was getting ready to close the park. How these people intended to get home I didn't know. My concern was to get them to leave peacefully and willingly so I could close and lock the gate behind them.

There were now upwards of 30 very drunk and very loud men. I was just 22, alone and hesitant. I made the call on the trunk radio. I would *not* put myself in danger by attempting to round up and hustle out these people on my own. I radioed the other ranger on duty, explained the situation and asked for his help to lock up the gates. His response: 'Well, if you women want to be park rangers, you've got to do all the park ranger work!' My response, although I can't quote it verbatim, was that it wasn't about whether I was male or female, but about making sure we empty the park quickly and safely. I wouldn't expect a male to act on his own in this situation either. It wasn't a gender issue, it was a safety issue.

This was my first encounter with gender-based discrimination and I pondered on it. Was this a one-off experience? Or should I always expect discrimination and prepare accordingly? Is the 'glass ceiling' for women so low they can't even be trusted to do basic work? I didn't know the answer, but it sure made me cross!

I didn't get it right all the time though. In summer visitor numbers rose and we needed more park rangers to run the place. We would bring in casual labour, mainly university students, to keep the place running. In my naivety I appointed three of my friends to the casual roster. I liked them and found them friendly and engaging people. If we just whacked a ranger's uniform on them and sent them out the visitors would also like them, and everyone would win!

Well, not quite. There were two *big* issues with this. Firstly, none of my friends, although lovely, had *any* experience in customer service. They didn't have the discipline, empathy or other essential qualities needed to deliver good customer service. I bailed them out of tricky situations several times.

Secondly, and much more importantly, I didn't realise the resentment it would create among my colleagues as I handed out 'jobs for the boys'. At the time, it made complete and obvious sense to me. It was four hours on a Saturday and Sunday afternoon for two months. It wasn't high stakes, it wasn't even particularly interesting, and they reported directly to me. So what was the issue?

I didn't stop to think that we needed transparency in the process. My colleagues might well have known other people who were equally eager to apply and were probably better equipped. There were most likely numerous sons, daughters, nieces and nephews who would have loved the opportunity. But my colleagues didn't get a chance to put them forward. They were aggrieved, and rightly so. It didn't go down well at all, to put it mildly, and it took some months and an apology to fully regain the trust of my people. It was a good lesson to learn early in my career about how to make the right decision the right way.

What I learned

- *Headed down the wrong track? Change tracks!* Life is different now from 50 years ago. Expect to make sideways moves many times in your career until you find your passion. And change then too, just before it gets stale.

- *Back yourself.* Even if you don't meet all of the selection criteria, it's still worth applying for the job you want. The interview panel will weigh some criteria more heavily than others, and often they will seek specific personal qualities rather than just a formal skill set.

- *Get a mentor.* A mentor can stop you making rookie mistakes, shortcut your learning and become a great ally.

- *Make your decisions the right way.* It's not enough just to make a good decision. People must perceive you have done it the right way.

Chapter 3

Always look for ways to extend yourself

I loved doing new things so I applied to act in John's role as Operations Ranger, overseeing the park's day-to-day operations when he took his annual leave. This would be a big step up. I would be manager of 18 rangers, all older (some as much as 40 years my senior), wiser and much more experienced than me.

Acting up

To my delight, John accepted my application. He showed trust in my potential and knew that if I had a shot at it I would give it everything. And I did, repeatedly! When he was away I put in long, long hours coming up to speed with some of the mysteries of Operations. Budgets! Spreadsheets! Reports! Meetings with contractors! There was a huge administrative burden that I wasn't prepared for. But I plugged away and leant on some of the more experienced rangers for guidance and advice. When John returned he was happy with my performance and from then on I applied for every acting role that became available across the state.

I knew that to progress quickly I needed to build my capability across a wide variety of situations, in different regions, parks and roles. I moved around the state a lot over the next two years. I knew the one advantage that I had over many of my peers was that I was unattached and childless. Many of my peers with equal or better qualifications and experience were married and settled, and had put down roots in their local area. They had babies, children at school and mortgages. I had none of these, and although I think I wanted them at some point, I knew that the opportunity to be mobile and learn from the best in the farthest flung corners of the state would quickly pass.

Each year I would take a six- to eight-week secondment to another region. One year I worked with NSW Parks and Wildlife on planning for the Sydney Olympics, another time I spent six weeks in Mildura, and other times I stayed local.

My selection of secondments was quite strategic, however. To date I had spent all my time in the metropolitan parks. Since we had merged with the national parks authority I knew that to have credibility outside of the metropolitan areas I would need to be immersed in national parks. These parks are very different ecologically and in terms of visitors. The focus in these parks is much less on visitor amenity and much more on protection of the natural environment. Chasing gun-wielding hunters back to their car isn't something you get to do in a metropolitan park! The closest you get is a golfer wannabe practising his or her driving skills in the middle of the crowded barbecue area.

I focused on broadening my skills and my understanding of national parks. I worked on the koala relocation program and caught, tagged, bagged and relocated koalas threatened by loss of habitat leading to overpopulation and starvation. (I still hear people call them koala bears! I reckon I spent as much time correcting that misnomer as I later spent correcting perceptions about polar bears.) I worked around the state, anywhere the organisation needed extra rangers.

My next break came when a role was advertised internally for a District Program Manager in Ballarat. Knowing very little about managing large-scale programs, and recognising that once again I would be on my own in a regional town where I had no friends, I applied and was awarded the role.

It was Monday morning on my second week on the job. I was a city chick in the bush, surrounded by 'blokey' blokes. I understood very little about life in rural areas. Peter, one of my peers, came up to me as we were getting ready for our weekly meeting: 'How was your weekend, Rach?' he asked cheerily. 'Did you get a couple of inches?'

I turned red, opened my mouth and turned around. That was how my girlfriends and I would talk! I was certainly not going to discuss my nocturnal activities in the tearoom on a Monday morning with someone I hardly knew. I beat a hasty retreat to my desk and buried my head in some paperwork. I felt ashamed for being talked to that way and shocked that Peter would be so bold and brazen. Fancy asking a young, single woman you hardly knew if she had *got a few inches* on the weekend? How rude!

Thankfully Marcia, who was my age and knew quite a few city chicks, had seen the interaction. She came over to me very quietly, bent down close to my ear and whispered, 'Rain. He's talking about RAIN!'

'Oh, my, God . . .' I exhaled.

I had a lot to learn! After a week it was apparent that rain was the number one topic of conversation in the bush. We were by then seven years into a 10-year drought, so it was never far from people's thoughts.

The power of influence

My role in Ballarat involved administering and managing the range of programs that were planned and in place across the Grampians. I again found myself knee-deep in very large, home-grown and complicated spreadsheets, managing programs like 'Rabbit Busters' (you can imagine) and 'Weed Control'. I had no staff reporting to me and had no direct power over anyone I was working with. There were four rangers-in-charge (RICs) who were equal grade to me, but I needed them to participate and contribute current information in order for me to do my job. Apart from the ability to wrestle with a spreadsheet, I knew that to succeed in this role I would need to very quickly develop the ability to influence those around me. I had to be able to get them to do things that weren't interesting or even related to their existing roles.

Rangers are like everyone who is deeply passionate about what they do. They relish getting their hands dirty on a project; they love to plan out new programs and deliver great outcomes for society. They *don't*, however, like to write up reports. It's the same everywhere. Salespeople who have to submit their outbound call sheet to head office know that mundane activity isn't going to get them a single deal. Project managers know that accounting for why they overspent on pesticide by $15 isn't going to reduce the number of rabbits in a park. So mostly they put it off. And off. Until head office notices. And then they'll be 'good' for another couple of months before they put it off again. Does this sound familiar?

It was precisely this type of environment I found myself in when I arrived at Ballarat. The first month went by in a blur, mostly spent talking to the project and program managers, getting a feel for their passions, projects and progress. At the end of the second month I fired up my spreadsheets and got to work on the reports to head office.

Have you ever tried to write a report without any data? Have you ever read a report that is so devoid of data you can't trust it? Well, that was my first monthly submission to head office. And... no one noticed. I lost sleep during the first week after my submission. I was waiting for the phone call: 'Oh Rachael, sorry we made a mistake putting you in that role.' But it never came.

What *did* come, however, was next year's interim budget. I still wasn't completely on top of the finances by this stage and I just forwarded the budget around to my RICs. And then the phone went crazy...

'What do you mean by this?'

'Why have you cut this program?'

'Don't you know that the weed problem in this park is out of control? Why have you cut the weed control budget by 15 per cent?'

Cut budgets? Me? Whaaaat?

I was very much under the pump, stressed and worried when I got through to the program team at head office who controlled and allocated the budget.

'Oh, well it all comes down to evidence doesn't it... There's simply no evidence that what you are doing is working... There are any number of projects and programs around the state that have a much higher profile than yours and, more to the point, we don't actually know exactly what's going on down there and we must prioritise somehow, so we use the information provided by the parks themselves.'

Here was the answer to my two biggest issues: what had happened to the budget, and how would I get my RICs to do what I wanted even when they didn't want to?

I'm sure you know what I did next. I did it fast. I got all my RICs together for a tactical meeting. I drew a line for them between their reporting activities and their budget allocation for next year. I put myself in the middle and explained that my job was to help them succeed, and that their success would depend on accurate, timely data that provides full justification for their work.

They quickly went to work, backtracked through a year of raw data, prepared their reports and entered the data into the system. It went straight to the budget allocation team, who were able to see the value of the work we were doing and, importantly, could see the return on investment.

The key lesson I learned through all of this was how to exercise influence when not in a position of power. When I sat back and reflected I realised there was a simple three-step process that was now only beginning to dawn on me.

Firstly, I had to understand the interests of my people. What is at stake for them, what do they have to lose and what do they have to gain? In this case it was very simple: they stood to lose their budget allocation for next year. In most cases, it's much more complex and will involve social and political aspects as well as access to resources, including people.

Secondly, I had to understand the levers I had at my disposal that could 'change the game' for my team. In this case, the lever was data. Good quality, lots of it, analysed and summarised in a way that made sense to people used to making financial decisions.

The third step, I realised, was my role in both the stuff-up and the solution. I contributed to the initial problem by not grasping the link between data and budget decisions. My ongoing role became one of facilitation between the RICs and the finance people. When I left that role a year later I had learned a lot about influence, but I had also left behind a much stronger and more financially accountable set of projects and a group of RICs who knew *why* reporting variances and reporting on progress were so important.

For anyone looking to develop their influencing skills, I would highly recommend taking on a role where you have *no* positional power to make people do things. You will learn how to position yourself, how to develop your value proposition, how to sell it and, importantly, how to sustain the relationship when for the other person it gets too hard.

In my experience, IT professionals often do this extraordinarily well. They don't run a 'line of business' so they're not responsible (and don't get the glory) for top-line revenue. They design and run company-wide programs that take years and eat large chunks of available cash. Yet they (the good ones) are able to sell the concept and idea to their diverse stakeholders. For a marketing director, investing in IT platforms means a smaller budget for marketing campaigns. For a human resources director, it might mean tightening an organisation's training and development budget. There are always trade-offs, but good influencers know how to make their trade worthwhile. (Delivering on the promise is also important, and somewhat fewer IT professionals are as successful in this arena!)

What I learned

- *Throw yourself into things you can't do yet.* This is seriously the best and fastest way to learn. You won't get everything right, though, so make sure you have a good safety net with mentors and coaches around you.

- *Understand and develop your influence.* Most of what gets done in boardrooms isn't about the numbers. It's about who stands to gain and who stands to lose. Understand it and leverage it to your benefit.

Chapter 4

Get out of your depth— it's a great way to learn to swim

In Ballarat I continued my practice of seizing every available acting role and this time I focused on senior management positions. My boss at the time was Chief Ranger of the Grampians district. He oversaw massive tracts of land, hundreds of staff and millions of annual park visitors. When he announced he was going on extended leave for 12 months I quickly applied to act in his role. The highest number of people I had had reporting to me up to this point was 12, so this would be a massive step up.

Headed for Chief Ranger

I spent the next year learning the ropes of being Chief Ranger. If I was surprised at the amount of paperwork at Jells Park, I was absolutely floored by the paperwork a Chief Ranger must manage. Fortunately, I was surrounded by a professional and skilled team who took on most of the drudge work, enabling me to work on the relationships with staff, stakeholders and media and to oversee our large projects.

After successfully managing the programs in Ballarat, it wasn't long before I caught the attention of Mark Stone, then CEO of Parks Victoria. The organisation, from inception through its multiple different incarnations, was male-dominated, particularly out in the field. At this time approximately 90 per cent of park rangers were men. The organisation had been aware of this for a long time, but without a good case for gender diversity it struggled with practical ways to address it. On the surface, recruitment was roughly 60 per cent men, but most women ended up either in head office or in corporate services roles in the regions, or they left the organisation.

What is the case for gender diversity? Or any diversity for that matter? It's a question that is dear to my heart, and I would gladly spend the next five pages setting out my views. But there are others much more qualified and erudite than I am who are better placed to do this. Suffice to say, I believe in equal opportunity for all—irrespective of gender, religion, race, age, you name it. I think that's uncontroversial, but sometimes it's hard for people and organisations to understand why it's important and what needs to be done—and then to actually make the transition.

Parks Victoria knew they had a problem and were actively looking for answers. They recognised that having competent and capable women in senior management roles would provide role models and mentors for the younger women starting out. So our CEO, Mark, took a special interest in how I was going. My willingness to be seconded to locations far away from home showed Mark I was serious about my career and prepared to work hard. Subsequently I was lucky enough to have very good access to him and his guidance. I often advised him on the organisation's key gender issues while he acted unofficially as a mentor. I felt flattered to be on the CEO's radar, but I also felt that I had something valuable to contribute. Mark would come to be a terrific mentor as I made the transition from staff to management and then into formal leadership positions. His guidance and confidence in me would soon be the catalyst for my decision to lead the Antarctic expedition.

Knocked back, but a new opportunity emerges

A year later a full-time role came up as Chief Ranger for the Basalt Plains district. This district borders Melbourne to the west and north and consists of mainly metropolitan parks, with a new national park thrown in for good measure. I desperately wanted this job. It would let me move back to Melbourne and reconnect with my friends and family. It would put me firmly in charge of a full district. It was the logical next step, so I put *everything* into my application. I was devastated not to be chosen. Chief Ranger roles don't come up very often, and I was at a loss as to what to do when my current acting Chief Ranger arrangement came to a close. I felt rejected and defeated. I knew who got the role and truly believed that I could have done the job just as well, if not better, than him. Certainly he was highly experienced, a good 25 years older than me, and would be a 'steady hand', but I thought the district needed me—young, energetic, passionate, driven and ambitious!

While I was licking my wounds and feeling sorry for myself I was very surprised to see another Chief Ranger role become vacant, in the West Coast district. This district is one of the most complex in Victoria, combining iconic locations such as the Twelve Apostles and the Great Ocean Road, buzzing coastal resorts like Lorne and Anglesea, several rapidly expanding towns and a vast number of parks, including newly established marine parks. The West Coast was the jewel in the crown for Parks Victoria and was internally classified as 'Level A—Most Complex'. It's the region that attracts large funding, has millions of visitors every year, contains international tourism icons, and has many very passionate and engaged locals. It is also geographically huge, spanning 400 kilometres from Torquay (south of Port Phillip Bay) to Nelson on the South Australian border, and employed 90 staff to manage the portfolio. I felt underqualified, underskilled and still demoralised from my last rejection, but I applied anyway. To follow my motto, I felt I had to try.

A week later I was again despondent. What are the chances of that district coming up again in a few years, I mused... probably bugger all. If the executive team didn't trust me with a small, uncomplicated district like Basalt Plains, why would they trust me with a massive operation like the West Coast? So I called Human Resources and withdrew my application, poured a glass of wine and threw myself a pity party.

That night my phone buzzed with a message from the CEO. He wanted me in his office the next day. Like all great CEOs, Mark knew when to reach out for specific expertise and I felt good and valued that once again I would be called in to provide a 'woman's perspective' on a situation, whatever the situation was.

I arrived at the Bourke Street offices expecting a round-table discussion, but Mark pulled me into his office, sat me down and gave me a questioning stare.

'What, Mark?'

He relaxed into his chair, gave me one more long look then told me he'd heard I had withdrawn my application for the Chief Ranger role.

I was stunned. I had no idea he was involved or really that interested. While I fought to remain poised and calm I explained to him my rationale—that I was just setting myself up for more disappointment and wasting the interview panel's time. I was still so bitterly disappointed and my self-confidence had taken a huge hit.

A glimmer of hope

Mark looked at me sagely, giving me a moment to recompose myself, and told me that sometimes we don't get what we want. He knew how much I wanted the role in Basalt Plains but was very firm that the executive team had put the right person into that job. He agreed that it would have been a nice introduction to a full-time permanent Chief Ranger role, but reminded me his job was to put the right people in the right place at the right time.

We talked about what the West Coast district required and what skills the new Chief Ranger would need. We both knew it would need someone who was prepared to live in isolation, prepared to put in very long hours with lots of travel, and prepared to restructure and turn the district around.

He asked me to reconsider applying. He believed I had all the necessary qualities and had already demonstrated my willingness to work hard and learn. Mark was very honest and frank with me and while he acknowledged I understood people and knew how to set a vision, galvanise a team and make things happen, he also reminded me that I didn't yet have all the technical skills. I knew that if I succeeded in the interview process and took the role I would be out of my depth. It would be an enormous personal challenge. A big restructure like this was bound to get nasty and I suspected it might even get personal. But Mark is a firm believer in stretching people and letting them show just what they're capable of.

His final advice to me still rings loud in my ears and he was absolutely correct: when you have a disappointment in your career, people will be watching you to see how you react. Do you take your bat and ball and go home, or do you learn from it, move through it and get past it?

There was one big problem I immediately foresaw. I was dating the regional manager of the West Region! David was on the executive team and carried direct responsibility for all operations within that region, including the West Coast district. I already had first-hand experience of nepotism, and my mistake in employing my friends way back in the early days had shown me how favouritism, or even just perceived favouritism, destroys teamwork. I didn't want a whiff of that around my career.

It all just seemed too hard, as I started to explain to Mark, but he calmly responded that he had already spoken to David. He told me David would not be on the selection panel. In fact, no one from Parks Victoria would be on the initial selection panel. Because it was such a critical, high-profile and politically important role, the organisation took the very rare step of advertising externally, both in Australia and internationally, and Mark personally interviewed the final two applicants. The recruitment consultants would handle the selection process and, quite simply, if I didn't get shortlisted by them I wouldn't be interviewed by the CEO.

Appeased, I agreed. I threw myself optimistically into reapplying for the role. I was shortlisted and sat through the panel interviews. I knew I was up against many others, some of whom were great friends, some who were tried, trusted and experienced, some who had amazing track records of success in internationally sensitive areas. After a two-month process I was awarded the role. It gave me great confidence to know that I was selected on merit. I was not a 'token' female Chief Ranger, the CEO's pet project or the Regional Manager's girlfriend. I had won the job fair and square, because of my energy, passion and skill in dealing with difficult people. I had just one month to prepare and there were a lot of decisions to make.

What I learned

- *Believe in yourself.* I was lucky that I had people backing me who believed in me more than I did. I took a valuable lesson out of this. How could people trust and follow me if I didn't believe in myself?

Chapter 5

Don't expect leadership to be an easy ride

First, my office. Where oh where in this vast geographic area would I base myself? I needed to be in the district, which stretched 400 kilometres from Torquay to Portland. But I also needed to make sure I could get to head office easily for face-to-face meetings with key decision makers. Around this time, the transition to email as a primary form of communication was in full swing. I was a late adopter of email and hadn't spent much time thinking about how best to use it. It was considered the answer to reducing travel time and expense. You can accomplish more at your desk than you can in the car, was the mantra of the day. I had a problem with this. You see, I already knew from a couple of experiences that email has no 'tone' button. Messages are often terse and can come across in completely the wrong way. I had seen email conversations escalate into full-scale warfare. Experience had also taught me that face-to-face communication that engaged physical expression, tone and body language was a much better medium for important conversations. Writing this now, 10 years later, it seems like I'm stating the obvious, but to us then it ran against the current and certainly raised a few eyebrows. So I decided to move the District Chief Ranger's office from Warrnambool (about 300 kilometres from head office in Melbourne) to Lorne, half that distance. In one and a half hours I could be in the minister's office in the centre of Melbourne, at head office, or meeting with key corporate stakeholders. The downside was that I knew I would be on the road a lot more and I committed to making the long trips in my own time whenever I could.

Into the cauldron

I knew the move would be controversial. Before I had even started my 60 staff knew things were going to be significantly different. Through the grapevine I heard all sorts of mutterings about an impending cataclysm.

'Regret what you did, not what you didn't do,' I kept reminding myself.

Next I needed to find somewhere to live. Once I knew I would be based in Lorne I rented a gorgeous house overlooking the water in nearby Anglesea. This was to become my haven for the highly eventful two years that followed.

Finally I needed to think about my style of leadership. Obviously Parks Victoria was looking for a change agent. Someone who would crash through or crash. This would be very different from maintaining the status quo. I would need to shake up the district, unsettle it, reshape it, and turn it into a powerful and effective group.

I had seen people take on roles like this and crash. Mostly they had crashed because they did all the mechanical and formal things right (for example, merging, restructuring and new role definitions) but left their people behind. People felt that 'change had been done to them', rather than feeling that they were part of the change. I made a commitment, first to myself and then to my people, that I would listen, engage, understand and address their concerns as they arose.

My first experience of this was to face my 13 direct reports and explain why I chose to move my office. I started by stating my position and reasons then gave everyone a chance to speak. I listed the objections and the 'reasons it was wrong' on a whiteboard, without challenging or defending myself, but asked probing questions to uncover their 'interests'. What was underneath the objection, what did the people feel was at stake? These interests I added in a separate column on the whiteboard.

Rather than address the objections, I worked through their interests, one by one. As with my RICs in the Grampians, I helped them see that not only would their interests be furthered rather than hindered, but that we could also easily deal with the objections. I was delighted with the outcome of this meeting. I felt my staff left feeling good about the prospect of being led by me and I had earned a small amount of trust by being open and listening and responding thoughtfully. I determined that this approach would be a key tool in my leadership toolbox.

One thing that astounded me from my first meeting was the number of people reporting to me. Why did I have 13 direct reports? I started to ask around, spoke to head office and tried to understand why the district was structured in such a top-heavy way. This certainly was not the case in any other district in the organisation. No one had a good answer — it's 'just how it is'. Unhappy with this response I looked closely at the people and their personalities. Of my 13 direct reports, six were clearly there because they needed to be so we could run the business effectively. The seven others were not; they were 'problems', not because of their roles, but because they had been traditionally hard to manage. Instead of making his direct reports manage their staff, the previous Chief Ranger had taken on the role of overseeing these 'difficult' people, shielding his managers from having to deal with the issues. He changed their reporting relationships so they reported directly to him instead of their line manager. This had to change!

I was determined to reshape and transform the region. For this my managers had to manage and my leaders had to lead. So I planned a restructure that would make better sense. I knew that simply putting these people back where they belonged wouldn't change anything; my people needed the skills and support to lead with authority and conviction. Fully supported by my central HR team, we spent the next two months coaching and training my people in how to have these difficult conversations, how to approach, manage and close out performance management, and how to drive excellence and results through getting their people on board or, if required, out of the way.

When my people were ready, I announced the restructure. Of course it met with resistance, but my management team really stepped up and made a good fist of it. I spent nearly two months with my now six direct reports, coaching and mentoring them in how to address these longstanding issues.

Four months later, when the structure had settled in, reporting lines were clear and people were being properly managed, it was time to roll out my master plan. The region had often languished in terms of performance, visitor satisfaction and biodiversity outcomes. It was obvious why. Poor leadership and poor reporting had constricted the region's budgets to a maintenance-only level. There were no meaty projects running and nothing was in the pipeline. It was time to ramp up our visibility and polish the jewel in the crown.

I set to work with great intensity and made sure our reporting was spot on, applying the same techniques as in the Grampians. After three months we had a 99 per cent completion rate for our monthly environmental project reporting, up from less than 50 per cent. We were clearly providing value to the state and its citizens, and we needed additional funding to make it even greater.

We came up with several great projects to increase visitor numbers, improve park infrastructure and provide safer and richer experiences to our visitors, and sent them through to head office. Each one was approved. Why? Because they had the data. Our analysis showed a clear return and our numbers were accurate and incontrovertible. We kicked off the projects and worked hard to make them a success. I was very proud of my team and all we had achieved.

And then it got nasty

But all wasn't well in the land of the West Coast. Not everyone had kept their job in the restructure and, as anywhere, not all parks were equal. One of the people who had left was from a small state park outside Warrnambool, a long way from Anglesea. This park had lower social and environmental value than other parks, and its budget was small. It was in maintenance mode. The residents had been writing to the media and to the minister to have this changed. Unbeknown to me, the ranger who had resigned as a result of the restructure had been busy agitating within the local community. He had stirred up the passion of the locals, providing them with internal budgets and other information known only to those within my team. Managing stakeholder expectations is a critical role in any organisation, and it's particularly crucial when working in government. No minister wants to be ambushed by a front-page story about something he or she knows nothing about!

So to get to the bottom of what the locals were concerned about, I arranged a public meeting. I put out a call in the local media for interested people to attend a 'Future Directions Planning' day for the park. Everyone was invited. I would meet with them all on a Sunday afternoon two weeks hence. By then I had run many such meetings. Typically, 10 to 15 or so of those who were passionate about their local park would attend. We would sit down, discuss plans, options and alternatives in a conciliatory way, agree on a way forward and move on.

Naively I expected this meeting to run along the same lines. So I was shocked when a hundred people showed up that afternoon. A hundred angry faces, complete with badges, banners and slogans. I had faced angry people before, but nothing like this.

I opened the meeting and quickly laid out our plans for the park, along with the reasons for the changes. Then the meeting turned in a direction I could never have anticipated. A disgruntled ex-employee had been 'digging up dirt' on me. The first question from a citizen on the floor was: 'What makes you think you are qualified to manage this park? You aren't trained in this, you've got a degree in PR! You're just here to spin us some unbelievable story. Go back to Melbourne and sip your lattes there.'

And the next: 'Everyone here knows you're not qualified, but not everyone knows that you only got this job because you're in a relationship with the boss...Well, they *all* know now!'

And another: 'So let me get this straight, you're 30, single and childless...Is that right?' I was gobsmacked by that one! What did that have to do with anything?

And still: 'Obviously you're not serious about your job. You moved the office from Warrnambool, the centre of the district, to Lorne to be closer to the city and restaurants. Isn't the bush good enough for you?'

They continued to get stuck into me. It was personal, and it was toxic. It was the first time I had been personally attacked (though it would not be the last).

After leaving the meeting I burst into tears in the car. Is this what leadership is like? Could I live with this? I was trying to help this community, listen to them and meet their needs. Soon my tears turned into anger. I was furious. Even though it was now near 8 pm on a Sunday night I received a call from my boss, Brett Cheatley, who by then was regional manager of the western region. Brett was wonderful. He listened patiently as I unleashed my fury, telling him, 'If this is the price I have to pay for a management role, then I will simply walk away.' He explained that it wasn't about me, it was about the uniform. He related some of his war stories and recommended I talk to the CEO in the morning if I felt that would help.

This episode changed me. It made me tougher and more resilient. I knew that if I could withstand personal attacks, professional attacks and gender attacks I could survive just about anything. Two years into my role as Chief Ranger of West Coast, I had received multiple awards, attracted significant funding, delivered some great projects, featured in media interviews and made a real difference to the district. I was proud of my achievements and I was planning more. I was no longer a 'novice leader' by the time I sat down to the breakfast that changed my life.

What I learned

- *It's okay to be unpopular every now and then.* Just make sure you go the extra mile to make sure people understand *why*.

- *Leadership is a choice.* There will be tough times and difficult decisions to make, but that's your job. You need to have a clear vision for your team and the ability to communicate that vision simply. Alternatively, if you really don't like scrutiny and pressure, think carefully about whether you would really enjoy leadership. It's not for everyone, despite what self-help books might tell us.

- *Leadership can be a tough road.* Expect resistance. Expect things to get personal, because they will. Soak it up and deal with it because it will make you stronger. If you fall down in a heap, don't give up; you need to build up your resilience and your own sense of self-worth.

Part II

Antarctica beckons

The 'true you' underpins all your relationships, whether at work or at home.

We hear a lot about the importance of being 'authentic' when we lead and manage. In fact, Authentic Leadership is a whole industry. The reason is clear. People who stay true to their values, who really know themselves and understand those around them, create loyalty and inspire trust. They make great leaders. Conversely, people who have one face at work and another face at home are quickly found out when the pressure is on. So understand yourself first, and stay true.

Chapter 6

Sometimes the right thing happens for the wrong reason!

It was a truly excellent breakfast that started my journey to Antarctica. The sort of breakfast that you don't want to finish. The coffee was sensational. Fresh, locally roasted beans, ground just right, brewed in a gleamingly clean espresso machine, matched with perfectly heated milk in a smooth-as-silk foam, served in a glass by cute boys in black t-shirts and little beards. The toast, local sourdough from the Italian bakers in Gertrude Street, freshly churned butter and perfect jam with just the right amount of whole fruit. All that passed too quickly, and I didn't want to leave just yet. So I settled in and turned to the unread bits of the newspaper. The car section? Not interesting at the moment—I had a nice government car to get me around. The finance section? Not really. While I have a good handle on business, reading advertisements for the latest derivatives trading platforms (this was 2003 and they were still the 'hot thing'!) didn't appeal to me. With only mild interest I turned to the careers section. It might have an engaging piece on a troubled kid who went back to school and landed a good job, or an inspiring article by a business leader. So why not?

How do you recruit for values?

I wasn't looking for a job. And if anyone from my workplace happened to see me I might have had some explaining to do. At 33, I was the youngest Chief Ranger in Parks Victoria, responsible for dozens of park rangers, many seasonal firefighters and the safe recreation of millions of visitors to the parks each year. I had a great track record in both my hands-on work and my more corporate roles. So I wasn't looking for a job. Rather, I had been grappling with an idea that I had read about recently. It wasn't a new idea by any means, but it was new to me and to my organisation. It went along the following lines:

'You can teach a person skills but you can't teach them values. So recruit for values and then teach the skills.'

The thing that caught my eye that morning was a photograph of penguins—in the careers section! It was captioned 'Men and women of Australia—have you ever wanted to work in Antarctica?' As I looked more closely at the advertisement I noted that the Australian Antarctic Division (AAD) was looking for an Expedition Station Leader. And, according to the advertisement, they were recruiting predominantly for a set of values.

I was intrigued. I ripped out the ad and mused, if I apply, I'll get to see how they do this. I'll experience first-hand the set of interview questions they ask to drill into personal values. I'll note them down when I come out of the interview and take them back to Parks Victoria.

I didn't learn until much later that their interview process was, well, unique. It was not a single one-hour interview or even a series of interviews. The Station Leader recruitment process stretched over five months and included a week-long boot camp in the central highlands of Tasmania. Oops.

The selection process

I did a *bit* of research on Antarctica to make sure I had a little background on Australia's role down there. When I say a *bit*, I really mean it. Yahoo Search and my old encyclopaedias were about it. Then I set to work putting a really good application together.

The initial application called for two very comprehensive character references. I chose people who I worked with: Brett Cheatley, my direct supervisor, and Annie Volkering, who was a layer above me in our hierarchy. Although I hadn't worked directly with Annie for several years, we had a great and open relationship. She had tracked my progress through the organisation and coached and mentored me along the way. She knew me better than anyone I'd worked with over the past 16 years.

I chose to go a step further and also asked Emma Danby to be a referee. Emma reported directly to me. My reasoning at the time was that it would make sense for the selection people to get an idea of both my leadership qualities and my ability to follow leaders. I saw the questions my referees would be asked. They were extensive and it would take real effort to answer them well. Fortunately, once I sent my application off it would be just between them and the Antarctic division.

I vividly remember the day I posted off my application. The night before, I had just sealed the envelope and was writing my name and address on the back when my phone rang. 'Rachael, you're needed on the strike team at the Harrietville fire at 6 am.' Even as Chief Ranger I still loved being 'on the tools' and physically fighting fires. There was something uniquely satisfying about slogging away at a fire with a team who were strangers in the morning but comrades by nightfall. A different management hierarchy was in place for firefighting. I might have been Chief Ranger in my day job but at the fires I was the lowest level general firefighter, one of many on the front line, all equal — and all very dirty! It was rare that my fellow strike team members even knew I was the Chief Ranger. I enjoyed the anonymity and camaraderie while it lasted, because eventually they would find out and everything would change. As our convoy drove to the fires I briefly pulled over and dropped the application into a postbox, thinking, 'Well, here goes nothing'. I spent the next two weeks fighting fires and didn't think about my application until I had returned from the campaign.

It turned out that 140 people applied for two Station Leader roles, one for Davis Station and the other for Mawson Station. Knowing so little about Antarctica or the culture there, I was completely indifferent about which station I might be placed at. I didn't ski, hated cold weather and had been to the snow once — on a Grade 6 school excursion. Besides, I didn't really want the job. I just wanted to learn how they recruited for 'cultural fit' rather than technical skill. After six weeks I still hadn't heard back and the application was becoming a distant memory.

The phone interview

When the Australian Antarctic Division (AAD) called me to schedule the first interview my first thought was, 'Oh yeah…I remember applying for that!' I was happy that I had progressed to the next round. Not ecstatic or overwhelmed or even excited. I knew this was just one very small step towards finding out how to recruit for values! I researched a bit more. Apparently, Australia ran expeditions to four different stations each year: subantarctic Macquarie Island and Casey, and Mawson and Davis stations on the continent. The leaders for the 58th Australian National Antarctic Research Expedition (ANARE) to Macquarie Island and Casey Station were chosen from applicants who had previously held the Station Leader position. Interestingly, the final assessment was simply a tick or a cross against each name — you were either suitable or you weren't. It was black or white. No ambiguity. They were looking for a very specific type of person; it was as simple as that.

I wondered about the form the phone interview would take. Recruiting for values, you really want to see how people operate under pressure. To my way of thinking a telephone interview would not be a good medium for determining this. So I based my preparation on the assumption that they would be looking to 'get a feel' for me. I made sure I could talk clearly and without hesitation about my life and career so far and waited for the phone to ring.

The telephone interview went without a hitch, and surprisingly I found that my background lent itself very well to the kinds of questions being asked. They probed into what I knew about safety, remote management and performance management, and I was able to respond with succinct answers backed up by real stories taken from my work at Parks Victoria.

Shortlisted!

I became slightly more interested when the news came that from the initial list of 140 applicants I had been shortlisted as one of 14 people moving on to the third stage of the process. To this point I had invested less than expected, but I knew that to go right through the recruitment process I would need to invest very heavily in both time and effort. I was at a crossroads. On the plus side, I hadn't yet learned what I wanted to find out — namely, how *do* you recruit for values such as integrity, respect and empathy? To pull out now would be kind of throwing away the effort and the goodwill of my referees. Also, the idea of Antarctica was beginning to grow on me. On the downside, I knew that the next few months were going to be chaotic. My Parks Victoria role was taking nearly all my energy, and now I had to carve out time off work and time at home to research, prepare and take part in the final selection round.

I reminded myself, 'Regret what you did, not what you didn't do', and pushed on with the application.

The AAD is very, very selective when choosing expedition leaders, for a number of excellent reasons. As the expedition's most senior representative of the Australian Commonwealth, the expedition leader is also deputised to act in special investigative and enforcement roles. The screening process would be broad and deep.

The screening process

Firstly, a complete and thorough medical test. I had some experience with medical tests. An important role of Parks Victoria is to provide the professional firefighting force under the auspices of the Department of Sustainability and Environment. At first I was amazed to discover we fought fires without hoses. Our approach was to starve the fire rather than beat it outright. A bushfire needs three things: fuel, heat and oxygen. Most fires that start in national parks are in remote areas that are not easy for fire-trucks to access. Our chief firefighting method was therefore to starve it of fuel by manually clearing the bush in front of the fire—by hand, with a rake-hoe! When I write it like this it sounds like a very silly way to fight a fire. It would be so much easier to stand back with a hose! But given this was almost always next to impossible we raked and hoed until we created a mineral earth break where the fire could not burn.

Most people have been in the bush and know how heavy and thick the undergrowth can get on the forest floor. Well, that is the stuff that professional firefighters work with. Standing in a line, we work for 12 hours straight, in blazing heat, whacking the earth with our hoes and dragging the debris aside to create a 'break' of 3 metres or so. We had to be fit and strong, and I kept my fitness levels high by running 10 kilometres three times a week. By this time I had 10 years of professional firefighting under my belt, including the terrible Alpine bushfires of 2003, and a pretty good fitness regime. I passed both the fitness and medical tests without raising a sweat.

The medical tests for Antarctic service are very standard. They don't screen for every illness ever known, but they do look out for health problems that might worsen in a short period of time. Given that there is just no way to evacuate someone from Antarctica during the depths of winter, it's prudent to select candidates in good general health. With good teeth. Good teeth are important—the station doctor has only two weeks' training at the dental hospital to qualify as the station 'dentist' so it's really not the time or place to ponder root canal surgery.

Then it was time for the security check. I had gone through a security check once before. It was a simple affair: two or three pages of questions and a quick phone interview. I was very surprised to find that not only was this questionnaire much longer and more detailed, but they were also going to dig deep into my past. So deep, in fact, that I worried some minor transgression on my part, such as making a late payment on a car loan, would be uncovered and scuttle my chances.

I had to satisfy the Federal Government's requirements to 'Highly Protected/Confidential' level. For the life of me I couldn't figure out why the bar was set so high. I got on the telephone to the AAD, not to complain, but to understand what it was I might be doing that would require such a security clearance level. On reflection I should have realised that if there was indeed work that required 'secret' clearance they wouldn't tell me about it, but that didn't occur to me at the time.

The answer was actually very simple. In Antarctica the Station Leader is the police officer, prosecutor, defender, deputised coroner, judge and jury. Because of the absolute remoteness and isolation over winter, there is no way to get outside help. Day-to-day communication relies on a satellite phone line and basic email. If someone were to die or, God forbid, be murdered on the expedition, it is the responsibility of the Station Leader to investigate the nature and cause of death and determine what actions, if any, must be taken. The Station Leader therefore must demonstrate outstanding integrity, have a blameless record, and be prudent and above reproach.

I trawled through my bank records and employment history, noted every address I had ever lived at and submitted the application for clearance. The first inkling something could be amiss was when one of my referees sent me a text to say she'd had 'an interesting conversation' with the guy undertaking my security check. Obviously I couldn't let that one slide so I was on the phone in minutes.

After a breathless 'What did he ask you?' and lots of 'Then what did you say?' she told me he had asked about my hobbies, drug and alcohol use, and the types of people I hung out with. He'd queried why, after working for 16 years, I had no assets to show for my income, to which she had replied, 'She travels overseas a lot and has a great quality of life. No, she has no assets, but she also has no debts.'

'And she's single?' he asked.

'Yes', she replied.

'Hmm...' he said. 'I think she sounds perfect for my son who lives in California.'

Seriously, you can't make this stuff up! That was my background and security check.

The psych test was the last selection hoop. And it was hilarious! Yes, I WOULD *prefer a beautifully written poem to a well-crafted handgun!* But in spite of myself I took it seriously. The Minnesota Multiphasic Personality Inventory (MMPI) was (and is) a respected personality test to assess mental health that has been extensively used by Western governments since the 1940s. I hadn't seen it before, but I had heard about it. I knew that 'moulding' your answers to what you thought the assessors wanted to hear would only identify you as a liar. By the time you get through the 567 questions, the system has generated a very clear picture of you and your personality.

One of the final questions of the MMPI test was, 'Lately I feel like I am being tested <y/n>'. I had a chuckle to myself. I was nearing the end of two months of extensive assessment and tests—financial, health, fitness, background—and if I passed this round there was even more to come. Well...yes. I *do* feel like I am being tested! I fought the urge to write, 'Wouldn't you?'

Transparency and honesty

Throughout all the tests and assessments I knew it was critically important to be 100 per cent honest with myself and my assessors. I didn't think I had any psychopathic tendencies, but if I did, I didn't want to find out when I was six months from the nearest professional help. Antarctica is the last place you want to be if you're not the right person for the job. I had to trust that the AAD knew what they were doing, and trust the process. If I didn't fit, great! If I did fit, even better.

I think this ambivalence towards the role worked in my favour. As I have said, I didn't grow up wanting to be an expeditioner. It wasn't a long-term career goal and I hadn't invested a large chunk of my life gearing myself up. It was an opportunity, a great opportunity. But if it wasn't for me, I wanted to know.

As the tests progressed I kept wondering, when will we get to the bit I'm interested in—recruiting for values? So far, I had expended two months of effort; endured multiple tests and probes; and spent countless hours running around collecting background material. When would we get to the part where we dig into the internal motivators, ethics and stuff like that? I didn't realise at the time, but through its rigorous background checking the AAD was already building quite a picture!

What I learned

- *Opportunities come when you least expect them.* So keep your eyes open. Your next million, next promotion or next house could come from your putting two and two together and taking a leap of faith.

- *Persist.* If you have invested in something that has huge potential, follow it through until the end.

Chapter 7

People notice when you try to be someone you're not

The next stage of the recruitment process was the leadership 'boot camp', or Assessment Centre, as it's correctly known, for the final 14 shortlisted applicants.

We received taxi vouchers and flight bookings in the mail along with a letter directing us to be in Hobart in two weeks' time for a week-long assessment to be held in a remote part of Tasmania. We were told what to bring and were given a brief outline of what the week would entail. It all sounded very exciting — James Bond meets *Survivor* — and definitely not what I'd normally be doing in an average week.

Tough competition

The 14 applicants met at the Woolstore Hotel in Hobart before we were ushered onto a minibus for the three-hour trip out to Bronte Park. As we drove I surreptitiously assessed the other applicants and struggled not to feel insecure. Twelve men and just one other woman. They were impressive. I was surrounded by some very, very experienced leaders.

The first activity at boot camp was for each of us to stand up, introduce ourselves and explain why we had applied for the role and why we thought we would be a good fit for it. I remember standing there feeling overwhelmed. Around me were a Commissioner of Police, a National Distribution Manager of Fairfax Media, a CARE aid group leader, someone who had spent two years in Papua New Guinea and a number of others who had already been to Antarctica.

I remember listening to them, thinking, 'Yeah, and I've worked in Ballarat...and Warrnambool'. I was completely intimidated, but at that moment I made the decision to continue to be wholehearted about the week. I thought, even if I don't have what these people have in terms of background and experience, I'm going to use this week as an opportunity. Where else would I get the opportunity to spend a week with a diverse group of some of the most experienced leaders in Australia? I'm sure I'm going to learn something from these guys. So whether I got the job or not, I was determined to treat this week as a gift, enjoy it and learn about myself.

There were a couple of people who were being highly strategic about the week. Initially we were very conscious of the mirror panels in the walls and the presence of observers, the interview panel, seated around the room. One or two people set out to present themselves as 'obvious leaders' simply through dominating the discussion and being assertive. The first scenario we had was to develop a waste management policy. I knew there were people in the group who knew far less than I did about waste management. I had been dipping my toe in and out of waste management (don't picture it in your mind!) for more than 10 years. I knew the environmental protection acts, I knew the technologies in use and the options available. Many of these people hadn't worked in a government organisation and so didn't understand any of the freedom of information or legislative requirements. But they saw the panel of observers behind the group and tried to dominate the conversation. I too was aware of the panel but I tried to approach it as I would any conversation. I sat quietly until the dominators had run down then quietly said, 'Well, I've got 15 years of experience in waste management in a government environment, and while I think some of the ideas presented so far are good and would work, we also need to be thinking about...' and I reeled off several key issues that had been overlooked. The group naturally turned to me and before long I was the de-facto leader of that exercise.

It was the same with risk assessments and the simulated search and rescue, which the Police Commissioner and I led based on our experience of similar scenarios in real life.

At other times I didn't have the expertise to lead. On the third day we set out on a 21-kilometre round-trip hike, including an overnight stay at a designated campsite. We carried our gear in backpacks but also carried a person on a stretcher who was pretending to be injured. I don't know who led us to get lost, but get lost we did. We were supposed to arrive at the campsite at 7 pm but finally struggled in, wet and exhausted, close to midnight. We needed to set up camp and get our food on the stove, knowing we had an early start in the morning. I knew nothing about tents, nothing about choofer stoves — I'd never even seen one before! Straight away a couple of the men started to set up the tents for our overnight bivouac. I said to the person who appeared to be leading, 'I don't know how to run a tarp or light a portable stove, but how can I help?' Collect firewood? Yep, I can do that. In my view, it is really important that leaders act when they have the expertise but listen to others when they don't.

Playing games

On the second night of boot camp we each had to stand up and give an impromptu talk about something we were passionate about. At that stage I had been living in country Victoria for two years, and coming off the back of the fire season campaign my passion became increasing the number of women firefighters. The Victorian fire services were still very male dominated and in my view would benefit from greater diversity, particularly in the senior ranks. I received a great response from my talk. People laughed when they were meant to and ooh'd and ahh'd where I hoped they would. I was pretty happy with my effort, but just before lights-out one of the boot-campers bailed me up.

'I HATED your presentation,' he spat. 'Just hated it. You deliberately chose that topic to try to profile women in male-dominated industries.'

I was taken aback. 'Uh, yeah, that was kind of the point. I believe in it and I'm passionate about it,' I replied.

'Yeah…well I'm on to you. You're a female and you're trying to influence the selection panel and guilt them into selecting you. You're manipulating them.'

Pfft. Whatever. I walked away. We obviously had different approaches to the week! I realised there and then that some participants were really taking a very competitive approach.

Instead of taking my talk at face value this guy was playing a strategic game. The aim of the presentation was simply to see if we had the self-confidence and presence to comfortably make a public address that engaged the audience. He met my apparent attacking manoeuvre with his best counterattack, designed to undermine and belittle my 'strategy'! As the week wore on I would see him do this with others and would come to understand a lot more about him. It was apparent that he desperately wanted the job in order to change his life. He wasn't happy with his work or home life. And he thought the only way to get this job was to pull down his 'competitors'—whatever it took.

My approach was much simpler. Be natural. Be normal. Build relationships, and if you're the right person these people will know it. Where he wanted the job for 'change', I wanted it for 'opportunity'. I had a fantastic life already, and I would have a fantastic life afterwards. Going to Antarctica wasn't going to change that; it would just make one year far richer than it might otherwise have been.

I think one or two others at boot camp may also have been game-playing, and it was interesting to see them revert to 'themselves' over the course of the week. They had no choice. The boot camp puts you under extreme pressure, and it's nonstop. We started formal proceedings at 8 in the morning and didn't stop until 11 pm. There is no privacy. You share a room, you eat together, you work together and by the end of the day you collapse into a deep sleep from the constant physical and mental exertion. There is no connection with the outside world. We could bring our phones but there was no signal out in the bush. There was no way to get a boost from outside or even to check in with people.

As well as being physically demanding, the boot camp tested our writing, negotiating and problem-solving skills. Each of us had to mentor one of the other applicants and also conduct a 'performance appraisal' with another applicant, providing them with direct feedback on how we thought they'd travelled through the week. A panel member watched the entire process, taking copious notes. We were asked to publicly state our position on alcohol on station and were given various safety and diversity scenarios to respond to. We even ate meals with the panel. There was no respite and nowhere to hide.

All of this was very deliberate. The conditions were designed so you couldn't pretend to be something you weren't. We knew we were under constant scrutiny, and under these conditions we had no choice to be anything other than who we were.

In one exercise we took to inflatable rescue boats (IRBs), often also called RIBs or simply Zodiacs. In teams of four we were required to paddle across a lake, but three of the team would carry a handicap: one wouldn't be allowed to speak, one was blindfolded and the other wore highly effective earplugs and could not hear. The team captain had to provide instructions that all three could understand to navigate their boat safely across the lake. Halfway across the leaders were given the instruction to turn their paddles around, hold the 'fat bit' and use the handle as the paddle.

My reaction to the challenge was, 'Sure, whatever. Let's get stuck in and give it a shot.' I was too exhausted to question the rationale and just went along with the directive. Some other people spent a lot of time trying to second-guess what the observers were looking for. One of the boot-campers just 'lost it'. He started shouting at his team, 'NO! Not that way . . . this way! Paddle like this!' After seeing this outburst I quickly realised the challenge was designed to see how we coped with ambiguity and with instructions that were difficult to follow.

Not playing games

One of the big gambles I took during the week was when deciding whether or not to provide a person with unsolicited feedback. We were engaged in an activity that involved setting down logs in front of each other to make a pathway through a 'minefield'. There was no real point to the exercise other than to see how we worked as a team. It was my turn. One of the other applicants was right behind me, looking over my shoulder. He became increasingly exasperated with the time I took to perform this apparently simple task. He finally exploded, 'Jeeesus! Not like that...THIS IS HOW YOU DO IT!', snatched the log from me and did it himself.

My immediate reaction was, no...that's not good. That's not how I expect to be treated. In fact, no one should be treated like that. I'm really not happy. I had an internal debate for a few minutes. Do I let it slide or do I say something, because really I'm competing against these people. If he continues to behave like this it will look bad for him and be one more person out of the selection pool. On the other hand, I must be true to myself and to the principles of leadership that I want to live by. Early and fearless feedback is one of those principles.

I approached my boot-camp mentor (another applicant) with my ethical dilemma and asked what he would do. He leant towards letting it slide. In his view there was no upside in addressing it, only a downside. I still wasn't comfortable with that and after another day I decided to provide the feedback. I waited until we could speak privately and provided my feedback to him. I explained that I didn't like how he went about correcting me and presented an alternative way he could have behaved, like, 'Hey Rach, can I show you a way that might be more helpful...' It didn't go down well. Feedback can be like that. He was cool with me from then on and he never sat next to me, or even near me, for the rest of the boot camp.

I don't know how it came out, but by the next morning everyone in the group had heard about it, including the selection panel. Towards the end of the week we had a formal interview with the panel and they specifically asked me about the incident. It threw me. What was the correct answer to give in this situation? This was a job interview after all. I had no idea. So I told them what I firmly believed: that I felt the applicant had been disrespectful to me so I had a private word with him about it, it was all sorted and it was between us. The panel didn't ask for any further details. They simply told me they only wanted to know if I had done anything about it. I guess I'd passed the self-respect test!

What I learned

- *Be vulnerable.* Understand your weaknesses and don't suppose that just because you're the leader you need to have all the answers. Leaders don't need to know everything—they just need to know where to go to get the information.

- *Step up when it's your turn to shine.* If you have the expertise or knowledge, speak out and step up into leadership, regardless of your position.

- *Sometimes you just have to be brave.* It can take guts to do something that's confronting. Be brave, prepare well and back your judgement. You are probably right, but if you're wrong and you approach it the right way you, and others involved, stand to gain from the experience.

- *Use facts and data.* Facts and data help you deal with the issue at hand and give you the opportunity to take out the emotion.

- *It's okay to bite your tongue.* You don't have to face conflict head-on all the time. Take the time, work out the best approach, and deal with it gracefully and directly with the individual.

Chapter 8

You know people by what they do, not what they say they do

Ithink the role of a leader is first to listen, and listen respectfully, before making a decision. The scenarios we played through, though, were challenging. They were nearly always ambiguous and often called upon our inherent sense of what was more valued—this attribute or that attribute. One challenge was particularly insightful.

The penny drops

We were given a list of values that included things like integrity, loyalty, being innovative and being hard-working. The task was to pick the value that was most important to you and then stand up and, in two minutes, convince the group that 'your' value was the most important. My immediate gut feeling was that if you've held a value for 30 or 40 years, a value that through role models or your own personal experience you most cherish, then I'm not going to be able to change your long-held belief in two minutes. Nor should I. I have no right to change people's values. So when my turn came I simply talked about integrity and why it was the most important of the seven listed values for me. I didn't try to convince. I didn't try to sell.

Others, though, took a completely different tack, two people taking it to the *n*th degree. 'Loyalty! How can you say that integrity is a more important value than loyalty? If people are loyal to each other all else will follow. Without loyalty you can't achieve anything. You're wrong. Completely wrong...' These individuals got really passionate and heated, and at times aggressive. They did everything they could to convince the others they were right and we were wrong.

As I watched I suddenly realised! 'This is how they're testing for respect and integrity. Have the respect to listen and affirm other people's views, but have the integrity to simply stand up and say what you believe without tearing down other people.'

All week I had been waiting for the time they would sit each of us down and ask us those magic questions around integrity and respect that I assumed were part of the selection process. Those elusive questions that prompted me to apply for the job in the first place. Those questions that I planned to take back with me so I would know exactly how to recruit for values. In my naivety I guess I was waiting for the question, 'So ... do you have integrity and what does it look like?'

It dawned on me only late in the week that those questions are irrelevant. At best they can be misleading, at worst they can be dangerous. The only way to really answer the question is to put people in a situation where they have no choice but to act according to their core values. The observers had seen us at our most tired, most frayed, most exasperated. By the end of the week the AAD knew everything they needed to know about our integrity and resilience, how we coped with setbacks and difficult situations, how motivated and energetic, innovative and conciliatory we were, and how we coped with authority, ambiguity and stress.

Interview on a double bed

The gender issue raised its head again, and when we were at our worst. We had just returned from our overnight hike. It was 4 pm, we were dirty, sore and very, very tired. One of the selection panel members met us in the mess hall. 'Right guys, you have 15 minutes to get clean and dressed and then we're going to conduct the formal interview.'

Whaaatt! It takes me 30 minutes just to do my hair! So we all bolted to our accommodation. Our pre-arrival reading pack had informed us that at some point in the week the AAD executive would be meeting us for dinner. I believe it's important to dress for the part so I had brought a nice outfit. I was used to travelling for work, and had packed a simple long, black skirt and blouse that didn't need to be ironed. You know, the ones you can just scrunch up and throw into an overnight case? I figured if we're going to have a formal interview I wanted to present as I would for any job interview — as professional and prepared. I quickly cleaned up, threw my clothes on, pulled back my hair in a ponytail and fronted up to the mess hall. To grumbles and whispers.

I was the only person in business wear. Several of the men were wearing clean jeans and open necked button-up shirts and the rest still looked dishevelled and were wearing outdoor gear. I could see criticism of the way I was dressed in the eyes of several people but stood firm. This is how I want to present, I thought. 'I'm proud to be a woman and I have no qualms about looking like one.' My name was called and as I was ushered out of the mess to the interview room I heard behind me, *sotto voce*, 'There she goes, playing the gender card again'.

Gender card? It mentally threw me as I walked out of the mess. Yes, I like to look feminine and I wanted to look professional that night. I told myself: 'I'm a woman and this is a business meeting. I am dressed the way I would dress in any other similar circumstance. I'm far better off being myself and not trying to be one of the men.' I had learned this early in my career. I had tried all sorts of different things when I first started managing in male-dominated environments. To a large extent, I had been flying blind, feeling my way forward in an effort to define the most appropriate 'style'. I developed a big voice, only ever wore pants, used assertive if not aggressive body language and talked about the footy. But it never felt right, and it failed every time. No, I had decided early on it was far better to just be myself. If I was to be an inspiring leader, people had to believe *me* and believe *in* me. I must be authentic. I could build the skills I was missing, but I would build them around my core self, not someone else's ideal.

The interview itself was surreal! I thought we'd go to an office but apparently there weren't any. I was led to an empty bedroom and shown a seat. Opposite me, three men and a woman sat on the edge of a double bed. It all added to the ambiguity. It was quite odd and I had to stop myself from giggling and blurting out, 'Well, this is a modern take on the casting couch'.

The first question made me laugh inside. 'So Rachael, tell us. Why do you want the job?' I paused, smiled and said, 'You know what? At this particular moment, I'm not really sure. I mean, I don't think I can quite articulate that'. Probably not the answer they were looking for.

The rest of the interview was mostly logistics: If I was successful when could I start? Did I have a preference for a particular station? Did I understand the salary structure?

It was much later in the year that I received feedback from the panel on the interview. They had noted what I was wearing. They were impressed that I presented as myself, and had made some attempt (albeit a small one) to look professional and not tried to look blokey, masculine or tough. They knew how important it is to keep your audience front of mind whenever you communicate, and that includes dressing for the situation and context. They appreciated that if I was to lead, it would be as me, not as an image of what an Antarctica expeditioner *should* be like. They also thought I had shown 'brave leadership' in addressing the issue with Paul and his disrespect, which made me happy!

Leaving boot camp on a high

One of the last things we did on boot camp was to nominate anonymously who, among our fellow boot-campers (excluding ourselves), we believed would make the best Antarctic Expedition Leader. As we were hanging out in the airport, ready to fly home, one of the guys came up to me and said, 'Just so you know, I nominated you'. I felt great and thought that was a lovely thing to say. Unfortunately I couldn't reciprocate! Before I knew it, five others had also approached me and said the same thing. I thought, wow, if this is the consensus among my fellow boot-campers maybe the selection panel will be of the same opinion? Oh no! This is getting serious.

Then it was a matter of, gosh, I better start getting my head around this and tell my family I have applied! Up to this point no one knew I had applied for the job, only my referees. My staff, employer, parents and friends were all in the dark.

I had taken a week's annual leave to attend boot camp so none of my work colleagues would know where I was. I was simply spending a week in Tasmania. Before boot camp I still wasn't sure what the AAD was looking for in a leader. Were they looking for someone who was highly experienced in remote dangerous expeditions, someone who had a taste, appetite and history of adventure, someone well versed in Antarctic science (like the American Station Leaders), or someone like me with more generalist skills and background? So I kept it to myself. I was worried it would be more embarrassing if I told everyone that I was applying and then didn't get the job. I thought there might be a bit of, 'Well, who does she think she is anyway!' So the whole idea of Antarctica was firmly under my hat and I figured I would work something out if and when the time came.

I returned to my little haven overlooking the beach at Anglesea. It had been a tough but rewarding week. I slept all weekend and tried to decompress. I hadn't reflected much during the week, because we had no time, and anyway, I wanted to stay in the moment and not try to second-guess the process. The single biggest thing I realised as I reflected on the week was that I *desperately wanted the job*. It was no longer an intellectual exercise about values. I knew I would be heartbroken to miss the chance to live and work in Antarctica. It wasn't about the penguins or icebergs; it was about the opportunity, and my readiness:

- I believed I could do it.

- I believed it would be fun.

- I believed I had the leadership and management skills needed.

- I knew it would be an amazing leadership crucible.

- I knew I could be successful.

In a week I had moved from ambivalence to extremely high expectations!

Breaking the news

Back at work I tried to temper my enthusiasm and hopes. I thought I was in with a shot at the role, but I knew there were other well-equipped leaders in the mix.

But I had to tell Shaz, Loz and the family. As a family we had grown very settled in our ways. Ben had finished his footy career with Carlton and was now happily married to his beautiful Samone and had a great teaching job. Jane was jet-setting around as a flight attendant with Qantas and had a gorgeous boyfriend, Tim. Mum and Dad were working hard and lived to see more of their kids. The pressure was on for grandchildren. The prospect of spending so much time away in what was possibly the twilight of my child-bearing years troubled me. And it would greatly trouble Shaz. To walk away from the chance of finding a partner and potentially becoming a mum kept me awake at night. I really wanted to lead the expedition but I would be almost 37 years old by the time I returned, which was cutting it fine to meet the right fella. It felt like an 'either/or' choice: either I work in Antarctica for a year, or I turn down the offer, stay home and keep dating. It felt like a head versus heart decision.

Then the words I'd lived my life by crashed through my thinking: 'I'd rather regret what I did than regret what I didn't do'. I had to have faith in myself. I had to believe I could take up this amazing opportunity *and* then return home and meet the man of my dreams and eventually raise a family. Maybe I could do both. It was a crucible moment.

I broke the news as gently as I could. Ben and Jane were great and Shaz put on a brave face. But I knew she was very, very worried, and I think may even have secretly hoped at that stage that I wouldn't get the role.

I requested a meeting with my CEO, Mark Stone, who was incredibly supportive. He saw this would be a fantastic way for me to fast-track my leadership development and return ready to take on an executive role at Parks Victoria. I agreed. He suggested I keep a journal. Not like a 'dear diary' where I simply recounted the activities of the day, but more a place to reflect on my interactions and decisions, and think deeply about issues that confronted me. Keeping a journal wasn't new to me. One of our leadership courses at Parks Victoria had recommended it and I had made a couple of half-hearted attempts. Mark reminded me that if I got the role I would be tested beyond what I thought possible. I would go to bed with my head spinning and wake up still without the answer. Mark's advice was that if I got into the habit of reflection, and journaling every day, I would learn faster, make better decisions and importantly learn more about myself.

I took Mark's advice on board, went out and bought a day-to-a-page diary to keep as a journal. My first entry illustrates I had a lot to learn about the art!

Tuesday 29th June 2004

Beautiful, enchanting, intriguing, temperamental...

But enough about me...how great is Antarctica!

The more I learn about it, the more I respect it—Antarctica is one of a kind!

I'm ashamed to admit that I still knew next to nothing about Antarctica. I knew the obvious things like where it was, that it was cold and that there were no polar bears down there. But I was now passionate about learning all I could. I found out about Amazon from a friend, went onto the World Wide Web (forgive me, it was still new to me!) and bought every Antarctica book in the store.

The Anglesea winter nights were cold, the weekends wet and I spent each of them devouring history, background information, novels and accounts of this amazing continent. I was staggered by the bravery and tenacity of pioneers like Shackleton and Mawson and reading their stories inspired me even more.

What I learned

- *You can't 'ask questions for values'.* There is no question you can ask that will tell you what someone's values are. At best, you can present a scenario and ask them how they would approach it. But be conscious that in an interview people are *performing*, and it's easy to keep it up for an hour or so. So set a probation period and make sure you get to see them work under pressure.

- *How you present yourself counts.* We are 'selling' all the time. You wouldn't buy a car from a shabby salesman or a house from an agent who looks unsuccessful. Dress and present yourself according to the perceptions of those you are trying to influence. This is not being 'unauthentic', it's simply presenting the best possible version of yourself, targeted to the situation.

- *Be gentle.* Sometimes we just have to break bad news to people. Stop, think about the impact on them and their families and speak to them from your heart. Don't make it sound better than it is, but acknowledge their fears and what they have at stake.

Chapter 9

First prepare yourself, then leave your comfort zone

L ate one Friday afternoon, about four weeks after boot camp, I noticed a missed call on my phone, but no message. It was a Hobart number, one I didn't recognise. I'd already knocked off for the week and had poured a glass of sauvignon blanc to celebrate the beginning of the weekend. Would I return the call or wouldn't I? I bit the bullet and called the number, even though by now it was close to 5.30 pm.

The appointment
'Hello, Rebecca speaking.' I didn't know a Rebecca and was tempted to hang up, but I said, 'It's Rachael Robertson. I have a missed call from you'.

'Wonderful! I'm the new recruitment officer at the AAD. I was going to call you back on Monday but I'll tell you right now . . .' She paused. For too long. There could only be *one* reason the recruitment officer was calling me . . . I held my breath.

'You've got the job! You're headed to Davis Station as Expedition Leader for 2005!'

I let out a whoop! Very uncharacteristic of me! Rebecca picked up on my excitement and became animated. 'We're very excited to offer you the role. You'll be only the second female leader at Davis Station in its 50-year history.'

We chatted some more about the mechanics of what would happen next and I hung up, elated. I kept the news to myself all weekend and started to make a list of the things I would need to do, think about, plan and prepare for. My mind was everywhere. I had gone camping once and seen snow once—where to start? My list was all over the shop. Peanut butter came after buying birthday cards. Buying a waterproof jacket came after handing in my resignation. I went to work on Monday excited, overwhelmed and nervous.

I received a fax confirming my appointment and then the Operations Manager, Richard Mulligan, called. He told me they were going to make the official announcement in three weeks. He also said I'd need to prepare myself and study up a bit on the detail of station life because they would soon send out a press release and I might be asked for an interview. He asked me how I was with handling the media.

'No problems', I replied. 'I've had some media training at Parks Victoria and last year I was the media spokesperson for the fire season.'

Richard wasn't expecting I would have to do much but suggested it might be smart to block out the day, just in case.

I arranged an annual leave day for myself, went home and printed out some of the hundreds of pages of information and instructions that had been emailed out that day. I read, and read, and read.

I found out Diana Patterson was the first female expedition leader to Davis Station nearly 20 years ago. By some fluke she lived not 10 houses away and we arranged a meeting.

Thursday 8th July

Dinner with Diana Patterson.

Diana gave me some great advice. The Yearbooks, 'Davis Experience' brochures and photo collages are all excellent ideas for things to do down there. I really like Diana, she is quite easy to talk to and very honest. I think she was a bit reserved with me to start with but soon relaxed and even gave me a big hug goodbye.

Very special night.

PS I saw pictures of my office and my bed!!

Media frenzy

I went to bed early the day before the big announcement. I didn't know what was in store but wanted to be prepared. But I wasn't prepared for the phone to ring at 5.30 am! It was the radio station 3RRR and I had been fast asleep. I came good quickly and gave it my best shot—luckily they were taping it and would be able to edit out my yawns. At 5.45 am I was deciding if I could sneak back into my warm bed for another half an hour when the phone rang again. This time it was Radio 3CR, another community radio station. These volunteers worked hard!

I gave up on the idea of going back to bed and started to make coffee. The producer of *Good Morning Australia* was on the phone next and we arranged for me to visit the Channel 10 studios the next day for a TV interview with Bert Newton. Wow! Bert Newton! Me on the TV—how funny!

Then it was the *Cobden Times* and AAP, and it wasn't even 7 am yet! In the middle of this noise and excitement I was trying to figure out what was happening. I had never encountered media coverage of a new expedition leader before. The AAD sends down four Station Leaders each year without a blip on the media radar. But I was certainly on their radar, with four interviews already done and a TV slot planned . . . all before breakfast!

The phone didn't stop ringing all day. The Warrnambool *Standard* was excited that their local Chief Ranger was going to Antarctica. Mike Carlton put me live to air on Sydney's 2UE at 7.45 am, 'Ross and Stevo' on 3AW at 8.15 am. Kathy Bedford from the ABC was next. I gave this interview from the car on the way to Channel Nine's helipad in Southbank to shoot a piece for the evening news with Peter Hitchener. Channel Nine flew me by helicopter from Melbourne down to Port Campbell, about an hour's flight away. It was my first time in a helicopter and I was simply beside myself with excitement. They ended up running a 'hero' piece that screened just before the weather segment. I was delighted with the story but even more thrilled when Peter Hitchener referred to me as a 'young Australian'. At 35 years of age I'll take that! Young indeed.

The print news picked up the story in earnest later in the day and I had some long and interesting interviews with journalists from *The Age*, the *Herald Sun* and several local papers.

Towards the end of the day I was exhausted, but Perth wasn't! They called at 7.45 pm for an afternoon drive-time slot with the ABC's Ted Bull. By the day's end I had conducted 38 interviews.

I pulled out my journal and started to write.

Monday 12th July

Today is the day it all became real. The media release went out and the media interest has just blown me away. I can't believe how fascinated people are and the fact Channel Nine did a 'hero' piece on me was amazing.

I'm feeling very excited but also very keen to get down to Tassie to start preparing. I probably have about three more days of positive energy left in me, so the timing is perfect. The 'farewell festival' at Parks has prepared me well for the media frenzy as people ask me the same questions—'how many people?', 'how long?', 'do you have email?' and so on.

I think my family is a bit stunned by it all too. People at their work have heard me on radio or seen me on TV and have commented. It's really nice to have so much support and the phone calls from Richard, Brett and Annie were really special. They've been a big part of my professional life for so long that to make them feel 'proud of me' means a lot.

Fui and Ed rang today—blasts from the past! I haven't seen Fui since Grade 6 and last time I spoke to Ed was probably our university graduation.

I feel very proud and privileged to be given this job and I'm so stoked that people are sharing it with me. It has been a truly wonderful day.

The attention continued for the next three days. My previous media experience was helpful but dealing with the media at this level was a new, exciting and exhausting experience. I attempted to give every interview the same level of passion and enthusiasm, but after 20 interviews I was starting to flag. I reflected on the nature of the interviews in my journal.

Thursday 15th July

Only three more to go thankfully. They have ranged from the friendly and intelligent (Virginia Trioli) to the straight out hilarious—Lauren from the *Cobden Times* asked, 'So I know you probably have to catch your own fish and stuff but what else do you eat?' The hardest one was the 3AW breakfast show. They were very intelligent but comic, which meant they could easily charm and disarm if they wanted to. They tried to engage me in discussions about sex—for example, 'Do they…you know what…down there?' Not my style to talk about that! I tried to steer the conversation on to community life in general. They also wanted to discuss our so-called exorbitant salaries, which I laughed off and explained we had internet shopping so we would spend money. The *Age* interview was interesting. I spoke to Catherine for 40 minutes and it was the 'blokiness' angle she settled for. Perth was easy and I really enjoyed 3RRR—it was a very different interview, very intelligent people asking insightful questions.

Overall it has blown me away. I think the reason it's been picked up so much is that I'm pretty normal, and this unattainable experience is actually within the reach of normal Aussies. I'm proud I can do that.

Leaving Parks Victoria

I knew that two weeks after the announcement I would say goodbye to Victoria and hello to Tasmania for three months of training. The six weeks between finding out I was successful and leaving were spent tidying up all of my affairs. In my brand-new will I left the little I owned to my sister Jane, and gleefully bequeathed her my entire CD collection, knowing how much she hates my taste in music. (The fact is, I have no taste in music. I listen to '80s songs on high rotation and that's it.) I eased out of the Chief Ranger role and handed over to my successor. I think I spent about two weeks travelling the state at the taxpayer's expense primarily to say goodbye to my friends and coworkers! The last day of work wasn't really work—my mind was elsewhere, far to the south.

Friday 16th July

Leaving PV last night wasn't as sad as I thought it might be. Probably because I had to drive home straight away for 6.40 pm and 7.40 pm media interviews. I didn't have time to be sad. I chose to invite only a few, special people so I could say thanks. I didn't want a production—just my true friends. I thanked them all but singled out John Goodman, Annie Volkering and Brett Cheatley. They have been a big part of my life and supported me for so long that I wanted to say thanks. I was presented with UGG boots (you can take the girl out of Dandenong...) and Brett made a lovely speech about how I had turned around the West Coast. It was short and sweet—just how I wanted it.

The response to my appointment has been overwhelming. I really expected many people to feel indifferent, even jealous maybe, for some reason. The PV crew have really embraced the idea. There was even a 'PV All' email sent out the day I appeared in the media. Following the notice about me was a note about payroll group certificates being sent out—so I managed to top 'money' as the most newsworthy item!

Len efficiently swung by at 6 pm to make sure I didn't leave the premises without handing over my building pass. That little thing wrenched me in the guts. This was it! Goodbye PV. It's been a blast!

The first crisis of confidence

I read and re-read all the AAD materials and all the books about Antarctica. The more I learned the more I realised I didn't know. My life and career so far had led me to know something about everything but to be an expert on nothing. It was obvious from my research that a successful expedition would require an expert leader—nothing less would suffice. I felt I needed a role model, someone I knew well, so I would be able to ask the question in my mind, 'What would X do?' I bought a suite of biographies on famous leaders, pored through *Harvard Business Review* summaries and started to build a picture of the 'ideal leader' in my mind.

I also started to feel a bit like I was going to Antarctica under false pretences. I wasn't that fascinated by climate science, I wasn't passionate about adventure or penguins...I was an opportunist!

Monday 19th July

Lifelong dream...not!

I'm feeling a bit stressed about the interview with Tracey Strong. She is an ABC producer and independent writer. She wants to do a profile piece on me, which is a bit frightening. When I think of other women who have achieved things they have all had long-held dreams—for example, Bridgette Muir knew at the age of six that she wanted to climb mountains, and most celebrities and high-profile people have been practising their art since a young age. Ditto sportspeople. I am such an 'accidental achiever' I'm worried I will disappoint. I have never had a life plan, a vision, clarity of purpose. I get through life taking opportunities as they arise. I suppose the positive thing is that I may inspire other people whose life hasn't worked out the way they planned. They might be able to look at me and see it's never too late to try something new. If something happens that you didn't plan for, like a marriage breakup or losing your job, then take it as an opportunity to have a go at something new!! You never know where you'll end up. I certainly never planned to live in Antarctica.

Note to self: Being bold and courageous feeds off itself. Once you do something bold it empowers you to try something even bolder next time.

I left my house in Anglesea and I was headed to Antarctica, but first was three months of training.

What I learned

- *Reach out.* Help can often come from the most unlikely sources. Find people you can learn from. Don't be afraid or timid. Make the phone call, connect with them on LinkedIn, shoot off an email and follow it up. Most people are more than happy to tell you about their successes and challenges or warn you about pitfalls!

- *Everyone has an angle.* When you do something interesting or different, people will react differently depending on their own experience and possibly their agenda. Go with the flow. Be true to yourself but 'tailor' your story or experience in a way that helps the other person get the most out of the interaction. You will both be happier.

- *Be bold!* Very few decisions we make in life are irreversible so 'have a go'. Work overseas, move interstate, start up your own business, try online dating—whatever it is, just take the opportunity. If you don't like the outcome, make another decision.

Part III

Preparing to leave

> *The biggest challenge for leaders isn't crafting a beautiful strategy or compelling vision; it's changing the way people think and how they behave — culture.*

This is why so many 'culture change' efforts fail. It's really hard to design and even harder to execute, and it's harder still to make it stick. There is lots of guidance available for leading attitude and behaviour change, but I reckon the critical points are: (a) people must own the change from the beginning and understand 'why'; (b) you need a team around you who believe it as much as you do; (c) get rid of 'friction', such as outdated processes, as they'll just hold the change back; and (d) listen to your people and understand the change from their perspective.

Chapter 10

Seeing what's wrong is easy—the hard part is the fix

The AAD is based in a beautiful little suburb of Hobart called Kingston. It's far enough out of town to have the luxury of being able to spread itself out, but it's close to the docks and waterside. The AAD facility would be my new 'office' for the next three months. I would commute daily on a minibus from our serviced apartments in Hobart. I was looking forward to the prospect of driving along the beautiful Derwent River, watching the yachts and keeping an eye out for the icebreaker that would eventually take us on our adventure.

Expedition leader school

The night before the first day of training we all arrived at our apartments and were milling about in the outdoor barbecue area. Not everyone was required for the full three months and the only people so far in Hobart were the other Station Leaders and their deputies.

It was an eye-opening dinner. Here was I, a girl from Dandenong, sitting down to a meal with seasoned Antarctic leaders. We were joined by Ross, who was to be one of my Deputy Station Leaders over summer. He had returned from Antarctica earlier this year so I felt comfortable that my deputy would be well versed in the Antarctic ways.

I had to share my suite with another woman, Eve, the doctor headed to Casey Station. I hadn't shared a home for over 10 years, but it wasn't the last time I would feel a bit awkward in those hectic few months.

First night in Hobart!

Am staying at Quest Trinity House and sharing with Eve, the doctor for Casey Station. Had a good dinner with Jeremy, Graham, Ross, Graeme and Micky. Feeling pretty good, although STUNNED to hear they haven't had another woman leader at Davis Station since Diana Patterson back in the '80s. Makes me wonder why . . .

I think Ross will be a real asset as my deputy. He has some good strong views on the role of both the Station Leader and the Deputy Station Leader. I think he will let me know what the troops are thinking and feeling.

I think I will learn more from Jeremy than anyone else, though. If people are asking to be on his station then I think that's a good sign. I like him.

Time for my first sleep on this big adventure. Tomorrow it's our first day at the division and I can't wait to meet everyone and settle in. Let the games begin!

I was highly impressed by the AAD on my first day. I had a laptop that was configured and worked properly, I had an office with my name on it, and even my phone extension was already set up. The key people responsible for our training met the bus at the front door and we spent the morning being inducted into the division.

For the first week or so it was just the expedition leaders and doctors at the training sessions. We were taught specific things relevant only to Station Leaders, such as our role as coroner and our legal obligations under the Crimes Act! We were also told, in no uncertain terms, that the *sole* purpose of Australia's funding and running these expeditions was to further our scientific endeavours.

Monday 2nd August

Wow!! Today we started the briefings in earnest and I have to get my head around some amazing things. I was quite comfortable with the legal stuff. The powers of arrest, search and seizure, cautions and rules of evidence are all things I'm familiar with as a park ranger. But the space and atmospheric science is a whole new ball game. It's unbelievably complicated—to me anyway. But I'm quite interested in learning more about it. I will make a great 'phone a friend' on *Who Wants to be a Millionaire* when this is all over. Although I DID impress the scientists with my knowledge of BODMAS!! And these scientists aren't easy to impress.

Yes, I'm confident I'll enjoy learning about the sciences. I need to know enough about the project, and about the instruments, to be able to manage issues. Such as...how to deal with light interference coming from the SMQ (sleeping and medical quarters) and LQ (living quarters).

I'm not stressed about not knowing the intricate details about each one—my job is to get the best out of the people, not second-guess their work.

I'm learning a lot about climate change science, particularly the work we do with ice cores. Antarctica is an important place to study climate for three reasons:

1 Because the snow and ice never melt in some places, Antarctica contains a very long term and accurate record of atmospheric makeup and conditions going back thousands of years.

2 Antarctica is a predictor of broader changes in the climate and weather.

3 Weather patterns in Antarctica determine the movement and flow of oceans and currents in the Southern Ocean. This has a profound effect on large-scale global weather patterns.

(continued)

Monday 2nd August (cont'd)

Geologists study meteorites down there too. I racked my brain wondering why Antarctica attracted more meteorites than other places—was it the magnetic South Pole pulling them in? Was it the size of Antarctica and the fact it was an easy target? Was it the freezing temperatures that somehow left the meteorites in an unbroken state?

Nope, it's none of the above. It's because snow is white and meteorites are black. So they are easy to see. Truly.

Who'd have known!

How Antarctic expeditions work

Nearly all the science takes place outdoors and there is only a three-month window when that is possible: summer.

We were to arrive at the beginning of summer and immediately commence our scientific work. The station would be full to overflowing, and managing the demand for resources such as helicopters, planes, quad bikes and lab space was going to be a challenge. Summer would also be the time for any major infrastructure work that may be needed, such as putting up new buildings and installing new scientific or communications gear such as antennas.

At the end of summer, the ship would return with new supplies and take the 90 or so 'summerers' back to Australia before the ocean froze around the station. Once the ship disappeared over the horizon, that was it. No way in. No way out.

With the exception of two scientists and two Bureau of Meteorology staff, the 18 who stayed behind simply did so to 'keep the lights on' until next summer. The 'winterers', as they are known, are mostly not scientists but ordinary people with simpler, everyday skills: diesel mechanics to maintain the fresh water production system; carpenters to refurbish worn-out equipment and furniture; plumbers to ensure that, well, everything flushed.

In addition to the trades people, the winterers would include a doctor, a chef and someone to lead, support and manage the team. Me.

It appeared to be quite a strange existence. The picture of summer the AAD built in my mind was one of mayhem, furious activity and the huge challenge of fitting everything into these three short months. The picture of winter was of nine long months of nothing much at all. It occurred to me that the seasons would have opposing challenges: managing frenetic activity in summer and managing boredom in winter. I would need to delve into and develop my kitbag of ideas and techniques to lead effectively through both seasons.

Meeting my fellow expeditioners

My fellow winterers started to arrive and by week four I had met all 17. I was happy to finally meet the people I was going to live with for the next year. People find it amazing that as expedition leader I had absolutely no input in the selection of my expedition team, but upon meeting them I felt they were a great bunch. They were as interesting as you would expect from such diverse professions. I liked my new team and we quickly started to bond.

Wednesday 4th August

Met my first two expeditioners today. I'm still getting used to the 'power' of the Station Leader position. EVERYTHING must come through the Station Leader — just like the Chief Ranger — but here it appears that everything actually does!! Although, that may change...

Some 99 per cent of our training concerned the mechanics of running the station and living in Antarctica. Sessions were organised for quad-bike lessons, first aid, crane operation and the like. Looking through my training schedule one afternoon I was surprised to see that Station Leaders were not given any Antarctic-specific leadership or management training. I thought that surely such a harsh and uncompromising environment would create unique management scenarios that aren't found in the average workplace. Obviously the AAD didn't agree. Towards the end of my time in Antarctica I would reflect on the leadership and management challenges and agree. They are no different in principle, but they are vastly different in application!

Not 'one of the boys'

One area of leadership, however, did receive reasonably constant attention: the behaviour of the leader him- or herself. Time and time again when the Station Leaders were gathered, someone from the AAD would exhort us to 'act like leaders'. What did this mean? What was he saying? I reflected on this one night.

Thursday 5th August

The unique nature of managing in this environment is starting to sink in. The Executive is very conscious of a Station Leader becoming 'one of the boys' rather than maintaining distance as a leader. I can understand how this would happen and how it could be an 'easier' way to operate.

But as Richard pointed out — the word quickly gets out. Station Leaders become a light touch and then find it very difficult to manage performance and get the most out of their people.

If I was to act as 'one of the blokes' and there was someone on station who had it in for me they could easily make sure head office found out. I think I will need to be very conscious of how much I mingle with and befriend my people. Or is Richard just trying to scare us into action?? I don't think so. There must be some history we're not being told.

Random Q: Why does the AAD need to put a letter F next to all the women's names??? Seriously, if they can't work out Sara, Kirsten and Rachael are females then I'm in more trouble than I thought.

We were deep into training now with an unbelievably long list of complex things to remember. We learned about the recent history of Antarctica since man started to suspect there was a continent at the South Pole. We learned about the Antarctic Treaty, which helps protect the continent from exploitation or damage. Each day was full of interesting lectures and presentations, and we had the opportunity to quiz our teachers along the way.

When a culture is broken

A couple of weeks into training I started to suspect there were some significant issues with the culture of the AAD and its expeditions. A number of clear 'us and them' distinctions emerged. One was between the AAD and the expeditioners on station. I likened it to what we sometimes saw in Parks Victoria—the rangers are on the tools, they do the work, they're important. But head office made the decisions and had the money and decision-making power. I've seen it in organisations where the 'scientists' fight the 'administrators'. It appeared to be happening here.

Friday 6th August

Another interesting day getting my head around the dominant culture of the AAD. I really need a better understanding of the corporate strategy. In the past Station Leaders have been seen very much as just operations, with little to no involvement with the various branches of the division, and scant knowledge of the inner workings of the AAD. This has built an 'us and them' culture.

I want to build a culture of 'us being a critical part of the division' rather simply being an isolated outpost. To do this I'm going to need far better understanding and insight into what it is we (the division) do.

I think this is going to be tougher than it sounds. I will need to show my desire to exercise and improve my corporate knowledge but not at the expense of learning the critical operations skills that will be crucial to the smooth running of the station and the safety of my teams.

(continued)

Friday 6th August (cont'd)

The need for cultural change seems obvious to me and there are some simple ways to achieve it. Things like fixing the clocks in the operations room, for example. The clocks are a great idea—everyone in ops sees the local time at each station. But none of them has the right time, and two of them don't even work! This sends a really bad message IMO.

P.S. Mel told me a great story last night about the Field Training Officers assessment centre. They weren't allowed outside for two days and had to eat standing up!

Another cultural rift was forming between the scientists and the rest—these were the people I was taking to Antarctica.

Saturday 7th August

More us and them—this time on station.

The scientists have been great with the briefings. I can see them really trying hard to make their projects understandable for us laypeople. However, I'm getting a real sense that there is a big cultural gap between the scientists and those who run the station. We keep being told that we are only in Antarctica for the science and therefore science is the priority. I believe and agree with this. But it also seems to have created a distinction between science and operations. Maybe aloofness. I can't afford to have this on my expedition. We must all work side by side and respect the important role each of us fills.

Questions of culture were beginning to dominate my thoughts in these early days of training. It was apparent to me that the expedition team must consider itself part of the AAD, a remote but integrated piece of the larger puzzle. The days of glory, fame and life-risking expeditions were over. Expeditioners were no longer explorers charting the unmapped continent at great danger to life and limb. As much as we were going to an extreme environment, I was becoming strong in my opinion that this was just another workplace and we should operate as such.

Monday 9th August

I'm a bit annoyed that some of the scientists have been put up in a separate hotel several kilometres away and they're not going to make it to our first expedition meeting. I'll give them the benefit of the doubt for now, but it's a potential sign of cultural segregation. This may turn into the first test of Station Leader clout.

At dinner one night I raised my concerns around culture with my fellow Station Leaders. I explained my philosophy of an Antarctic station being similar to a mine site or a branch office in a far-flung location. I was met with stony silence and a few grunts; my dinner partners were unwilling to talk 'culture'. After dinner one of the Station Leaders bailed me up in the lift.

'The culture's not broken. I've been down twice, once as Station Leader, and it's just fine. We need to be separate, boys will be boys and you can't stop that.'

'Well that might have been true 50 years ago,' I replied, 'but now you *must* comply with EEO, OH&S and all the other legislative requirements for a workplace.'

'Says who? What happens on station stays on station.'

I was nonplussed by this braggadocio and swagger. But it made me even more determined to run a professional, respectful and successful expedition. I would do it *my way*, whether or not the other Station Leaders agreed. I believed strongly that a 'professional workplace' should be the new model for Antarctic life. I also wondered why he brought up 'boys will be boys'. This wasn't an end-of-year footy trip. If my expeditioners thought they were in for a year of drinking, carousing and taking it easy, they were going to get a rude shock!

Mutual respect—the foundation of our desired culture

I started to envision the culture for my expedition team and gave it a name—'OneDavis—OneAAD'. I wanted my expeditioners to feel and act as part of the broader division. I wanted us to be tuned in to the head office requirements for communication, news and updates, completion of tasks and, importantly, a safe and harmonious workplace. I also wanted my expeditioners to operate as one team. No more scientists versus tradies. No more most important to least important.

To succeed over summer and survive over winter, we would all need to have the utmost respect for each other and operate as a cohesive unit. To do this we would all need to know each other's business—how each individual contributed and what made them special. I was fairly blunt about it. I didn't expect them all to love each other; that's impractical. You can't take 18 strangers from all backgrounds and walks of life, throw them together in total darkness, around-the-clock, and expect they'll all love each other. It's Antarctica, not a John Lennon song. But I did expect we would all respect one another. We would respect personal space, time, experiences, opinions, skills...everything.

I facilitated three 'culture change' workshops with my expedition. The first was to agree on the set of values that our expedition would count the most important and would live by. We used the second and third workshops to unpack the values and explore what they looked like in practice, using scenarios that were likely to occur in Antarctica. I made sure that each scenario contained a real tension between the values. It was important that the values weren't just a laminated wish list on the kitchen wall—my people needed to understand the trade-offs required. In one of the scenarios we described a situation where the person had to choose between being trustworthy and loyal to a fellow expeditioner and raising a safety issue with the Station Leader. It was a heated workshop! As much as you can't wave a magic wand and change people's values, you *can* work on behaviours and create a set of norms, of rights and wrongs. I didn't win 100 per cent agreement on all of the scenarios, but it was useful for everyone to see the challenges of the culture we wanted graphically played out in front of them.

What I learned

- *Positive change comes from the ground up.* A great culture takes time, commitment, energy, effort and constant vigilance. Leaders must model the behaviour they want all day, every day. However, it's the people who will make the change, so there must be input and involvement from them, not just a top-down directive. Staff must own the norms and behaviours, and for this to work they need to be involved in developing and setting expectations.

Chapter 11

Understand the game, and play your hand carefully

Ideoded to ensure that *all* expeditioners would have ready access
to information about the science program. In previous expeditions,
the scientists were expected to run their own programs in isolation.
But this, I believe, was a mistake. Scientists needed the support of
the tradies and engineers, and if the matter was urgent, as would
sometimes happen, the person would need to drop what they were
doing to help the scientist out.

Adding to the complexity was the issue of budgets. Where the science
was paid for out of the individual science program budget, labour
and materials for the engineers and trades would come from the
Engineering budget. When faced with the question, 'Do we continue
to do the "programmed" work, or do we drop everything to help out
this scientist?', my view was that we drop the program work to help the
scientist, because we were here for the science. A lack of knowledge,
and pressure from the engineering program manager back in Hobart,
could potentially derail this.

Cooperation through shared understanding

To help alleviate the problem, I decided that every individual should
know and understand all of the science program . . . a big ask!

To put out a communiqué that plumbed the scientific depths of each
program would have been an exercise in futility. The concepts behind

the science projects were complex, the language often unfathomable. So I asked each scientist to come up with two or three sentences explaining their science project. In plain English. In a form that an electrician or plumber or even a Station Leader might read and understand, so they would willingly drop what they were doing to lend a hand.

Now, these scientists, all card-carrying PhDs, were highly expert. Many of them had been working in an incredibly specialised field for decades and knew an enormous amount about their field of study. I was asking them to explain their work in a couple of sentences to people whose formal schooling may have finished in Year 10, who may have had no exposure to scientific concepts in their lives.

They couldn't do it. Of the 40 or so scientists who were coming to Davis, only two were able to summarise their projects in this way. There was a lot of pushback. *Why* was I pressuring them to 'dumb down' their highly complex research? It was incredibly difficult for them, and me, to find the right balance between simplifying their research hypothesis so it was clear and understandable, and not dumbing it down so much that it actually became incorrect or meaningless. They were all justifiably proud of their work and didn't want it oversimplified — totally understandable.

Monday 30th August

Today I met with the Program Leader of Biology, and he was totally inspiring!

I could have talked to him all day, and as he explained the climate change data I really felt like I understood it. He also encouraged me to continue with the changes I'm trying to make, like creating plain English versions of the science work so that everyone can understand them.

Still only two summaries. Forty-seven to go. (I think!)

Sharing leadership around

As more and more expeditioners started to arrive at training I quickly found my days consumed by daily interactions with my new staff. Unlike the other stations, almost all of my expeditioners were first-timers to Antarctica. They were unsure of what to do next, how to prepare, and they required a lot of guidance and support. Many of these early interactions were extremely fruitful and important. I relished the opportunity to get to know each and every one of them at a personal level. However, many such interactions were highly transactional and mundane, and served little purpose other than to inform people about what was coming up next. As the rate of these interactions accelerated I felt myself sliding into 'management' mode. I was doing less leading and much more managing than I wanted.

I was concerned I would become the 'go-to' person for every request regardless of whether it was important and whether I was the best person to ask. If this was allowed to continue unchecked I would spend all my time managing the little things and lose the opportunity to keep my head above the daily grind and focus on the big, important things I would need to do to lead the expedition successfully.

I quizzed the other Station Leaders about how they handled this situation and the predominant response was just to stick with it. 'This is how it is. They need to know all this stuff and they'll be easier once they understand more. If it all gets too much I just lock my door', was one response. Again, I wasn't satisfied with this. I didn't want to spend the next three months and then a year in Antarctica being the font of all knowledge on station, but equally I didn't want to run from my staff.

I began to toy with the idea of creating a small leadership team. I hadn't heard of any expeditions sharing the management beyond an appointed Deputy Station Leader, so again I was headed into uncharted territory. How positively Antarctic of me!

Wednesday 18th August

Finally had a day to start organising some things for my team. Sent out the first newsletter and arranged the first meeting.

I'm still trying to work out the roles and responsibilities of a station leadership team. This has never been formally done before so there is no guidebook or framework to follow. I've created leadership teams before so I know what I'm doing, but I have to make sure I get the right balance of leadership and management responsibilities.

The AAD supported the move to use a wider group to guide decisions. Unsurprisingly, the concept was discounted by some of the other station leaders. Traditionally it was seen as very much a command and control leadership role. 'I tell you what to do and you do it.' I was told quite emphatically that it wouldn't work, it couldn't work and I would erode my position as leader by surrounding myself with a team. I thought, obviously this new kid on the block has very different ideas about how a station should operate!

Friday 20th August

I met with Richard and he supports my ideas for wider involvement in decision making using an on-station leadership team. But he also kept mentioning the importance of maintaining Antarctic traditions like celebrating midwinter's with a swim and so on. Innovation meets tradition.

It's going to require a fine balance between making changes to operate more professionally at the stations and keeping up the traditions. Some of the traditions no longer pass muster with today's society, mixed gender and the like (for example, compulsory shaving of heads on the way south—why? who knows).

Richard brought up the issue of Station Leaders not being 'one of the boys' again. I don't think he's specifically targeting me. One of the other Station Leaders, who is returning for a second season, told me 'the secret is to try not to ever say no...'. In my mind this isn't good leadership. So I can see why Richard is banging on about it.

At this stage I am determined to manage with integrity and stay true to my own leadership style. I realise this will be bloody hard at times and no doubt there will be tears. I expect there will be many times when I will want to throw my hands in the air and say 'sure, do it your way'. But these are the times I'll need to stay strong and remember that I want to be a certain type of Station Leader.

My goal is to run a professional station with a strong leadership team and a happy, healthy community. I have to be careful because talking about professionalism may suggest I think the AAD is unprofessional. I don't. I just think there is a new, better model for station management that I can implement. Maybe I'm wrong? Time will tell!

Information is power

My mind was like a sponge. I had moved into learning mode and was absorbing and assimilating information faster than it was given to me. I have never been particularly mentally agile; there have always been people around me who are much smarter. But I had an incredible thirst for knowledge about everything that might or might not be useful in Antarctica. So I quizzed people, asked questions, went to extra briefings.

I was convinced that the more I understood what was happening, at Davis, out on the ice and back in Hobart, the better I could lead. Time and again during training I was told 'You don't need to know that'. It frustrated me no end.

Friday 27th August

I'm worried about the lack of wintering experience among my expeditioners. Of the 18 going down, only two have been there in winter before, and one of those hasn't been down for 20 years.

I wanted to get my head around what they did for work during winter so asked Richard for a copy of the 'works program' for my own benefit. I want to know what my guys are up to but I'm told 'You don't need to know that. The guys know what they're doing so just let them get on with it'. I don't think I conveyed WHY I need it to support delivery of the program.

It's happening a lot. Today I also got a 'you don't need to DO that'.

I'm trying to bring innovation and change to the station but also to lead the team the best way I can, which means I need to use the tools that have worked for me in the past. Things like org charts and FAQs help clarify and communicate things and I find them useful. But it's seen as criticising the status quo and what 'has worked'. I'm not criticising. I just want to lead well and lead in my own way that I know works for me. Maybe I should just say 'No I don't need that, YOU need me to have that'. Grrr...

Tuesday 31st August

Another day, and more office politics, continually being told 'you don't need to know that'. Bloody frustrated! Aaargh!

I know it's not them being mean, they are trying to protect me from too much work by reassuring me that I don't need to know the detail. But all the same, I'd like to make that decision myself!

My job is to build a supportive environment and I can't do that when I don't know what people are doing. But obviously people are reluctant to relinquish any power.

P.S. Most of the team are thoroughly insulted by Nikki Gemmell's new book on Antarctica that portrays expeditioners as ugly, bearded and sex-crazed! I'm certainly not bearded!

I'd had enough! If I, as the leader of the expedition, was constantly being 'put back into my box' I could only imagine what my fellow expeditioners were experiencing. I decided there and then to absolutely break through this culture, if not for the broader AAD then for my people. I wanted to ensure they had all the information they would need. It needed to be easy to find and easy to consume. I turned to the 'Davis Station Handbook' that had been provided. It was a scant 24 pages, roughly cobbled together from bits and pieces, snippets of information from disparate sources. It covered station-specific items such as meal times, muster points for emergencies and included a map of the various buildings.

I determined to compile a comprehensive handbook. One that would be useful for all expeditioners. One that my people could turn to first for guidance. It would be practical but also informative. It would contain all the things you would expect on entering a new workplace—who does what, when and where, how we are structured and organised. But it would also explain what we are doing and why. And it would absolutely contain the summaries of all science and trade programs.

As with many changes I had tried to bring to our expedition, there was resistance. I anticipated opposition from the usual suspects, fellow Station Leaders and past Station Leaders, for whom the existing handbook was more than enough. Water off a duck's back...by now I was kind of immune!

Thursday 21st October

What a day. I'm really getting the sense now of what it's going to be like living with my team 24/7 with no ability to get away. I had a run-in today with Michael over some of the contents of the new handbook. I really needed some time out, but I had to front up tonight for the sea-ice briefing with the rest of the team. I had no choice but to go. I really need to develop a thicker skin. The division is generally not supportive of our much more detailed handbook—but I should just accept that, and probably not be so judgemental.

Just re-read the Field Manual and can't believe it has a recipe for how to cook penguins (in case you get stranded without food). Seriously...

We plugged away at the handbook for weeks. I harangued the scientists for their summaries, and had my emerging leadership team dig deep into the accumulated knowledge of Davis Station and the AAD to create a truly comprehensive handbook of life on station. We decided to include the names of every one of the 120 people who would be working at Davis Station over summer. But a week prior to embarkation I was met with resistance that was both unexpected and demoralising...

Wednesday 27th October

We had another big flare-up over the new handbook today. Why is this so problematic for everyone??? The new handbook is 80 pages of A4, and we need 120 copies...so what's that, about 1000 pages? We need these printed and bound and the little laser printer in the office isn't up to it.

I asked Stewie to get the printing done down at Snap Printing in Hobart. It should be no more than $1000. The expedition is costing $20 million so I didn't think twice about the request and Richard said he'd find the dollars in his budget anyway.

As I was coming back into the office after lunch I heard Sophie complaining to my boss about me and the handbook. She was saying that 'the whole of AAD thinks it's a stupid idea' and that she wasn't going to approve the expenditure.

I'm so annoyed because once again I feel she is grumbling about me behind my back. I felt like going in, ripping it out of her hands, taking it into Hobart and paying for it myself. I can't believe this pettiness. I feel disrespected.

I have sent her an email telling her I'm aware she is unhappy about it and setting up a time to talk it through. I really should have spoken to her not emailed but I'm just too cross. She won't change her mind but it will at least put her on notice that she's been caught out. I will talk to her tomorrow but I will remain firm and explain that I'm hurt and disappointed that she didn't feel she could talk to me about it directly and instead went over my head to my boss.

I guess there are two lessons for me today:

1 Develop some bloody resilience and don't get so upset.

2 Let people know that it's 'not OK' to bitch and moan about someone. (Work on this in Antarctica.) It's disrespectful of yourself and the other person, and the person you're moaning to! 'No triangles'—let's have the courage to provide direct feedback. Not sure how to communicate or implement this yet.

What I learned

- *Change requires alignment.* Cultural change will fail if you focus only on the people, or only on the process and systems. Get a group of senior people on board then provide them with the tools to support and easily communicate the change. Make sure your systems and processes are ready.

- *Empathy goes a long way.* People may have legitimate fears when you announce a change. Your role as leader is to uncover these fears, work out what people have at stake and address it with compassion.

- *People need to know why.* Introducing a change requires you to communicate the 'why' more than the 'what'. Once your people buy into the reasons, the actions are much easier.

- *Practise 'No Triangles'.* If you want to build respect in a team there can be no triangles. If you have a problem, go directly to the person concerned, not to a third party. It's the professional, decent and respectful thing to do.

Chapter 12

Ask 'why?', then keep asking why

A ll through training we had been pushed to our limits mentally and socially. But much of training was also highly physical. First fire training, crane operation, working from heights, then boat training.

Fire training? With all that cold and ice?

Fire training

The lowest temperature recorded on Earth was −89.2 °C (−128.6 °F) at Russia's Vostok Station, halfway between Davis Station and the South Pole. The highest temperature recorded at Davis Station is 8 °C, which had occurred the year I was in training. The average temperature of inland Antarctica is −57 °C.

Now, I knew that for fire to burn it needed fuel, oxygen and *heat*. So why all the fire training?

Humidity. Antarctica is technically a desert. It is the driest continent on Earth. It never rains, ever. It only snows. The extreme low temperatures result in near zero humidity—a big cause of cracked lips and skin among expeditioners.

There is next to *no* risk of anything burning outside buildings in Antarctica. It's just too cold, and there's no fuel. The huge, indeed massive, risk is within the station buildings themselves. These are heated to a balmy 23 °C by large diesel heaters that run all day, every day. Any moisture that might have been in the air from humans inside is sucked out. Any moisture inside timber frames, furniture, clothing and bedding is quickly evaporated out, leaving a highly flammable mix of combustible materials.

The fire danger is complicated by the 'single use' nature of the buildings. The planners cleverly designed the station to have completely separate buildings. It's better that one small building burns down leaving five unaffected than that one large building burns down leaving nothing. But each building serves a specific purpose. If we lost our accommodation building, for example, we would have nowhere to sleep, except the science labs perhaps. If we lost our food store building, we would have little food until the ship returned at the end of winter.

So indoor fire fighting is a critically essential skill, and every expeditioner is required to be fully trained. Our fire training took place over a full week and was an amazing adventure. Incredibly, after 15 years of professional firefighting I had never even used a fire extinguisher. Until day 1 of training I didn't even realise there are different fire extinguishers for different types of fires!

Monday 27th September

Today was a big day. First day of fire training and then I came home to respond to the million emails that arrived during the day. Didn't get to bed until late but it was good to stay on top of my admin. I can't believe that my expeditioners don't have email yet—but at least it cuts down the 'noise'.

Really enjoyed the hands-on work with the fire blankets and extinguishers. And it's good to have everyone back together now their role-specific training has finished. I'm enjoying the banter and haven't noticed any strong cliques yet.

Tuesday 28th September

Day 2 of fire training and several glitches!!

First the bus almost left Ian behind and then did leave Griff and Andrew behind! Then Gina turned up and had to be sent home in a taxi...she's not on the fire team. Joy!

I had heard that the expeditioners from the other stations hadn't been trained in the right gas detectors—they were being shown units that were different from the ones on station. Tasfire said the reason was the 'Drager' units we were supposed to use were too complex (!!). Even though Tasfire had two of them they were reluctant to instruct us. A bit more investigation revealed the Tasfire boys simply didn't know how to use the units comprehensively, or so I was told, and I think they were too embarrassed to say so. So I stood my ground and insisted the expeditioners be trained on the type of unit they'd be using down south. And I won!

The irony is that one hour after using it we dropped it down a concrete pit and it broke! Hilarious!

But a good day learning about confined spaces.

Wednesday 29th September

Today was a tough day learning to use the breathing apparatus (BA). The BA stuff was really hard and I felt totally freaked out when I had to go into the shipping container full of fire. I almost stood myself down but lovely Eric the trainer encouraged me. Once I was inside I stopped worrying about the breathing.

The guys were all so caring and helpful and I didn't mind them showing me the ropes one iota. As I said to them, 'it's your time to shine'. Know when to lead and know when to follow.

It was tough, pitch black, hot, uncomfortable, crawling through tunnels and up ladders—awful.

> ### Thursday 30th September
>
> Another big day. I pulled up very stiff and sore from yesterday's effort, several bruises. But today was tougher on my team—emotionally and physically. They were doing the actual fire fighting, I was just supervising. They were very flat at dinner and one was in tears.
>
> We were flat-out all day and the last scenario was a debacle. The guys left the pumps unattended to help out Kirsten and consequently the water support stopped!! I felt so bad for them but it's a good experience. It's the sort of thing you want to do in training and not in Antarctica!
>
> After the highs of yesterday the lows of today were hard. The fact that we showed so much emotion shows me they really care (or are overtired?!). I'm proud of them. I hope they never get sick of me telling them that!

Falling apart at the seams

We were becoming more and more fatigued as the fire week progressed. And this was only training! Tempers started to fray, patience ran thin and more and more errors started to occur. We reached ignition point on the last day of the week. You know that feeling of dread you get when you wake up in the morning and things haven't been going right? You turn up at work just wondering what new hell might be there for you? This was one of those days, and boy, did we have some hell! By the end of the day I and some other expeditioners were in tears, my team was fractured and I had no idea how we were going to survive the year together without a murder being committed!

Friday 1st October

A marathon day of firefighting, with lots of emotion and my first real test of leadership. The day was going well, a bit up and down until the fuel-farm scenario. Then it turned to shit. Brian and Paul were really difficult and argued with Pat till they were blue in the face, and he was the Fire Chief for this scenario. It's a command-and-control situation, dudes! Not the time to debate tactics with your commanding officer.

Then, THEY were bawled out by our instructors, at which point they reacted badly. Paul continued to debate the issue with the experts.

Two expeditioners expressed concerns about working with him in Antarctica. I spoke to him and suggested he might rethink the trip altogether. I was worried about him and the broader team as his peers appeared to lack confidence in him. If they were unwilling to work with him in Hobart what chance did we have in Antarctica? I'd been told very clearly by Richard that I had the overriding say in who was on my team. I had the power and authority to stand people down from the expedition—and it's been done before by other leaders.

Keep reminding myself that we have to live together for the next year. I need to weigh up the impact of any decision to stand him down with that in mind. What do I bloody do? I have no idea.

Spoke to Paul—he couldn't see what the fuss was about and then disengaged from the rest of us for the night. He will be back on Monday, but a lot of harm has been done. We now need to take the emotion out of it and deal with the behaviour. The expedition team also seems to be taking sides, so I need to nip that in the bud before it sets in.

It would take me all weekend to figure out what went so horribly wrong, and what had me on the verge of saying no, I won't have this person on my expedition. We were so close to the end, it would really set us back if Paul wasn't to come with us.

We had worked together virtually seamlessly now for over eight weeks. I knew we could cooperate when the pressure was off, but when the stress levels were high it seemed we became highly dysfunctional. The pressure would be on in Antarctica and I couldn't afford members of my team to go off tap. It was a nightmare.

For the first time I started to think about *who* these people really were.

Why we acted the way we did

Paul was a scientist. Most of the time he was quiet and thoughtful. Like all good scientists he dealt with facts and data. For him ambiguity was something to be resolved. A scientist can't confirm or reject a hypothesis based on intuition. It has to be clear, unambiguous, grounded in fact.

Pat, on the other hand, was a plumber who'd worked all over the place. He was full of energy and excitement. Pat was used to turning up in unknown situations and quickly resolving them. He would use intuition, experience and rule of thumb to get to the bottom of problems and resolve them.

For Paul, the fire training scenario of the day presented too many grey areas. He felt highly uncomfortable and wouldn't feel at ease until he had total clarity about the situation. For me and Pat and some of the others, this persistent questioning and perceived challenging of the instructors came across as stubbornness.

As I reflected over the weekend I finally understood the source of the problem. It boiled down to how each of us thought, processed information, made decisions and understood the world. I could fix this for now, but we would need to develop a good strategy to harness Paul's desire for facts and to help the rest of us to avoid jumping in with obvious, but potentially wrong, solutions.

Saturday 2nd October

I had a big sleep-in today—feeling miserable. I think part of the issue is the perception that Paul argues a lot. My experience is that he's not actually arguing, he's clarifying and checking facts. His science brain needs accurate information to make sense of the world. Whereas the tradies are more hands-on—just start fixing it...they are happy with estimates.

I think I'll counsel Paul about what is more important, being correct or being right? Being ignored or being accepted and respected?...

Sunday 3rd October

Still feeling sad, although I think the solution is dawning on me. We all need to understand how we think and make decisions. I went online and took a good look at the Myers-Briggs personality types again. It was helpful to map Paul's and Pat's personalities. They are opposite ends of the personality types – Paul is highly 'S' and 'T', for sensing and thinking. Pat (and most of the other expeditioners) understand the world and make decisions with 'N' and 'F'—intuition and feeling. It's important that we all understand the differences.

Remembered the time from our 'get to know each other' BBQ in the early days. Baz was telling a story about somewhere he'd been, Alaska I think, and how it was so damn cold that as you put your foot into a puddle the water turned to ice. 'It must have been at least −23', he told us. The scientist interrupted him and said 'Water freezes at zero, so it must have been "at least" zero'. Sigh...

Monday 4th October

Well we JUST survived fire training and I survived my first real test of leadership.

I considered all my options and in the end did what has always worked well for me in the past. I talked to each of the affected people individually and affirmed their value to the expedition. We talked through the different modes of seeing the world and making decisions and I think it was very helpful. It was the first time most of them had seen a framework like Myers-Briggs and it was amazing to see the 'a-ha' moments for each of them. I made sure everyone had a chance to 'get the shit off their liver' and tell me how it made them feel.

In the end we came through stronger, although it will still take effort for Paul to really assimilate and for us to cut him some slack when he starts up about facts and data. Empathy! To help him deal with ambiguity I've put him in charge of the social club! We'll see how that goes.

I'm proud of my team and myself. But I'm glad I had two days to get my head around the issue. No way I could have made an on-the-spot call if I'd been asked to . . .

Tuesday 5th October

I'm really feeling the loneliness of leadership. Even though I'm not alone in terms of personal relationships, I am alone in terms of leadership. I have to carry a fair emotional burden and this weekend was rough, pulling the team back together from the meltdown last week. I doubt I'll be able to confide in anyone on the other stations. So I think the enormity of the challenges are starting to hit me a bit. It's going to be a huge adventure and right now I have the most surreal gift but it's going to get tough. I'm envious of the friendships my people are creating, as I know I probably won't have that peer support available when I get there.

What I learned

- *Understand why.* When people are acting oddly, or differently from the way you'd act, ask yourself 'why?'. We all react differently to various situations. What stresses out one person no end will not faze someone else in the slightest. Don't try to change the person; just try to understand why they are not behaving the way you expected.

Chapter 13

Adventure is not without risk

The last area of training was to become familiar with the boats we would use in Antarctica. The funny thing is there are only about three weeks of the year when the boats can be used. Even though summer is formally a three-month season it takes ages for the sea ice to disappear. The ice starts to melt early in the season, about mid December. But it's thick, and it's another eight or nine weeks before the bay is clear and we can use the boats. Very soon after that the cold returns and with it the sea ice. I was doubting the value of boating training but thought, what the heck. It could be useful, and I'm being paid to learn. If you listen to the stories of sailors they'll tell you the sea is a capricious mistress — you never turn your back on her. We nearly didn't make it.

Boat training and a near-death experience

Tuesday 12th October

Big day today. I'm feeling stiff and sore all over. We took the IRBs out into the ocean and practised our Man Overboard drills, flooding and restarting the outboards, flares, beaching, trailering and docking. My back muscles are aching from pounding over waves. This training has been harder for the women than the men I think. It's all so new. The men looked like they had grown

(continued)

Tuesday 12th October (cont'd)

up tying knots and backing trailers! They picked it up so quickly they were able to pitch in and help out, whereas Kirsten and I were still struggling with the basics. You then have to be content with not one but four instructors—which even though they were trying to help actually made me feel even more stupid!

Pizza and Plankton tonight at the local pizzeria.

Boat training is a hoot and it still spins me out that I'm paid to do all this. The variety and diversity of our training is unlike anything I've seen before.

I was nervous at first having to do all this stuff, but now I seem to be relaxing into it. I think I put myself under too much pressure to exceed expectations so that people think I'm a good leader. But I'm starting to realise I'm a good leader whether or not I am completely proficient with a forklift, IRB, crane or extinguisher or backing up a trailer.

Thursday 14th October

Today I think we almost died.

We were out at sea and were entering a sea cave when a big wave broke over the boat, soaking us all and filling the boat with water. Before we had time to react, the first wave had pushed us deep into the cave. We tried to back out but then the cave filled with another massive wave that pushed us up near the top of the cave. We were close to panic as the water level kept rising. One of the rubber hulls snagged on a ledge and the boat was totally swamped and wallowed about in the pitch-dark cave. We all ducked as water pushed us up to the cave roof. But just as quickly as the water level rose it subsided and we were sucked back out of the cave. Thankfully the outboard was still running, but the boat was very unstable due to the extra load of the water in the boat. We bailed out with our hands as fast as we could. Our instructor opened up the scuppers and revved the engine hard to drain the boat as fast as possible. Thankfully it drained and soon we were headed back to Hobart. In the driving rain and hail coming back across the bay we all felt miserable, wet and cold.

Boating rule #1: Never turn your back on the ocean.

I asked Tim our instructor, 'That was a bit gnarly, hey?' He sheepishly replied, 'That's the closest I've ever come to dying. It was stupid of me and I'm furious with myself for taking you in there.'

I started to rationalise with him and tell him it was OK, we were all safe, no harm done. But nup. I was just too tired. Not interested. I've got 17 other people I need to take care of and, sorry buddy, I just won't add you to that list. You'll have to deal with this one yourself.

The expedition nears

By early November we had completed training and felt prepared for what lay ahead. There was still much to do. We had to find and pack personal supplies that would last 13 months. I knew how many t-shirts I would wear in a week, and I could multiply that by 4.25 for a month's worth. But how many would I need for a year? How quickly would they wear out? Were the washing machines nasty top-loaders that wreck clothes or were they gentle front-loaders. That could make a huge difference. How fast do pyjamas wear out? How many toothbrushes, hairclips and pairs of sunglasses would I need? How much deodorant do I really use? How much sauvignon blanc would I consume in a year?

Before I spent too much time on these questions I sat back on a Friday afternoon and wrote in my journal all the things we had been taught in our training. I couldn't believe we had achieved all of this in three short months.

Glaciology

Climate change

IRB boating (4 days)

First aid (3 days)

Fire training (5 days)

Search and rescue

Air operations

Flight planning

Water desalination operations

Science project briefings

Sea travel procedures

Ice travel procedures

Quad-bike driving

Hagglunds ATV driving

Forklift driving

Pallet racking

Hydroponics

Home brewing

Special Police Constable powers

Deputy Coroner powers

Antarctic Treaty Inspector responsibilities and powers

Fire investigation

Crane sling loading

OH&S legislation

Polar medicine

Space and atmospheric science

Antarctic history and heritage

Environmental authorisations and permits

Antarctic biology

Fuel spill procedures

Alcohol awareness

Blizzard procedures

Survival techniques

Ice climbing

Crevasse awareness

Scientific instruments

Manual handling

But more than anything else, I had learned about myself and the sort of person I must become.

Friday 5th November

I can't believe how intense this last three months has been. On one hand it's been highly technical and practical. But on the other we have been forced together in a way that has required us to understand each other and reconcile our differences. It's caused me to recognise that I have a lot to learn about leadership, particularly leading myself, managing my emotions and getting the most out of my team. It's going to be an incredible year. To make it through mentally and emotionally intact I must be stronger, smarter, braver and more in tune with myself and my people.

We were sent home to pack and say our goodbyes. I cancelled my lease and set about moving my belongings into long-term storage. There wasn't much! For a 35-year-old woman I had accumulated surprisingly little! Packing up was fun and easy, but it troubled me that I wouldn't have a place to come home to.

Saturday 13th November

Back in Melbourne. It's important that I spend some good time with Mum before I go. She will miss me the most of anyone — no matter what I say or do. But she'll be there when I get back . . .

It was great seeing her face when I stepped off the plane. And when I got back here she had put fresh flowers and a box of tissues in my old room! Is it any wonder I have the confidence to do the things I do when I am so loved? We went out for dinner to a little Malaysian joint in Syndal. It was great fun and we did laugh at the $50 'no expense spared' send-off! I teased Loz that on my return we'd lash out and spend $60 on a meal for the three of us.

But it's good to be home, even though it signals the home straight. Not long now.

Sunday 14th November

BBQ dinner with the family and friends. I loved seeing Nicki again and meeting Max. It was sad saying goodbye to Aunty Pammy and Shauna. I didn't know Pammy was upset until Uncle Pete told me tonight. Sam had morning sickness. I'm going to miss the birth of my first niece/nephew . . . that makes me sad.

We all wore Davis Station gear for a family photo and had lots of laughs. It was great to have everyone together and the usual family jokes and discussions in the lounge room.

Tuesday 16th November

Last day in Melbourne and the day dragged on like I couldn't believe. Every minute felt like an hour. I'm itching to get back to Hobart. My emotions are very close to the surface. I'm crying or laughing constantly! It has been an amazing three months and I've learned stacks—especially about myself. I feel more confident than at any other time in my life. I can't believe I'm the same person as the little 17 year old who left home for Warrnambool all those years ago.

What I learned

- *Leadership is a lifelong journey.* No matter how accomplished your résumé looks there is always room to grow. There will always be something new to learn about yourself. There are always new techniques to try. There are always better ways to deal with issues, conflict or motivation. Keep striving, testing and refining yourself.

Chapter 14

Try to stay positive: even the stormiest seas eventually subside

My supplies for the year were packed into a 1-metre cube, as were those of my fellow 120 expeditioners. It was surreal to watch the crane lift our gear on board. There would be no chemist, Target or David Jones to duck into and replenish my supplies. I hoped anything I had overlooked or undersupplied wouldn't be critical.

At the dock

My whole family came down to wave us off from the dock. It was a highly emotional occasion for all the expeditioners, but particularly for Stan.

Stan, a 65-year-old carpenter from Adelaide, was one of my summerers and was returning for his seventh summer expedition. He had just celebrated his fortieth wedding anniversary with his gorgeous wife Madge, who adored him. They were an old-style couple and she did everything for him. She would pack his lunch everyday and make a thermos for smoko. At home, dinner was at 6 pm and lights-out at 9 pm. Each trip, Madge would come aboard with Stan and make up his bunk for him, and they would sit together and quietly say goodbye away from the hubbub of the dock.

But things changed after 9/11. Now only expeditioners and ship's crew were allowed on board. No general public and no relatives meant no stowaways or sabotage, no sneaking bombs on board. I wasn't happy with this, no one was, but these were the rules. It was hard for Stan and Madge, though. I tried to bend the rules for them and spoke to the captain, but he was firm. Welcome to the 21st century, Stan and Madge. I made an effort to get close to Stan over the next few days. Although his special routine had been disrupted I wanted to make sure his final trip to Antarctica was memorable for the right reasons. I asked him if he was okay with the fact that his wife hadn't been allowed on board.

He told me, 'Yes... eventually. It took ages but eventually I worked out how to put on those damned fitted sheets by myself.'

We set sail

As the lone piper played 'Amazing Grace' and families threw brightly coloured streamers, I stood at the stern and watched my loved ones slowly shrink to small dots on the wharf. Even when I couldn't distinguish one from another, they never stopped waving the banners they had made for the occasion. Everyone was teary and as we exited the Derwent River and crossed into Storm Bay the decks were empty. Everyone had gone to their cabins to regroup.

Wednesday 17th November

Well we are sailing. What a roller-coaster day of emotions. I didn't sleep at all last night because I was just so excited. I can't believe it's almost two years since the breakfast that changed my life. I'm feeling all sorts of emotions as I sit here on my bed on the *Aurora Australis*. I'm tired but happy.

Saying goodbye was awful. I completely lost it when the piper played 'Amazing Grace'. But I wasn't alone. Mum and Dad cried. Dad more than Mum. He tried so hard to say something poignant but it all came out mumbled. Jane was probably the most upset I've ever seen her. She wanted to cuddle me all day—and I wished she could too.

When we were sitting at the Chancellor Hotel waiting to board a ladybird flew in and landed on her shoulder. Ladybirds are our all-time favourite things. We watched it and smiled. For two people without a religious or superstitious bone in our bodies we still felt it was a good sign.

Friday 19th November

On board the *AA* and we're all settling into a routine which revolves around eating and sleeping. I was feeling quite sick with mal de mer today—what a quaint name for such a horrid affliction! We're out in the Southern Ocean but it's calm and the seas slight.

The captain came on the speaker and 'invited' us to a 'compulsory muster'. What an oxymoron. I almost declined his kind and thoughtful invitation just for the fun of it, but didn't. For entertainment tonight Frederique gave a fascinating talk on long-line fishing and the effects on the albatross. It's bad news for these amazing creatures.

P.S. Saw my first wandering albatross today—beautiful bird.

Monday 22nd November

Groundhog day. Have played all the songs on my iPod four times and finished the Chocolate Royals.

We start planning meetings for the resupply tomorrow and I'm looking forward to the change of pace.

Seas are big and wind howling. Difficult to write. Sick as a dog. Are we there yet?

The Southern Ocean

The calm seas had given way to a raging storm, 60 knots over the deck combined with 11-metre swells—this was a true Southern Ocean experience. It's why they call it the Roaring Forties!

The good thing about icebreakers is that...they break ice, which is particularly handy when you're headed to Antarctica. The bad thing about icebreakers is that in order to break ice, they have a unique set of design specifications. Icebreakers must rock up and down, they must have a very round hull and they can have no external protuberances. The 7000-tonne ships break thick ice by sliding up onto it, allowing the weight and shape of the ship to crack the ice beneath and the momentum of the ship to cleave a path through. At the next piece of hard ice, up she slides up again. To achieve this rocking motion the vast bulk of ballast is centred fore and aft. Think of a pendulum—that's how they move.

And protuberances, such as the side stabilisers that enable a large ship to keep an even keel without rolling from side to side, have no place on an icebreaker. They cause too much friction and are easily damaged by the ice.

Take away the fore-and-aft stabilisation and the side-to-side stabilisation and you've got a very uncomfortable ride. We're not talking about a gentle list from side to side, we're talking 30 to 45 degrees either side of upright! The resulting motion is like a corkscrew, but maybe not so predictable. Perfect for ice. Very, very uncomfortable at sea, particularly in big seas, particularly after a week of storm-force wind, driving rain and absolutely massive seas!

Wednesday 24th November

I can't move. My tongue is thick, my head is throbbing and I ache all over. What the hell have I done?

Into Antarctic waters

The ship came through the storm intact and we settled back into some form of normalcy. The first thing we all did was have a good clean-up. Bunks, bedding, bulkheads (walls) got the once over with bleach; clothes were washed and we all showered ready to resume our preparations. It was peaceful, we were out on deck watching the Antarctic birds. Excitement and anticipation filled the air.

Our days were filled with planning meetings for the resupply. I used the relative lull to connect with my winterers, both individually and as a group. We talked about our hopes and aims for the coming year. We talked about our roles and responsibilities, and our relationships on station. I made a particular point of ensuring that my winterers understood one another's personalities, preferences and styles. I didn't know if I would have another chance to do this and wanted to make the most of the time we had. I figured that if my expeditioners could predict how each other would respond to any given event it could only be helpful.

Friday 26th November

ICEBERGS!!!!!

Today is the first time I really feel like we're in Antarctica. As I sit here in my bunk it's surreal to watch the icebergs going past my window. They are various shades of blue and white and all shapes and sizes. The size and scale of the bergs is incredible. Antarctica is just awesome, the colours are so vivid—I thought icebergs were white but they're not. They pick up every hue from the sunlight and ocean and range from deep blue through to jade to stripes and everything in between.

It is simply breathtaking to stand at the bow and look out onto this huge expanse of ice ahead of us. When I look at it I get a fierce urge to protect the place.

The ship made rapid progress deep into Antarctic waters. The temperature plummeted and we all scurried to fish out our brand-new cold weather gear, freezer suits and glacier boots. The ship had the atmosphere of a six year old's birthday party. We had people acting the clown with excitement.

Our excitement reached fever pitch when we saw our first penguins. We were punching through thin pack ice, easy work for the icebreaker. There was no sea swell and our ship was steady as a rock, carving its way through the ice above the Antarctic water. The constant throb of the diesel engines and the thin plume of black exhaust were the only reminders we were on a ship. We spent every available moment on deck watching the amazing scenes unfolding before us.

Saturday 27th November

PENGUIN SIGHTINGS!!!

'Keeping watch' on the bow was something none of us had to do but we all did anyway. I had just ducked down to change my camera memory stick when I heard Kirsten squeal 'Penguins!'

Right in front of us, about 100 metres away, were 30 or so Adélie penguins. We were heading straight for them as they sat on a large piece of ice about 2 meters or so above the pack ice. They just looked at us as we got closer. They didn't move a muscle. When I thought it would be too late they must've said 'Shit, let's get out of here' and madly scrambled off the mini-berg and hit the ice. We laughed until we cried, but it was a mixture of terror and humour...Cookie reckons Adélies invented the 'chicken' game just to mess with people.

Towards dinner time we came across some emperor penguins. My god they are huge and playful! I could have watched them playing for hours!

Gradually we started to hit serious ice and we were able to see the icebreaker finally doing its thing. It was fascinating to watch the ship slide, slip, crack and part massive chunks of ice. As I sat in my berth one afternoon I heard an almighty tearing sound and looked out to see a huge chunk of ice flip on its side and grind its way down the side of the ship. A normal ship would have been torn open like a small tin of tuna, but the *Aurora Australis* didn't miss a beat. I finally appreciated the strength of the double hulls, round belly and funny shape of the icebreaker.

We were now two weeks out of Hobart but it already felt a lifetime away. We had a rhythm, our own tone; it felt like we'd been together as a team for years. But not everything was running smoothly. Unbeknown to me, some issues had been fermenting on the voyage.

What I learned

- *Focus on the positive.* When you feel like giving up focus on what you have, not on what you have given up. Look forward to the time when the worst will be over.

Chapter 15

A handpicked support team can be essential

At Davis Station, the 'green store', the big green building that served as our supply depot, was apparently in disarray. Supplies had been accumulating for decades and no one had any real idea what was inside. To my mind this was a probity issue for the AAD; obviously, unnecessary supplies were being sent. But it also worried me that it was a huge waste of money — money that was much needed to fund the science program. Back at Kingston we had negotiated an increased budget to cover a store person over summer, someone who would conduct a full inventory stocktake and organise the return of surplus requirements.

Going off half-cocked

I wasn't sure where this person was coming from, but the most likely scenario was that a 2004 winterer would be flown across from one of the other stations and would stay on at Davis for the extra few months before going home early in 2005. When my deputy, Ross, heard through the grapevine about a Mawson winterer doing the store work I wasn't surprised. But I was concerned about the timing. It would be critical that they met the ship, as a key role during resupply would be to direct pallets of supplies when the ship was unloaded. I emailed head office: 'When is the Mawson store person coming over?'

The ship uploads and downloads emails twice a day and has a satellite phone for use in emergencies. I thought no more about it until the next morning, when I got the reply from head office: 'What person?' Grrr! Twenty-four hours later and still no further ahead. This went on for three days. I kept quizzing Ross, 'Who is this person?' We had no time to lose so I radioed Mawson and started the arrangements to have the person in question flown over to Davis.

Eventually I received this reply from Hobart: 'No one, particularly a highly qualified and specialised scientist who has just spent the last 12 months at Mawson Station, will be arriving at Davis to act as a store person. You will need to make do. We don't know where you're getting your information from.' I knew that in the absence of information, misinformation flourished. Someone had mentioned something somewhere that was repeated, fed up and down the food chain until it finally arrived, half-cocked, totally wrong, at my desk. And I'd believed it.

Alcohol and culture

Some aspects of the cultural change we had started were proving very difficult for many of the expeditioners. I was adamant that alcohol be managed, and of course illicit drugs were prohibited—we were to live in a Federal Government workplace, combining work and home. We would run shifts 24 hours over summer, with people knocking off work at all hours of the day. Should they be able to relax with a glass or two of wine or beer? I had no issue with that, but I had heard many stories about expeditioners, particularly over summer, drinking themselves into a stupor. One of my changes was to open the bar only at 7 pm and to close it at 11 pm during resupply.

Monday 29th November

The last few days have been tough and for the first time I wondered what I was doing here. The fallout over the vacant store-person role is amazing and I got a rocket from head office after I acted on incorrect advice about the store-person. Plus, one of my summer deputies has been acting strange with me. I found out last night that it's because a confidential discussion I'd had with a fellow station leader during training had been repeated. I'd made a comment about keeping this person 'on a tight rein' and it had gotten back to them. Out of context. I'm furious at the 'Rachael said this about you' crap.

I'm also copping it from several expeditioners unhappy with the cultural change regarding alcohol. They think I'm joking and making up stories about the bar closing at 11 pm — interestingly, Cookie over at Mawson is doing the same thing.

I've also inherited some expeditioners who joined us on board when we stopped at Casey, who tell us they drank themselves stupid every night over summer last year — apparently they were allowed to take extra grog! Apparently, they think Davis people are 'nerds'. Amazing. I cried for the first time last night and worried that I wouldn't be seen as a good leader if I didn't drink with the troops.

But I called a station leadership team meeting to discuss managing alcohol at the station and was really pleased with the support.

I can see why past Station Leaders don't drive cultural change — it's really hard and incredibly lonely. I believe I have enough support among the winterers to get me through but it will tough.

Leaders shouldn't expect to be able to please all the people all the time. I have resigned myself to not being the unanimous-best-ever Station Leader I want to be. Some people won't like it.

Davis resupply

We were close to Davis Station now. Punching through thick ice had slowed our progress but we were still on track to arrive on time. The changeover would be extremely busy. In three days we were required to safely dock the ship, unload our expeditioners and their gear, perform an orderly handover and restock the ship with the returning winterers, along with all their waste products. Unlike the old days, nothing is left behind on Australian Antarctic expeditions. Everything is either burned or returned. Including bodily waste.

Tuesday 30th November

Today is our last day of sailing. Our ETA at Davis is sometime tonight and I'm excited. The butterflies in my tummy are back. I introduced my station leadership team to the summerers for the first time — they are my secret weapon! At the meeting I tried to set a tone of busy and exciting — let's have fun and stay safe. Lots of cheers and lots of excitement.

There is a funny culture of referring to the Station Leader as 'God'. I don't like this and will need to change it somehow. I want my role to cover a range of styles; coach at times, dictator at times, facilitator at others. The God moniker will not help this.

The enormity of the resupply task is daunting — three days doesn't seem like enough. I need to make sure the handovers are COMPREHENSIVE. I could imagine the current winterers just want to get on the ship, but if we don't get through everything in three days I'll have no issue holding the ship back until I'm comfortable the handover is complete. I will tell them that when I meet them tomorrow.

Unloading a ship in Antarctica is an unusual experience! There are no piers or docks, no tug boats or pilot boats to guide entry. The captain simply noses the ship through the ice until it gets close enough to the station, and then turns off the engines. Then the fun begins.

On the ship our helicopters were reassembled and made flight-ready. We assembled and load-tested the cranes. We opened the huge cargo doors and sorted through the huge pile of machinery and supplies, some of which had been 'upset' on the journey over.

On station the leaving winterers were busy with their own preparations. Light trucks were fuelled up and the antifreeze flushed from every crevice. Our first view of the winterers was the sight of a white Toyota Hilux ute gingerly making its way across the ice trailing a large, snake-like black tube — our diesel refuel line.

The penguins were unbelievably cute. Their main predators are leopard seals and killer whales. They have no land-based predators so when they see people, trucks and machinery they don't react in fight-or-flight mode. They just sit there and look quizzical. Sooner or later they walk or slide up to a person or truck for a closer look before they continue on their way.

The diesel line *really* confused the little Adélie penguins. It ran from the shore, several kilometres out on the ice to the ship, and fell right across their normal transit path across the now-frozen bay. Not 10 minutes after the line was laid I looked over to see three or four Adélies stand right next to it, then walk up and down along its length, stop again, look at it quizzically and repeat this. The fuel line was only half as high as the Adélies, but with no purchase on the ice, no thick legs for jumping and no arms to climb with, they were stumped. It reminded me of the *Dr Who* cartoon from the '80s where the Daleks, confronted by a set of stairs, respond, 'Well . . . there goes our plan for universal domination!'

Kirsten and I watched from the boat and provided the voiceover.

'Hey Roger, what's that?'

'Dunno. Hey Fred, what's that thing?'

'Dunno. Let's see if we can get around it.'

'Nup. Can't. It's big. It's long, goes for hundreds of penguin miles in either direction.'

'Well, let's just look at it for a while.'

We entertained ourselves for 10 minutes until one of the expeditioners took the initiative and built a ramp out of snow. No sooner had he done so than the gathering penguins pushed and shoved their way over. Smarter than we thought!

'Wait a sec . . . There's a bridge! Woohoo!'

Wednesday 1st December

It's Davis, it's home! There's no snow, no plants or trees, it's just a barren brown landscape for miles around. The station looks just like a mining camp! I stood at the bridge of the ship shaking my head at the desolate, brown moonscape, wondering when I'd signed up for a year in Coober Pedy? The captain walked up, slapped me on the back and said: 'Don't worry about it Rachael. There's help behind every tree!'

Thanks buddy, you're really helping me out here.

The station itself, though, is way better than I thought or had hoped for! The SMQ (sleeping & medical quarters) is fine and I think once the summerers go in three months' time there will be heaps of room. Everyone seems happy.

The outgoing leader, Bob, was strange and a bit dismissive at the start of the day, but by the end of the day he was warming up to me. Lots on his mind. My winterers seem a bit quiet.

I've been put up in a shipping container with Kirsten because all the winterers' accommodation is still full! I didn't expect this, but it's an absolute first. I've crashed in many dodgy places but never a shipping container! I checked out my room for the year and it looks great. An ensuite would have been nice.

Thursday 2nd December

Second day of changeover and I worked from 6 am to 11 pm. We've got 24 hours now to complete the handover. It will be stressful but a relief to get things the way I want them. I probably should be more concerned but I'm not. I really just want to settle in and get into my room and my office and unpack my things.

We are probably under-prepared but I figure we'll work it out.

Fired up my email for the first time in two weeks and have 280 emails to get through.

Twenty-four hours of daylight is messing with our heads. It never feels time to knock off for the day and I have to force myself to go to bed and rest.

The final day of changeover was frantic. I felt like I was a celebrity being followed by the paparazzi! Everywhere I went, I was followed by a trail of people, all looking for advice and answers about how to do this or that in this highly foreign environment. Some people would stand up when I walked into the room and treated me with great deference. I wasn't used to this. The teams I led at home understood that I was most certainly *not* a god and *not* the font of all knowledge. My preferred mode of decision making was through facilitated discussion and consultation. It appeared to me that the expeditioners were looking for a strong, decisive, even heroic leader.

Finally the changeover was complete. All 84 of us gathered on the sea ice to wave goodbye to last season's expeditioners. I couldn't imagine their emotions. Antarctica had already started to feel like a home away from home, but these people were leaving their home of the past 13 months.

There were tears all round. The three short days with the returning expeditioners had created a special bond and we were all amazed how sad it was they were going. There was a pack of 10 to 12 expeditioners surrounding me, each with a question or a problem to solve. I dealt with them all and then had a moment on my own. I was the last to leave as the ship dislodged itself from the ice and slowly backed out of the bay. Over the past three days the sea ice had already broken up and retreated about half a kilometre, so it wasn't long before the icebreaker spun around in clear water and accelerated over the horizon, leaving its telltale wake of dark smoke hanging in the thin Antarctic air.

I turned around and faced the station. This was it! I was now officially in charge of up to 120 people, in the most dangerous and remote workplace on the globe. My heart swelled with a mix of excitement, trepidation, abject fear and joy. I didn't know whether to laugh or cry, and walking back to station I think I did both.

By the time I got back the place was deserted. We were all exhausted. It looked like daytime but it was 11 o'clock at night!

Friday 3rd December

Handover day. I'm here and I'm in charge. I can't believe it. I'm very emotional.

I opened Mum and Dad's card and got all homesick. I'm not sure why but I know I'm very tired and have a lot to think about. I guess this is the moment I've been training for. It will take a few more days to settle in and sort out my stuff.

I'm still confident about it all but it will be a long year. I wonder what my troops are feeling tonight. We're all in our rooms and I'm missing a few boxes of stuff. I can't wait to ring home tomorrow.

I am finding more and more that I need my crew to take some of the load. I am yet to have a meal without someone interrupting and wanting a meeting about something or other. It will be exhausting over summer unless I can get my two Deputy Station Leaders to pick up some of this.

Up to me to manage this.

What I learned

- *Change requires a team.* We nearly always require a 'guiding coalition' of people to make change stick. Without this the initiative can be construed as the whim of one or two individuals and quickly sputter out. Gather your supporters and use their skills and influence to augment your efforts.

Part IV

Summary in Antarctica

We can become so busy managing that we forget to lead.

Sometimes the sheer load of work pins us down and we find ourselves living from moment to moment, just dealing with the crises. But leaders must habitually 'get on the balcony' and watch the activity from there. From here you can spot small brushfires and act; you can see how things are going on a broad scale and appreciate the efforts of your team. Effective delegation, strong and clear personal boundaries, and an unwavering commitment to personal reflection are key tools.

Chapter 16

Make the right decision the right way

Summer in Antarctica is all about the science; 84 scientists descend on a small patch of dirt at the bottom of the world to conduct their experiments, take readings and just do science stuff. Most of the scientists must get off station to perform this work. This is often a day trip, but sometimes they would be away for two, three or four days. Critically, they had to be transported to where the science work would take place. For some scientists, the work was conducted around the station, but for most, their science ground was 200 to 300 kilometres away.

Allocation of scarce resources

The transport mode of choice was air. We had two helicopters at our disposal and two specially modified aircraft were to arrive soon, having spent the winter back in Australia. Now, I'm no mathematician, but two four-seater helicopters and 84 expeditioners, all champing at the bit to get off station and count the penguins, doesn't compute, particularly when a round trip of 400 kilometres takes up most of the day.

So, as in most organisations, managing this was all about the appropriate allocation of scarce resources. The trick in managing scarcity is not just to make the right decision, but to be seen to make it the right way. People might be upset with the outcome, but if they understand the process they are more likely to accept it.

I went to a lot of effort to ensure our flight schedules catered for all the science teams. We had spent hours and hours on our way down working out flight plans, food drops and schedules. People were reasonably happy with the outcomes. Everyone would get to go off station to do their work. I had heard so much grizzling about perceived favouritism and some people getting more flight time than others that in exasperation I developed the Flight Board. It was a simple whiteboard divided up into quadrants with masking tape. Each section outlined who was flying today, and at what time, who was flying tomorrow and their expected departure time, and who was flying next week. The bottom quarter listed the incoming flights from other stations. It was like the departures board at any airport. Not revolutionary, but gee it helped. Having that transparency gave the scientists reassurance about who was getting flights and when. One of the team commented on my 'brilliance' in implementing such a useful tool. But it wasn't brilliance, it was self-preservation! They were doing my head in at times and the Flight Board stopped much of the niggling. All was good in our world.

Until the weather threw a spanner in the works.

The first few days of flights were perfect. They made good time, were incident-free, and the helicopters flew in no wind and bright skies. The station quietened right down. We had 20 or so people in the field, all doing their thing, and those on station were preparing for their field trips. Perfect! Then the Bureau of Meteorology scientists came in to see me one morning...

'Boss, we've got a problem.' (Why do some people start their bad news with that phrase?) 'We've got a big system moving in from the west. It's got the lot — big winds and heaps of snow. Total whiteout.'

'How long?'

'It'll be here tomorrow and blow over in three days.'

We got our scientists back quick smart and strapped down the choppers. The blizzard came on time and hung around, but it wasn't anywhere near as bad as expected. But we lost three days of science and the scientists didn't like it. Some were unhappy they had been pulled from the field; some were unhappy their flight wasn't going out that day; and some were worried they wouldn't get out on the ice on schedule the following week. It was the first instance of what would become a common dilemma. Antarctic weather changes faster than almost anywhere in the world, even Melbourne! Scientists can be intense at times, but imagine sharing a mess hall with 84 of them, all disgruntled! They understood the weather was totally outside anyone's control, but it didn't ease their fears that years and years of research might be at risk because of the 'A' Factor—the curve balls, mostly weather related, that Antarctica can throw at you, any time, any place.

Leadership style—you scratch my back…

I had two Deputy Station Leaders over summer, both of them experienced in Antarctic ways but both very different. I had already had a couple of heated discussions with one of them, but now he was seriously confounding me.

Ross was a firm believer in leadership by quid pro quo. If something needed to be done and the person didn't want to do it, his style was to offer something of equal value as a reward. He had a fantastic memory and somehow managed to keep track of 'favours done' and 'allowances made' stretching back to before our departure from Australia! It worked for him. He developed great relationships with the team and was the go-to person whenever you needed a favour done, such as a roster switch or help making your Kris Kringle present.

I firmly believed it was an unsustainable way to lead. People soon understand that no doesn't really mean no. It doesn't even mean not yet. In fact, there is no 'no'. Instead, people he directed quickly learned to seek some compensation in response to even the simplest request. This would lead to quarrels about perceived inequity of favour versus reward, but it also caused other, bigger problems. The weaknesses of this approach were highlighted during the flight scheduling incident.

Like some other challenges I encountered in Antarctica, I was blissfully unaware of the flight scheduling problem until it was too late. Sitting in my normal spot at dinnertime I had four scientists approach me. I could tell by their body language that something was wrong. They stood over me as I was eating and I could feel the heat of their anger.

'Boss, we need a word.'

I quickly grabbed my two Deputy Station Leaders, Howie and Ross. If we were going to fight, then three against four were slightly better odds. In the meeting room Dave, their spokesman, took the initiative.

'This … this … bloke,' he growled, pointing an accusing finger at Ross. 'This bloke shouldn't be here.' I bit my tongue and waited.

'We've been bumped until next Saturday. If we don't get out on the ice this week there's no point in our having come to Antarctica in the first place!'

I had read about their science project and knew they needed to take three readings six weeks apart. If they missed this week, they would miss the window to get the first reading. To me, they were top priority and should be on the first chopper out of Davis once the weather cleared.

'I'll sort it out. I'll come and see you in half an hour.' As they left I turned to my deputies. 'What's going on?'

'Well,' replied Ross, 'I moved them because I thought three other projects were more important.'

As I delved deeper into the situation, I realised that, firstly, the other projects were not more important and, secondly, the other projects had been moved up the sequence as 'favour returns' for those scientists picking up extra shifts helping in the kitchen. It was their payback for helping out the team, but this simple 'gesture of thanks' had caused huge ructions.

Not only was the decision wrong, but the *process* for arriving at the decision was wrong. To someone on the outside of the trading and swapping, it was favouritism and nepotism rolled into one—a sure recipe for discontent.

Saturday 18th December

Ross continues to confuse me. He is a wonderful person, very kind and caring, but his leadership style is vastly different from mine. He thinks the way to get people to do what you want is to promise a favour in return, to offer them an incentive. He doesn't see how this approach actually creates conflict and is unsustainable.

I'll sit with him tomorrow and work through the incident and talk about how his decision actually created the problem.

The scientists are mostly all happy again, time-critical science is going to get done, which is the important thing from my perspective. There are a few grumbles from people who have been 'un-bumped' but I spent some time with them explaining that 'our' decision was incorrect. I'm conscious of openly showing leadership solidarity and taking one for the team, but that doesn't make it any easier.

A Chinese welcome

Davis Station is one of four Australian research stations in Antarctica. It's the furthest south and houses the largest number of scientists over summer. But in size it pales in comparison to the American bases. Where Davis has up to 120 expeditioners on station in summer, McMurdo Station houses up to 1000. Serviced by three airstrips and 100 buildings, McMurdo even has hairdressers and an ATM! There's nothing like free enterprise. We, by comparison, had no use for cash because there was nothing to buy. We were partly envious of McMurdo. They appeared to have all creature comforts on hand, including three TV channels (a US military channel, an Australian channel and a New Zealand channel) and broadband internet.

Along with Australia and the USA, a surprisingly large number of nations have permanent research stations in Antarctica. All the usual Western suspects, such as the UK, Germany, Japan and France, are represented. In addition, many Eastern and emerging economies are present — China, India, Russia and Romania to name a few. Just around the corner from Davis Station are the Chinese at Zhongshan, operated by the Polar Research Institute of China.

Pretty soon we were getting requests for visits from neighbouring stations. Our closest neighbour called at 9.45 am one morning with a request. The Chinese were bringing in a patient with diarrhoea and trouble urinating. We didn't have much to go on other than that, so we prepared a stretcher team and had Doc and the anaesthetics team at the ready. I was stuck in the green store so sent Jason out to greet the chopper.

Jason was our summer plumber from country NSW. He was down-to-earth and a bit of a knock-about kind of bloke, and he took the role of welcoming our first international visitors very seriously. The chopper landed just as I left the green store and I hustled out to meet them. From 50 metres away I could hear Jason. He was speaking very loudly, very slowly and using lots of hand movements.

'HI, I'M JASON. I'M. THE. PLUMBER.' (I would ask the reader to picture the appropriate hand movement to indicate plumbing—maybe he was pulling a large wrench.) 'I. MAKE. THE. WATER. YOU KNOW? WATER... TO DRINK.' (Again, picture a hand turning a tap, filling a glass and raising it to his lips.) By then I had nearly arrived and saw one of the funniest things from the expedition.

Jason continued loudly: 'I MAKE THE WATER. WHAT DO YOU DO?'

The first person to step forward and greet Jason looked very distinguished. He was dressed in a sparkling clean, bright red tunic emblazoned with the PRIC logo (unfortunate acronym). He bent forward from the waist, straightened up, smiled and said in a beautifully cultured English accent: 'Hello Jason, my name is Dr Lee. I am a professor of glaciology leading the research into the environmental processes that affect the rifting and calving of icebergs on the Amery Ice Shelf. I am pleased to make your acquaintance.'

We fell about laughing and before long the Chinese and finally Jason joined in. As we walked back to the station, I put my arm on his shoulder and said, 'Jase? Rule number one?'

'Yeah', he replied, smiling sheepishly. 'Never assume. Got it!'

Sunday 5th December

This is meant to be a day of rest but I'm exhausted!

The Zhongshan team arrived and Jason set the tone of the day. What a cracker! The patient turned out to have a bladder infection but they were worried because he is their trip leader for their traverse to Dome A, which leaves tomorrow. We fed them and they entertained us.

They ate fishcakes with apple, tried every sauce we had on station, ate heaps of lettuce and mopped their plates up with lettuce leaves. They must be short of fresh veggies already. Our supplies are planned to run out in about February to coincide with resupply and the return of the summerers to Australia.

We lent them a starter motor for their other chopper, which was out of action. The plan was they would use it for a week and then return it but I got a fax saying they were keeping it until the 20th January! Apparently the Chinese are the Homer Simpsons of Antarctica, borrowing and not returning items.

But it was an entertaining day and a bonus of being at Davis rather than the other stations that don't have the international interactions.

Somehow I've lost track of how many expeditioners I have. People are flying in all the time from other stations and flying out to the field. Last count I had 68 on station and 30(ish) in the field.

What I learned

- *Resource allocation must be transparent.* It's not enough to make the right decision. We need to be seen to make it the right way. People might be upset with the outcome, but if they understand the process they are more likely to accept it.

- *Leadership means accountability.* When you're the leader, you're it. When things go wrong you take full responsibility, even if it isn't your fault. If your people make the wrong decision but have followed the correct procedures, applied due diligence and had good intentions, then you must back them, even if they got it wrong. If they get it right, give them all the credit anyway!

- *Innovation requires safety.* Doing things in a new way is more likely to fail than doing things the old way. Make sure your workplace values failure as a learning opportunity as much as success. If people are too scared to take a risk because they think they'll suffer if it doesn't work out, your people will never innovate.

Chapter 17

Step up onto the balcony—but you'll need time and support

After the first week of life on station we had settled into a good routine. We all knew what we had to do and my deputies had started stepping up to 'protect' my time. I had spoken to them during one of our catch-ups and told them that for my own sanity, and so I could keep a helicopter view of the station, I needed to be freed from the daily barrage of requests so I would need their support.

Loyal deputies

They were surprised at first. Previous Station Leaders appeared to favour the more heroic model and being the font of all knowledge, wisdom and decisions, and my two DSLs weren't used to this. I told them I trusted their judgement but if they needed me I would be there behind them.

It got off to a bit of a clumsy start. Howie would spot someone making a beeline towards me at dinner, jump out of his chair and almost perform a crash-tackle intercept! He was extraordinarily kind and loyal. And Ross was a ferocious ally and excellent deputy. He took his leadership duties very seriously. Before long, most people took the hint and we gradually managed to direct people to their line manager on station in the first instance.

As summer progressed it started to warm up and before long we were enjoying beautiful weather. It was stunning. We had gotten so used to the cold that when the thermometer hit 9°C we were outside in t-shirts playing in the melting snow and ice.

Our science programs were progressing well and I felt the station was running smoothly.

Tuesday 7th December

I'm still not used to the 24-hour daylight and wake every morning at sparrow's—but that's partly excitement too. Things have quietened down and I'm right on top of my workload. I even had time to reply to all my hotmails and bid for a couple of things on eBay! (Although delivery will be a challenge—there's no postage calculator for Antarctica.) Good old Mum and Dad will look after it.

I went down and visited the trades buildings today and it's amazing how much the guys loved having me visit. Or so I think? I spent a great deal of time with them and they showed me all that they're up to. I even sat in on their toolbox talk. It's important to make time to 'kick the dirt' with the guys.

Regular performance reviews are mandated across the Australian Public Service and Antarctica was not exempt, certainly not in theory. I received pushback for the scheduled meetings from some of the very experienced expeditioners. Did they really have to go through this? I got the distinct sense that these reviews hadn't been taken seriously by some former leaders, who had treated it as a 'tick and flick' compulsory duty. There was a big gap between corporate Australia and corporate Antarctica!

Thursday 9th December

Another day down. I completed all the performance reviews for the winterers, which took most of the day. I got the feeling that none of them had ever had a performance review before. Most were relieved that it wasn't as scary as they'd thought it might be. It was very funny that they all brought me gifts!! Mainly chocolate. And they ALL complimented me on my hair. Hilarious!

> But I think it shows the camaraderie that is developing in the team. They are all in good spirits and quite playful.
>
> It was also a good opportunity to remind my winterers that I wouldn't be seeing much of them over summer and it wasn't because I didn't care. It was because I trusted them to get on with their work and to come to see me if they had any concerns. They all understand me a bit better now and realise that my style is to look after them and let them look after their teams.

Food and other supplies

All up I had spent about an hour in the green store over several quick visits. Each time I was amazed at what I found. The last straw was when I was looking for toilet paper. I went to the inventory register on the computer and located the rack and bay of my pallet. I had avoided using the forklift up to now, after my less than 'excellent' training result, but this time I had no choice.

I gingerly nosed the forklift into the bay, raised the lift and retrieved my pallet. Only it wasn't toilet paper. Instead, in front of me were 34 boxes of shower-curtain rings, very neat, tidily arranged and all unopened. Davis Station had moved from shower curtains to solid shower doors in 1989! I searched the labels and to my horror saw that the most recent resupply of curtain hooks had come down on my ship! I was looking at 16 years' accumulated hooks for 60-plus showers. Why anyone thought they needed to be replaced every year was beyond me. Why anyone thought they needed to keep sending them down was beyond belief. It must have been a glitch in the electronic ordering?

I phoned down to my store manager and asked him to come up to the green store quick smart. I needed to understand the breadth and depth of this issue. Simon arrived immediately and agreed. 'Yes. Not only that, but in my quick review I noticed we have replacement wastepaper baskets also going back several years.'

As he enumerated several other oversupply issues, two thoughts were running through my mind. Firstly, the last thing the AAD wants is for there to be a shortage of anything, other than perishables like oranges and lettuce. But hardware and furniture were surely a different matter. Secondly, the enormity of the task dawned on me. This was a *big* warehouse. If we were to clean out all the unnecessary equipment and supplies, (a) where would we put it all? (b) how would we get it back home? (c) what would the AAD do with it? and (d) what if it somehow leaked to the press, who are always hungry for a 'waste in government' story?

Bugger it, I thought. We were going to sort this out.

I assembled a 'strike team' to methodically work their way through the green store over the next week and identify and mark anything that could be considered not required. There were the obvious items, such as the ones mentioned, but there were also more ambiguous ones that could get me into trouble.

The distinction between 'best before' and 'use by' on food labels had never occurred to me. Back home, I wouldn't eat anything that was past either date. But Antarctica is different. Sure, we would need to observe the 'use by' date, but 'best before'? One of the pilots had formally complained to me about being served food that was 'out of code'. He reminded me of my responsibility for managing the workplace and the obligation to serve up food that was suitable — the last thing we needed was an outbreak of food poisoning. I rang my boss in Hobart and he told me to pull all the out-of-code food from the shelves and turf it into a shipping container to be returned to Australia.

My stocktake team moved quickly, and before lunch there were 14 mixed pallets of supplies that were no longer required. Most of it was food. Five-year-old biscuits, 20-year-old tins of baked beans, out-of-date flour, sugar. There were more shower ring–type items. Two boxes of shoelaces from 1991 and 1993 were deemed surplus to requirements because we had three newer boxes. Incandescent light bulbs (we were totally fluoro), floor-standing fans (!!!), and boxes and boxes of fan-fold computer paper were quickly added to the pile.

An older and highly experienced scientist came to me almost in tears. 'You can't do this. You can't waste all that good food.'

'What do you mean? It's all out of date.'

'No it's not. "Best before" doesn't mean *anything* in Antarctica. Down here, with absolutely no humidity and no insects, mice or rats, 99 per cent of this stuff will last forever, and it will be fresh!'

To prove his point, he reached out and grabbed a packet of Scotch Finger biscuits. He pointed to the best before date, '13 April 1998'. 'Try them', he said. I did. They were perfectly crunchy.

Other expeditioners gathered around, shaking their heads.

'What if our resupply gets stuck and can't get here?' said one.

'What if there's a nuclear holocaust?' said another.

I sighed. Overdramatic as it seemed, they kind of had a point. The shower-curtain rings and their friends were certainly going home though!

Saturday 11th December

Well, my next big test of leadership down here and my first big night and I reckon I passed both.

At a guess I reckon almost 30 per cent of our food is out of code, and I've got a big issue on my hands. It was a lot of pressure in a highly charged environment to come up with the answer. The irony is that by isolating the out-of-code food, we'll have to put in an extra order for resupply, adding to the cost and the warehousing effort. Tomorrow I'll draft an email back to AAD outlining the extent of the problem and what we're attempting to do with it. We need a proper reordering method, not just sending down the same thing as last year and the year before. That's what has gotten us into this mess.

For the first time I hung out in the bar tonight; I've been too busy up to now. Well, that's not entirely true. Part of me wants to socialise but I think it's important to keep some distance. But tonight was different: we had our 'D for Davis' party and everyone dressed up. I went as a doctor and danced for four hours! Sam and a couple of others commented that it was the first time I had let my hair down. I hope now they see that I am a fun person, but with a big responsibility.

Sunday 12th December

Very quiet on station today. Almost everyone was out on the ice enjoying the weather. I attended a craft workshop and made a necklace! I'm so not a crafty person but it was fun.

A crew came back from Deep Lake, a lake that is so salty it never freezes, even in winter. They were excited and told amazing stories about the incredible colours. I really want to get out there before the end of summer.

I was bored today for the first time. Odd and strangely worrying. This is our busiest time of year and I'm already wondering how we're going to fill our time and not kill each other when there's nothing to do over winter.

The food issue really tested me but I believe I showed good leadership—I was decisive yet empathetic and I listened to my people. It's a big issue that won't go away soon.

Monday 13th December

Had a phone hook-up with Kingston today to talk about the food. It has all turned out better than I'd hoped for. Now we only have to return the hardware and one pallet of food. Next year they are going to send down a full-time, experienced store person and leave space on the ship to clear it out for good.

I'm getting tired of fighting with some of my leadership team over fatigue management for the troops. I don't understand how they can say the welfare of our people is the number one priority and then ask them to work seven days a week! Crazy! I need some time off so I've scheduled a trip for Wednesday. I need to walk off my irritation! Ross is still a puzzle to me. Sometimes he is so wonderful and helpful but other times I am just totally bewildered. We're just different I guess.

I'm now making a concerted effort to get as many people off station as I can, especially the ones working hard who may not get the chance to explore this beautiful place. Each night they have been coming to me asking if they can go here, there or everywhere. With 24 hours of daylight it's become a standing joke that they can go out as long as they are back before dark!

Wednesday 15th December

Yeah! Finally a day out in the field. I had navigation training and it was hard yakka but great fun. Every time my shoulders hurt from the survival pack or my legs ached from walking I just reminded myself I was actually at work. It was great to get some fresh air and some exercise; I feel fat and think I've put on a few kilos.

Eating lunch outside was a great experience. The air was so crisp and the deep blues in the ice made a terrific contrast to the white snow. A bunch of Adélie penguins came up close to check us out and see what we were eating. I had to fight the urge to throw them my crust—that's a BIG no-no down here.

The silence has to be heard to be believed. Is that an oxymoron? I have never 'heard' anything like it—total, absolute silence. No leaves blowing, no birds chirping, nothing. I realised how much white noise we have in our lives. You really notice it when it's not there anymore... total silence.

Thursday 16th December

Another good day at the office. Not too stressful. The highlight of the day was finding out a bird had crapped on our webcam. Kirsten's mum emailed to tell us. It was hilarious. Up there with the quote from the head of the AAD saying 'I didn't realise Antarctica was so far away' in response to why the planes had been delayed. He'd never been here. Crazy!

Friday 17th December

Today marks one month since we left Hobart. It seems much longer, but oddly also shorter. So much has happened and we've been so busy—it seems like another world.

I had a ball today on the quad bikes. As I was scooting across the ice on Long Fjord with the wind whipping my hair and the sun on my face I could hear Dad's voice in my head, 'Just look at Dachoo'—his pet name for me since my sister was born and couldn't pronounce Rachael. I got a sense of the real Antarctica, away from station.

I fell off too so I'm a bit sore and know I'll be stiff tomorrow—so am turning in early.

What I learned

- *Line management is king.* All requests for information or resources *must* go through line managers first. When people start to go around line managers to a more senior manager it erodes the supervisors' authority and sets up a culture where staff may 'shop around' until they get the answer they want. It's like getting a 'no' from mum so hoping dad will give a 'yes'. Again it comes back to the concept of 'no triangles'.

- *Use data.* When faced with an issue that is charged with emotion, always dial it back through facts and data. Avoid using (and watch out for other people using) words such as 'everyone', 'no one', 'always' and 'never'. It's rarely 'everyone' and 'never' is a big call. These words are used to build a case or strengthen a position but can easily be discredited, or confirmed, with facts and data.

Chapter 18

Ambiguity and leadership go hand in hand

One of the biggest challenges for an expedition leader is to set the right tone for our combined work and home environment. There are obvious, generally accepted standards for the workplace. We are firm about bullying, choice of language, viewing of unsuitable material and, in general, being politically sensitive. 'Political correctness' has had a bad name since the expression emerged in the 1990s, but I really believe it in it. I don't use it in conversation, though. I use the term 'respect', which is basically what political correctness boils down to. It is mostly self-evident how to show respect to your colleagues when you're at work, but at home you make your own rules.

What you did at home back in 2004 was largely your own business. You could shout at the cat, drink yourself silly, swear like a sailor and basically do whatever you want, and your boss wouldn't know or care. As long as you fronted up to work on time and got through your work, then what happened at home stayed at home. This demarcation has been eroded since the advent of social media, smartphones and the permanent connectedness we now 'enjoy'.

Still, in 2004 work and home were very, very distinct. But when your workplace is your home, as at Davis, that distinction completely disappears. 'Home' is reduced to the small room you sleep in. This means that most of your normal home activities take place within the workplace.

Shades of grey ... well, blue really

I had started to experience some of the unacceptable behaviour Richard had warned us about back in training. Behaviour that was unacceptable in the workplace was being played out at night (well, after 6 pm as there was still no night!), in the bar, in the theatre — in our workplace.

I made it clear to my expeditioners that they could do whatever they liked in their room, but outside of the room it was a Federal Government workplace and professional rules applied. But of course those normal rules didn't and couldn't always apply. We had a bar and we served alcohol at dinnertime — and that's not in the government handbook! It was a grey area, an issue that could not be solved by hard and fast rules, one that could only be managed through mutual respect.

Before leaving Hobart I had heard stories about a recent expedition where the women expeditioners were sent out camping on the plateau so the boys could have a 'porn and prawn' night. I was floored at the time. What decade were we living in? So I kept my eyes and ears open, or so I thought.

Respect was sorely missing on the night of Saturday, 18 December. The day had gone well, dinner was over and many expeditioners were looking forward to Blake's screening of the home movie of his trip through Thailand. After dinner I said good night and retired to my room to write my daily Station Log and rest and reflect on the day. Thirty minutes later there was a knock on the door.

'Rach, you better come down to the theatre. There's a walk-out. It's messy.'

I hurried down to our small cinema. It was really just another square, flat room but at least it was completely blacked out so we could watch movies. The door was shut and on the door was a hand-written sign 'This movie contains graphic content. Don't come in if you are offended easily. If you are offended easily, fuck off now!' That was a bad sign! The door opened as I approached and two expeditioners hurried out, ashen and with a look of disgust on their faces. I stopped at the door and poked my head in. I couldn't believe it. Blake's home movie was a full-on account of his sex-trip to Thailand. Everything was on display, close-up and personal. I quickly shut the door, horrified.

Many thoughts ran through my mind. This could easily become a station-wide issue. How many of my expeditioners had been exposed to this? It wasn't just distasteful, it was illegal. It is illegal to screen pornographic movies in a workplace. I thought about how the AAD would respond once they heard. I thought about the reams of paperwork I would face dealing with the complaints. But most of all I thought about my people. Those still inside obviously had an appetite for this at some level, or perhaps they just felt too intimidated to walk out, but there would be many now locked in their rooms trying to purge those images from their minds.

I asked my colleague, 'How long to go?'

He poked his head in just as the film was ending. 'It's over.'

I sighed. At least I wouldn't have to go barging in and pull the plug on the projector. Instead I went looking for casualties.

In the bar two guys were playing darts. They waved and went back to their game. Okay, I thought, they're all right. I went into the mess. Empty. The entire place was deserted. I thanked my colleague and quickly went back to my room and drafted an email to Hobart. I had to get on the front foot 'up' the food chain. They needed to hear it from me first before it filtered up from one of the other stations, all mixed up and misinformed. I spelt out the exact scenario and the expected impact on the station, and recommended Blake be given a formal warning.

I tried to sleep but couldn't. I would need to address this head-on in the morning. The cinema held 40 people and there were only about 50 on station that night. I needed to know who had been exposed to the movie so I went looking for Blake. The theatre was empty and I tracked him back to his room.

I found him smiling and enthusiastic about the showing of the film. What?! What was going on in his head that made him think I would condone it, especially in a workplace?

I explained to him that what he had done not only went against our code of conduct, but was illegal and it was within my powers to have him removed from the station and sent back to Australia at the next available opportunity. He insisted it was just a bit of harmless fun, and the sign on the door was obvious—they knew what they were coming to see. It was an adult choice. Everyone had a ball!

How do some people go through life and still not have any idea about what is socially acceptable? I talked through what I remembered about the laws governing what is permissible for public display, the AAD policies around appropriate behaviour and finally the cultural norms we were trying to instil. I think most of it was lost on him, but he did get the bit about being sent home. Still professing he had done nothing wrong, Blake gave me a list of who had been in the room when he started the movie. I think he had been so engrossed in his own performance he hadn't noticed people walking out!

Strike while the iron's hot

It was late now, but I knew I had to deal with my people right there and then. One by one, I visited each person on the list to let them know I understood what had happened and was dealing strongly with the issue. They were surprised to find me at their door. At least I had changed back out of my pyjamas! The reactions were mixed: some people defended their adult choice to watch the video; others were apologetic, indicating they had no idea of the content and hadn't read the sign on the door. They figured it was going to be just a garden-variety holiday film.

The point was it wasn't a judgement by me on the merits or otherwise of pornography. As I'd said all along, what you did in the privacy of your own room was your business. But this wasn't private, and this wasn't a bedroom. It was a very public screening in a workplace. No shades of grey. It was black and white.

It was 1 am by the time I finished checking in on all those who'd been in the theatre. With just three exceptions my people said they had made the choice to go in, knowing they might be surprised by the content. They had made an adult decision to watch, and when it was clear that it was just a showcase of Blake's sexual conquests most had made an adult decision to leave. Few had stayed to the end, which was when the worst of the movie was played.

Unsurprisingly, Antarctic expeditioners are a resilient bunch. I was lucky. The impact wasn't going to be as bad as I'd originally thought. And it *was* luck, pure and simple. We were all grown-ups and could make adult choices, but it was also a workplace where legislation on bullying and harassment applied.

Saturday 18th December

A quiet day and a terrible night.

Terrific Indian dinner — Kirsten is an amazing cook! Then came back to my room to relax while Blake's movie played. After all the work on setting and communicating what it is we stand for I'm terribly disappointed that so many people would go to Blake's movie after seeing the sign on the door. Although someone did tell me the door had been propped open at the start to let people in, which means they wouldn't have read the sign and were expecting holiday snaps from Thailand.

I have requested over-the-phone counselling for the three people who were badly offended. Hopefully the counselling will help and I won't have to go through the EEO processes.

Blake still didn't get it after I talked to him. I'm so angry but also fearful about tomorrow. It will be a black mark against my leadership I'm sure.

In the morning I addressed the expeditioners at breakfast. But I had another challenge, as Blake was one of the aviation team. Taking him off station would severely curtail our science operations. The AAD and

I were faced with a moral dilemma. Send Blake home and send a clear signal about appropriate behaviour, or accept this was a serious but one-off event, counsel Blake and continue to run the science program. The AAD agreed with my concerns but thought it would quickly blow over. They were keen for me to let it go. I was less convinced but in the end agreed. It was in poor taste, it was unbelievably disrespectful and it was illegal. And he was going to get away with it. Shades of grey indeed!

Sunday 19th December

After the debacle of last night my guys cheered me up no end today.

Someone had created a poster and stuck it on the outside of the green store. It looked totally official, government logos and signatures—the works.

It was a mocked-up 'Heritage Listing' for the 'Out-of-Code Food'. With all the negative emotion it was great to see people laughing about the food issue.

It was quiet today, but I know that as soon as the planes arrive it will go crazy. Everyone will suddenly 'need' to be flown somewhere.

White Christmas

The lead-up to Christmas was challenging for me. I place great stock in celebrations. At home, my birthday is referred to as 'the Festival of Rachael' because I somehow manage to string it out over a week. This was my first Christmas away from my family and friends in 35 years, and it felt hollow. I knew I had some presents to open but it just wasn't the same not being with them. I began to feel quite homesick.

I pulled myself out of the funk by staying busy. I would do all my work then go looking for extra work. The whole station seemed like they were coping in the same way. Just stay busy! Try not to think about it.

Friday 24th December

Christmas Eve. Feeling alone and lonely so I stayed busy today. Took three phone calls today from radio stations in Australia wanting to hear about Christmas in Antarctica. I told them what I could but took the opportunity also to tell Mum how much I loved her and how much I missed her. I knew she would cry but I knew she would also feel proud of her little girl.

We had so much fun preparing Christmas Eve dinner. Chris and I were in charge of the deep fryer and it was great singing 'London Calling'—I hope '80s music makes a comeback, I love it!

Saturday 25th December

What a wonderful day! It started with a surprise present from Kirsten and a beautiful card. I worked as slushy in the morning, cleaning the plates, prepping the food and generally helping get the kitchen up and running. Had great fun making doughnuts in the deep fryer! It was great just to do something where I didn't need to think. Dip the dough in, watch it cook, take out the doughnut, roll it in the cinnamon. Over and over. A real change of mental gears and a great relief from dealing with crises, issues and personalities!

There are no reindeer down here so Santa arrived pulling an ice sled behind his quad bike! He had a massive collection of presents—gifts from people at home and gifts we had made for each other in the last few weeks.

Heaps of people back home had heard the radio interviews. It was great to have my expeditioners come up to me, full of pride and tell me their mum, dad or loved one had heard the interviews. Somehow it made them feel connected not only to 'back home' but also to me and our mission.

It's so surreal to spend a day like this with so many unrelated adults, and it was sheer joy. Not a single moment I didn't savour. Particularly right now as I indulge myself with Belgian truffles and a hot chocolate in bed!

I spoke to my family on Christmas Day on the telephone. I had about 15 minutes available but by the time I'd spoken to everyone I'd spent 20 minutes. I let Mum know I really loved the new handbag she had sent down. I gently explained that, while it *was* lovely, it would serve absolutely no purpose in Antarctica! We don't carry money as there's nowhere to spend it. I don't need a wallet, loyalty cards or mobile phone, and don't carry keys as there are no locks on the doors. The only personal effect I carry is my lip balm, and that slips nicely into my pocket. We had a great laugh about it!

Many handmade cards were distributed on station. I still have my card from Josh, one of the meteorologists. It was a lovely card, full of beautiful thoughts and sentiments, but his writing reminded me of a colt learning to gallop, or a 14-year-old boy after a growth spurt — all arms and legs. He wrote like I did in Year 12, full of huge, elegant and poetic words, all in context, but very much overdone.

What I learned

- *Leadership is often about managing ambiguity.* The grey areas aren't taught in business school, and many situations in our workplaces do not have a black or white response. Leaders must use their judgement, experience and wisdom to make a call in these situations.

Chapter 19

Feeling stressed and overworked? It could be your boundaries

One of the great things about the way the AAD prepare our expeditions is that they go to great lengths to make sure we never run out of anything. Sometimes it doesn't work out quite right, as I had seen from the green store debacle, but they always try to err on the side of caution. With resupply anything from three to nine months away, we just couldn't run out of important supplies.

Sex on the ice

Which is why I was shocked that after just two months on the ice we had run out of condoms.

Many people were, and still are, intrigued about how normal daily functions operate in Antarctica. It was commonplace for journalists to ask me how we went to the toilet, whether we had showers and what we ate. Less commonplace, perhaps because of the delicacy of the topic, was what we did about sex and intimacy.

I can picture the accountant back in Australia with his spreadsheet, trying to work out how many condoms we would need:

1 Firstly, many people, say 50 per cent, are in relationships with people back home, so I'll assume they won't need any...

2 Then, we'll have a certain number of people who just aren't interested in pursuing any kind of lovin'...

3 Then, among the people who are interested, many will bring their own supplies...

4 So, maybe out of up to 120 expeditioners we could assume, maybe 30 would try their luck in Antarctica...

5 But the young PhD candidates and the single tradies could be heavy consumers...

6 Hmm...30 people, let's say 300 condoms?

7 Let's make it a round number and prepare for the worst. I'll order 2000—that way no one can say we didn't create a 'safe workplace'.

After just two months our seemingly generous supply of 2000 condoms had an inventory level of zero. When I found this out I was staggered. What are these people up to when they go out on their little jaunts to remote corners of Antarctica? Is there any science going on at all?

Some of the 'welcome back' conversations I had now started to take on a new meaning.

'How was the trip? Did you get all your science done?'

'Yes Boss...we were hard at it.'

Good grief!

I heard via the grapevine of one relationship that was blooming, and causing all sorts of ructions. For some reason Antarctic expeditioners adopt an extraordinarily strong 'moral compass'. As a unit they didn't appreciate a married man and a single female scientist spending lots of time together. And when the couple openly displayed their affection at a dinner party many expeditioners were indignant.

A blooming relationship

On Boxing Day I could see them being more and more isolated by the rest of the team. Was it because these two were getting something no one else was? Or was it because the others were being strong in their commitment to their spouse or partner and felt everyone else should be? As on remote mining sites, there is a perception of rife infidelity in Antarctica over summer. Some people assume that with all these fit and healthy, but lonely, people with lots of time on their hands, the temptation to not remain celibate must be too great.

Nothing could be further from the truth. Occasionally two people will meet there and fall in love, and the rest of the community is thrilled. It's more normal to have couples in a community, so we're always very happy for the new couple, as long as they are discreet. Public displays of affection are an absolute no-go and anyone showcasing that they're 'getting something the rest of us aren't' soon incurs the wrath of the community.

So while sexual relationships are certainly not unheard of, they are relatively unusual, which meant the fact we'd gone though 2000 condoms in two months confounded me no end. This wasn't an Olympic Games village. What was going on?

I reflected on my role in managing the issue. My hunch was that some of the younger people who had a minimal student income back home were stockpiling a personal stash to take back with them. But apart from the mysterious disappearance of 2000 condoms I had no right to intervene in this aspect of my expeditioners' personal lives. They would have to work it out.

I did raise the issue of the condoms at breakfast to lots of laughs, jocularity and fingerpointing.

Tuesday 28th December

What a boring bloody day! The wind was gusting to 40 knots (65 kilometres per hour), making it unsafe for the choppers, so we didn't fly up to the plateau as planned and my long-awaited field training didn't eventuate. So instead we sat around all day waiting.

This morning was hysterical. I can't think of another workplace where the boss stands up at breakfast to talk about condoms!

I think people were stockpiling, not in the hope of scoring, but to take a supply back home because by lunchtime there were over a thousand condoms back in the store — returned, unopened. Still 1000 out in circulation though, which is making my mind boggle!

(continued)

Tuesday 28th December (cont'd)

The not-so-discreet fling has everyone talking. I'm leaving it alone. For now. But will watch it closely.

I'm getting fat. I haven't exercised since we've been here as the gym is always full and I'm always busy. Plus, I'm eating a lot of comfort food and starting to bust out of my jeans. Come winter when it's just the 18 of us I will go for a run on the treadmill everyday. Need to get back into shape, not just because I like looking and feeling healthy, but because it will be good for my mental balance. Plus if I grow out of my clothes there ain't no Witchery down the road to pop into and buy some bigger sizes!

Sleepout and New Year's Eve

I was determined every expeditioner should have the opportunity to camp out during summer, even though it wasn't part of their official duties. I wanted to make sure everyone had great stories to tell when they got home. So I dressed it up and called it 'field training'. Some expeditioners had no reason to stay out on the ice overnight. The plumbers and carpenters, for example, worked solely within the station. If they were required, for some reason or another, to help out with a science project, they were always out in the morning and back in the evening.

I announced the concept of field training one evening to the expeditioners. The idea of taking two days off to have fun on the ice, watch the penguins and observe this beautiful continent met with wide enthusiasm. There were several people at Davis that summer who had made three or four trips to Antarctica and had never been out of sight of the station. They appreciated an 'officially sanctioned jolly' immensely.

Part of my reasoning was selfish. I knew that come winter, when we would have the time to spend days or weeks away from the station, the climate and conditions would prevent it. I was no camper, but the opportunity to go out on the ice and snuggle up in a massive sleeping bag for the night was something I was looking forward to.

Thursday 30th December

I'm back in bed in my own room and I'm so tired I can't even remember the day.

We camped out last night on my field training excursion. Because of the high winds we couldn't fly to the plateau, so we just walked out onto Lake Dingle instead. I was surprised at how warm I was. Even though the ground was hard and I didn't get any sleep I certainly couldn't say I was cold.

We pitched tent in broad daylight, went to bed in broad daylight, tried to sleep in broad daylight and got up and decamped at 5 am, in broad daylight.

I don't know what I was thinking, but until we actually got there I thought I would lie on my back and look at the stars!!! Duh! But it was more fun that I expected and we were back in time for a breakfast of pancakes and poached eggs. Gotta love Kirsten and her kitchen skills!

Big preparations today for tomorrow's party. It seems we're having a party every week at the moment!

Friday 31st December

I just survived NYE Antarctica style. We had a live band playing rock hits — lots of talent on station! There were only a few pissed idiots, and I kept an eye out for random acts of stupidity.

Danced on the pool table tonight! The boys joined in and took their shirts off. Lots of wild abandon, in good fun. Usually they just watch the girls dancing with their arms crossed.

Everyone thought I was drunk … on four glasses of tonic water! So funny. I guess it looked like vodka or gin. I thought I would have a one or two drinks tonight but after only half a glass of bubbly I started to feel queasy.

(continued)

> ## Friday 31st December (cont'd)
>
> I used to over-consume in the past, but now I don't really need it to have fun. Somewhere along the line I got comfortable with myself just as I am. I don't know when this happened but it did. I think the fact I can dance around and be silly without being fortified by a wine or three shows me I've grown as a person. I certainly couldn't have done that 12 months ago.
>
> As I look back on 2004 I will remember a great year. It started well and ended well and I really don't recall any bad times. Finishing up at Parks in July was big and then the months in Hobart. And now I'm in Antarctica.
>
> How do I feel looking ahead? Excited, relieved and strangely relaxed and happy to be here. I thought I'd be counting off the days by now but I'm not. It's not that stressful and I think boredom will be more of a problem.

It's boundaries, not time management

A really tricky issue that had plagued me in Hobart and that now arose on station was dealing with constant interruptions and requests for advice, decisions or action. My deputies were taking some of the load but it wasn't enough. I was convinced that I wasn't managing my time well. I reckoned I should be able to do the bulk of my work in around 10 hours, but it was taking me upwards of 14 and sometimes 16 hours a day.

This left me sleep deprived, mentally exhausted, grumpy and short-fused in the mornings. People look for stability and predictability in leaders. They should have a very good idea of how their leader reacts in a given set of circumstances. But operating under sub-optimal conditions meant my people couldn't predict my response, and they became more and more risk averse and cautious around me.

It wasn't that I snapped or growled at people. My way of dealing with this kind of stress was much less obvious. As a good ex-Catholic girl I internalised everything. I swallowed it and it festered inside, breeding resentment and a slow, seething anger. I often still marvel at many Mediterranean people I know. You know, the ones with short fuses—they 'go off' at the drop of a hat but two minutes later are smiling and laughing again. It takes me a long time to get angry, and a long, long time to cool down again. Up to now in my life, by the time I had gotten angry enough to do something, it was often too late—the issue had turned into a crisis.

The absence of my lifelong friends and family and the lack of distractions and entertainment in Antarctica turned into a blessing. Alone in my room at night I would reflect on my day, my interactions with people, and my life. I think few others get or take this opportunity. Days were packed with action and excitement and nights were packed with introspection and reflection.

It was during these nights that I realised that my ingrained internalisation program, the one running inside my head that kept telling me to 'suck it up, be a good quiet girl', was destructive and was getting in the way of my being a good leader. Somehow I needed to find my voice. I needed the skills and techniques to 'push back' without letting the pendulum swing too far in the other direction. It would be a question of balance and I would need to approach it carefully.

I started by trying to understand the facts, and there are no facts without data. So one day in mid December I made a tally board in my head. I wanted to count the interruptions and requests and gauge their impact on my time.

The first day there were 70 requests, and that didn't include 'urgent' emails. They ranged from the simple 'Can you open Fort Knox so we can get some wine out?' to the more complex 'Can you decide which science program gets the magnetometer for the trip to the plateau tomorrow?' But each interruption demanded my attention, and the swing back into my other work took time. I kept my board for a week, and by the end of the week I knew what I had to do.

My problem wasn't time management. There wasn't a pattern of goofing off or being distracted. I knew how to prioritise my work and wasn't getting bogged down in trivial matters. My problem was my boundaries. In some areas of my relationships with the expeditioners my personal boundaries were so permeable that they might have well not existed at all.

Sunday 2nd January 2005

For the last two weeks I've been trying something new and it's working a treat. I'm meeting questions with questions, instead of answers. My people are adults and it's my job to help them make good decisions, not to make their decisions for them.

I think people are still a bit freaked out by my, on one hand, dancing on the pool table and, on the other, being (or trying to be) inscrutable.

But I need a new tactic to handle the interruptions. I need better personal boundaries. From now on if I am watching a movie and someone asks me to do something, or if I'm relaxing with a cuppa or if I've got my head deep in a conversation or in my computer, I have a new response: 'Does it have to be done now?' It's like saying 'Not no, just not now'. People are shocked because it's a new 'me', but they quickly understand. I think they will need to retrain themselves just as I am retraining myself.

And the bloody complaints. Complaints about the food, quarters, schedule, roster. You name it. I want to deal with issues, not tissues! So I put it back on them: 'By complaining, what are you asking me to do about it?' Instead of trying to solve the problem or be an agony aunt I think I'm getting them to see that a complaint is an escalation. Don't escalate an issue if you don't want it escalated!!!

So I think I'm learning to be a better leader by protecting myself. I certainly don't feel like I've got to let off steam anymore.

What I learned

- *Set personal boundaries and keep them.* If you are 'always available' to people, then they will always approach you. If you have an important personal commitment at night and don't want to be interrupted by work issues, then turn your phone off. If you don't have 'five minutes' now, then say so and invite the person to come back at a time when you can give them your full, undivided attention. It's not about you, it's about them. Your team deserves a leader who is fully engaged, not distracted and glancing at their email or smartphone while someone is speaking to them.

Chapter 20

Good leaders know when to show emotion

For the first six weeks of our expedition all air transport used our two Squirrel helicopters. The Squirrel is a tough, versatile helicopter that can carry up to four passengers and a small amount of luggage. They have a range of around 500 kilometres, give or take 100 kilometres, depending on the weather.

The planes arrive and the pace picks up

But a great deal of our science work, called 'deep field' work, took place much further away than the helicopters could go. Deep field work took place far inland on the huge layers of ice that cover the continent. Here the ice is more than 1500 metres thick and is incredibly dense. It has been laid down as snow over countless centuries and packed down into ice by each succeeding snowfall. Scientists calculate that if all the ice were to melt, the global ocean levels would rise by more than 5 metres. Climate scientists speak about catastrophe for our way of life if oceans rise by half a metre!

The scientists working out in the deep field areas did mostly seismic research and glaciology. At other stations ice core sampling is the norm. Scientists extract large cylinders of ice, digging deeper and deeper with each pass. By applying sophisticated equipment to the ice core, the scientists can date the ice and determine the makeup of the Earth's atmosphere at the time the ice was formed. Pretty cool stuff.

I must admit that the actual science of deep-drilling ice cores was beyond me. But what wasn't beyond me was my responsibility for the safe delivery and return of these scientists to and from their chosen location. The only way out to these areas, other than a hazardous and weeks-long overland trek, was by plane. We were awaiting two planes — CASA C-212 Aviocars — and they were late.

The planes were originally due to arrive in late December but an issue with the regulator, combined with poor weather, meant they were already two weeks overdue. My deep-field scientists were becoming increasingly agitated. What had been an eight-week window to perform their work was now at best six weeks. They would need to work around the clock to catch up if they were to achieve their objectives.

By now I was fully up to speed with managing flight operations. Overseeing and monitoring refuelling, take-off and landing, and weather broadcasts, and generally keeping all concerned happy, is a complex affair. With the arrival of the planes I would now need to seriously step up the speed and efficiency of flight operations.

Wednesday 5th January

I'm buggered. The CASAs arrived and things got really busy. I think they will settle down but for now it's crazy. I hope we manage to get our systems and processes up and happening so it can run itself a bit.

Got bawled out today by head office for not informing them about Margaret's fall. She slipped over on the ice and bumped her head. No blood, no stitches, no concussion. Not a big deal and no need to panic. What can you do? I didn't even think about reporting it. I know how annoying it is for them but I guess I didn't see it as an 'incident'.

I think one or two people at head office are suffering relevancy deficiency syndrome. They are so important for half the year getting people ready but when we are actually in Antarctica they are largely irrelevant to us. Maybe this is where the us-and-them culture gap has come from. It's almost like some of them are hanging out for gossip and are upset when they don't hear it first!

The CASA C-212 Aviocar is a multipurpose aircraft with a short take-off and landing. Ours had skis as well as wheels for landing gear and had been converted to suit the unique requirements of Antarctica. When kitted out for civilian use the CASA can take 24 people. We were using ours like army paratroopers. Troop seats lined the walls, leaving a large area in the middle of the fuselage for cargo and supplies.

Depending on how much gear was being carried, our CASAs could take a payload of 1000 kg (12 people, or eight with gear) up to 750 kilometres inland, with an extra range margin of 100 kilometres if something was to go wrong. On a continent the size of Antarctica, 750 kilometres gets you nowhere near the middle, but it was sufficient for our scientific requirements.

The morning after the planes arrived I was besieged! It seemed like everyone suddenly had an urgent need to leave station! I got up early expecting a big day and during the short walk to my office I had beaten off 10 or so requests. 'We have a schedule, we have a flight plan based on the scientific imperatives. We have been over this with a fine-tooth comb and no, there is no negotiation today', I said as I walked into my office.

Thursday 6th January

Up at 0700 (oh-seven hundred) and finished at 2200. I need to practise my 24-hour times!

In my lunch break today I signed heaps of letters for stamp collectors. It made me think about the status attached to the Station Leader role. People around the world must see this role as very exalted and special. I wonder if people like the Prime Minister feel the same way—that they are too close to it to actually get what the fuss is about?

I'm really enjoying working with the CASA pilots. They are a highly professional outfit and are also a lot of fun. I'm learning an incredible amount from them and the engineers who came with the planes.

(continued)

Thursday 6th January (cont'd)

We deployed 20 people into the field today and that's the last we'll see of them for a while. The CASA will drop them some supplies next week and we'll keep in touch via the radio sched. I can't wait to get rid of more of them! (As much as I love them!)

PS I notice a hint of jealousy among the helicopter pilots. So funny. They are no longer top of the heap!

PPS I think if I wasn't hyper-organised this flight business would get totally out of control really quickly. As it is I still had moments today when I struggled to keep all the plates spinning.

How not to prepare for a sleepout in Antarctica

Despite their renewed sense of urgency and the months they had had to prepare, it appeared only some of the scientists were actually 'ready'. One sparkling clear morning I was doing the final prep and check for a team headed out for three weeks on the ice. There were five going out this morning, but there were only four waiting at the plane.

'Where's Stewie?' I asked.

'Oh, he slept in. He's just having a quick shower.'

I thought, these guys have been waiting two months for this day! How can he have slept in? 'Okay,' I continued, 'let's run through some final checks. Ration packs?'

'Yep.'

'Glacier boots?'

'Aww, forgot ... we'll go get them.'

'No, don't—not yet. Let's work out what else you don't have. Stove?'

'Yep.'

'Have you tested it?'

'Aww, forgot ...'

'First aid kit?'

'Hmm ...'

And so it went. If their very lives didn't depend on each piece of forgotten equipment it would have been hilarious. But I laughed anyway and made a mental note to ensure the first-time scientists really understand the nature of the environment they were headed out into and prepared themselves properly.

The next day was quiet. All the aircraft were away at other stations or in the field. There were only 40 or so people actually on station and it was blissful. I took some extra time to think about the dynamics of this incredible workplace.

Saturday 8th January

A return to normal today. Well, sort of normal. Sam had just come back from being with the Russians for the last week. Apparently they had commented that I must be 'a very strong woman to run a station'. It made me realise that in an international context my background is very different.

The Station Leader at Zhongshan is a former submariner (he'll have the close-quarters living thing down pat). It's amazing that until recently the AAD also mostly recruited from the military. It's only been in the last 20 years that things have changed. But it's ironic because many military people would by design be quite precise and regimented and would expect the same from their people. This would be the worst style of leadership for Antarctica — or really any leadership role other than military! There's a time and a place for a 'command and control' leadership style — but it ain't Antarctica. A person who thought only in black-and-white terms would also really struggle. You need to find the grey areas and be confident with handling them. It's a great training ground for adaptive leadership.

(continued)

Saturday 8th January (cont'd)

In Antarctica you have to be flexible, adaptable and able to deal with ambiguity. I'm still learning that bit!

It's funny how the AAD is weak on some of their processes, where I'm quite strong on processes and systems. One of the things I have done is implement the whiteboard system for flight scheduling so that everyone can see who's going where and when. I didn't realise it was an innovative approach to solving an old problem until several of the old-timers commented on it, and how it made a big difference. To be honest, I only did it to get a bit of peace around here! Who knew?!

Unauthorised cricket and a taste of things to come

Three deliveries of fresh food were scheduled for our year in Antarctica. Fresh is of course a relative term. When a lettuce is picked, packed, delivered to a market, collected by a distributor and trucked to the supermarket we still call that pretty fresh. We're happy with that level of freshness at home. But when that supply chain is extended by a month and involves docks, crates, pallets and a three-week voyage across the Southern Ocean, fresh takes on a whole new meaning!

So fresh fruit was a major treat for the month or so it lasted, and only fruit with real staying power would survive the journey south. Which is why we had no bananas, but we did have oranges. They keep well and we had enough for the rest of summer. That was, until it was time for cricket.

It was late, probably 2 am. They were drunk, which is never an excuse, but perhaps it is a reason.

They (who will remain nameless) had decided that it would be 'fun' to play cricket, indoors, with oranges. Let's face it, what red-blooded young Australian has never whacked a piece of citrus with a stick! I know I have, and I hate cricket.

But this was a different time, a different place and with different rules.

Matt, one of my winterers, was first on the scene in the morning. The mess was one thing, and it was annoying. But what galled the winterers was that these irresponsible summerers had destroyed our winter food supply.

Sunday 9th January

My winterers were all growly today because of the oranges. Several of the boys visiting from Casey got through nearly a third of our oranges last night. There are pieces of orange all over the mess hall. I found those responsible and made them clean it up straight away, but the mess is only part of the problem. I can see why my winterers are pissed off. It's our home for a year, and the next resupply has already left Hobart. Anything that gets broke, stays broke.

I'm so angry. Surely, they knew that those oranges were the last ones we'd eat for almost a year? I actually think it was just thoughtless—they simply didn't think. They were shocked at my reaction as I rarely get cross, but I reckon using emotion appropriately shows strong leadership. So when I told them in no uncertain terms that their actions were selfish as 'they would be back home soon and could eat bloody oranges every day if they felt like it, but we couldn't because they'd just destroyed our supplies', the penny dropped and I saw remorse on their faces. Good. I'm glad.

With some of the summerers' lack of understanding (or is it empathy?) of the winter, it's easy to see how us-and-them scenarios are created. Right now with 120 people in and around the station it's quite easy to ignore someone who is pissing you off. We also have a dynamic where the winterers are 'united' against a common foe—summerers. They roll their eyes and many of them have said 'I can't wait till they go'.

I agree it will be different when they go but it means we will probably then turn on each other. With months of darkness ahead and no other distractions we will fight among ourselves, I'm sure.

Monday 10th January

In bed at 7.30 pm. I'm overtired and getting irritated by things that really shouldn't irritate me so I figure it's best I go to bed. Oh the joy of leadership—you need the self-awareness to know when to step in and when to step out.

The station leadership team meeting was flat today but I just didn't have the energy to bother about it.

I found the WHOLE PLACE annoying today and for the first time I feel lonely. Even though there are 80 people here at the moment I still feel alone. I'm not really close to anyone, which has also been my choice. I'm not even sure what's pissing me off really. Probably just tired. Jeremy, Janine, Mike all corrected me on trivial issues today. Maybe I should just stop writing and sleep! And exercise. But not now. Zzz

Tuesday 11th January

Felt awesome all day today. 12 hours sleep made all the difference. I can't believe I wrote all that drivel yesterday. What a self-indulgent thing I am when I'm tired. Lucky no one will ever read this. Lesson to self: YOU MUST GET YOUR REST!

What I learned

- *Strong leaders know how to show emotion.* The right emotion at the right time tells people how you really feel, not just what you're thinking.

- *Look after your body.* Make sure you take time to rest during crazy busy times. It might not seem like you have the luxury of time but it is critical to maintain your mental acuity and keep your emotions in control.

Chapter 21

Think ahead and know what you will do in an emergency

There is nothing tougher than living in a community of strangers, in freezing temperatures, around the clock and with no escape. Well, actually there is. The one thing worse than this is living in the same environment with the same strangers, but this time you're stuck inside a tent, around the clock, with no running water and no toilet. Oh, and someone forgot to pack the toothpaste!

The plane crash

Two scientists and two pilots were on their way to the Amery Ice Shelf. Our pre-flight checks of the plane, expeditioners and likely landing area were all clear so I sent the plane off with the confidence of a seasoned air-traffic controller. I noted the time in my log and wrote up the time for the check-in from the pilot once they had safely landed.

I didn't get that check-in. What I got was:

'VLZ Davis, VLZ Davis, VLZ Davis. This is Victor Hotel Bravo, Do you read? Over.'

'Victor Hotel Bravo, this is Davis. We are reading you loud and clear. Over.'

'Davis, we have an incident here. Over.'

'Repeat please, Victor Hotel Bravo.'

'Davis, we hit something and our landing gear is damaged. Over.'

'Please advise condition of passengers and crew. Over.'

'No injuries. Over.'

What a relief, but I knew that the safety of the expeditioners was still at risk.

'Victor Hotel Bravo. Can you please switch over to the satellite phone and I'll call you now.'

'Roger. Out.'

This was it. My worst nightmare had come true. Prior to and since arriving in Antarctica I had often lain awake wondering how I would react in an emergency that threatened the lives of my expeditioners. And here it was. VHB was down.

Our planes were brand new. This was one of the reasons they were so popular. We had upgraded from the Twin Otters only this year. The CASA-212 was bigger, faster and quieter, had better avionics and was … safer! The aircraft was put to use by military forces around the world as a medium-sized transport. But it was unproven in Antarctica.

There were many radio sets on station, all tuned to the same frequencies. This brief exchange could have been heard by anyone and I needed to take control of the situation. So I rang the chief pilot on the satellite phone and tried to understand exactly what had happened.

A bolt had sheared off the nose landing-gear after presumably hitting a large piece of ice. The plane could still be flown but as the landing gear had collapsed the nose was dragging in the snow, making it impossible to taxi and therefore impossible to take off.

They were 400 kilometres away, and in rapidly worsening conditions.

I got hold of Bruce, my aeronautical engineer, who talked through the incident with the pilot. He turned and wrote, 'Get the diesel mechanic up here please'. I hustled down to our expert fitter and turner.

'Keep it under your lid', I said to him. 'VHB is stranded and we need you up in the ops room!'

Quietly, he followed me up and together he and Bruce mapped out a plan to manufacture a replacement bolt for the stricken plane. While we had lots of spare parts stored on station, this bolt wasn't one of them, and there was no hardware store down the road where we could pick one up. It would need some very skilled work to manufacture a replacement on the spot.

Crisis assessment

I collected the rest of the aviation team and my deputy leaders and we discussed how to conduct the search and rescue. The stranded expeditioners had 10 days' food and plenty of water on board and could shelter either in their tents or on the plane. They were not in imminent danger. However, they were alone, isolated and cold—in the harshest environment on the planet.

We mapped out a rescue mission using our other plane. We could send it out with supplies, mechanics and the tools to jack up the aircraft, fix the problem and bring her and her crew home. But first we needed to speak to the Civil Aviation Safety Authority (CASA). This Commonwealth agency is responsible for the safety of all civil aircraft in Australia and its territories. They manage regulatory items such as aircraft registers, operators, licences and registrations. And they also play a key oversight role in any aircraft incidents.

Our contact at CASA was adamant. Because we could not establish the cause of the accident we could not fly the other plane out. This was the first time these particular aircraft that had been especially fitted with skis had been used in Antarctica, so we didn't know if the crash was caused by a design fault, pilot error or some other unforeseen circumstance. I agreed with CASA when I viewed it in this light. It just might have been a design fault and I certainly didn't want eight people and two planes stranded! Until we knew the cause of the incident we had to sit tight. The forecast was for three days of bad weather ahead. I was worried about four of my people living in a tent through a blizzard and foul weather.

I was also mindful that incidents in Antarctica attract media attention, always. I didn't want the media to get hold of the story before we'd had a chance to contact the families of these people and reassure them they would be okay and would be back on station within a few days.

Saved by a blizzard

So the forecast blizzard conditions were a mixed blessing. On the one hand, it would delay our attempts to retrieve the team, but on the other hand it would take the immediate pressure off as a search-and-rescue would be impossible. It would buy us the time to make a good decision and do whatever we had to do well. Thankfully, we could stay in contact using the satellite phone. I arranged to speak to the stranded expeditioners twice a day to keep them updated on progress at our end and to hear how things were going at their end.

Wednesday 12th January

My biggest day in Antarctica to date. VHB had a 'bingle' on landing and I have four people stranded at Rofe Glacier (400 kilometres away). The front ski hit a large block of ice and the bolt that holds the nose-gear attachment sheared off. We will try and get CASA approval to go out tomorrow with a replacement bolt to attempt a rescue.

I think we handled it well. It was important to stay calm and keep the train on track. I think it's important to over-communicate to the troops so the speculation is kept to a minimum. I sent out an 'all-station' email and plan to send one every few hours just to keep the other 116 people on station well informed.

I'm happy my people are safe but this is huge. It's like a really bad Gilligan's Island—they set out for a four-hour reconnaissance flight and now they're stranded!

It was now 24 hours after the event and alongside my station leadership team and the technical specialists involved, a team had mobilised in Hobart to provide support. Skytraders, the operator of the aircraft, were on standby, along with the team who designed and fitted the modifications. It was a national effort involving dozens of people, but I knew my role was pivotal. It was critical that I make good and sound decisions about the safety of my expeditioners. Less critical, but also important, would be how I led the rest of the expeditioners through the emergency. How I presented myself to the team, conveyed the news, and managed the inevitable gossip and misinformation would make all the difference.

I had sent a quick email the day of the crash but knew it wasn't nearly enough. I was only too aware from the store-person debacle that in the absence of real information, misinformation becomes truth. I also knew the station community would be watching me. They would take their cues about whether to be worried from me. Many people wouldn't be sure how anxious they should be and my actions, language and behaviour would be under close scrutiny.

Crisis leadership

It taught me a lot about the role of a leader through the tough times. It was not enough to just be 'in control of the situation'. I needed to be *seen* to be in control. I decided to be highly visible. I had to be seen about the place often, if not constantly, to give people a chance to ask questions and seek answers. I had to instil optimism but temper that with reality.

So I chose my words with great care. I spoke about an 'incident', not an 'accident'; and a 'retrieval', not a 'rescue'. I was being completely honest when I said I held 'concerns' for our colleagues but I wasn't 'worried'. These words convey very different meanings: while a leader's concern will be accepted by people, a leader showing worry will only increase the stress levels.

I decided to provide complete, accurate and timely information to create a sense of calmness and confidence. Information was critical. I kept my expeditioners informed about how the retrieval efforts were going and what impact this event would have on them and their roles. I divulged things that I typically would have kept on a 'need to know' basis, such as what our response to the media would be. My expeditioners were fully informed of our discussions with CASA, how the expeditioners were coping and what head office was doing to develop search-and-rescue options from other stations.

The information served three purposes. Firstly, it ensured there were no knowledge gaps — they had all the information I had. Secondly, it sent a signal that I trusted them with the information and valued their input. Thirdly, it created a sense of solidarity — 116 expeditioners and countless others against the elements, all pulling together.

I cancelled all new science flights and explained why. All air transport, including helicopters, would be focused on the retrieval. I explained that once the situation was resolved and everyone was safely back on station, the leadership team would meet to prioritise and reschedule further flights. This clear and regular communication helped focus people and also removed some stress from the leadership team, who didn't need to answer questions around 'when will we get to fly out to do our sampling?'.

People make an extraordinary commitment, and give up a lot, when they decide to undertake their scientific research in Antarctica. The small, roughly eight-week window of opportunity when the weather is suitable to undertake field research can come and go in an instant. The twin imperatives of cost and time put the scientists under significant pressure to complete their work. Any disruptions, be they weather or logistics, just add to an already complicated challenge.

Keeping morale strong and ensuring the rest of the works program stayed on track were considerations in every decision made. While the emergency response was clearly the highest priority, it is important during challenging times that the leader is perceived to keep their 'eye on the ball'. That is, they are expected not only to manage the crisis or challenge but also to ensure the critical day-to-day business continues.

Saturday 15th January

Well it looks like we'll be able to get VHB home tonight. We finally got clearance from CASA to send out VHA with the replacement bolts. The guys back home have done an incredible job testing the shear loads, and they determined that VHB must have hit a big (massive) block of invisible ice. The bolts are over-engineered to the max so I felt safe sending out VHA — just for good measure I got the VHB crew to sweep the landing area first!!!

VHA left with the bolts at 1715 hrs and arrived safety not long after 1900.

I'm just exhausted. Have existed on two to three hours of sleep for the last three days but I'm going to try and pin down what I have learned before I forget it.

What I learned

Deal appropriately with emergencies:

- Be calm in a crisis, or at least appear to be calm even if you are doing internal flip-flops. Take a deep breath, still the voice inside and be calm.

- Be highly visible. Be seen about the place so people can ask questions.

- Provide lots and lots of information — more is better. Don't gloss over it or hide it from people.

- Provide the same information to everyone — it encourages a sense of solidarity.

- Choose your words carefully. Some words excite passion, others calm.

- It's okay to admit you don't know something, as long as you confirm you have a plan for finding out the answer.

- It's okay to show emotion. People will appreciate your honesty.

The Robertson clan send-off.

The view from my cabin was spectacular.

Davis Station, or 'Coober Pedy' as it was known in summe

The colours in Antarctica are extraordina

Our first tomato—split 18 ways!

e B & S Ball. That's not my green satin dress,
ase you were wondering.

CASA-212 showing front ski assembly.

Two juvenile male elephant seals practise beach fighting.

The emperor penguins were fascinated by us and the quad bikes.

he Hagglunds—all-terrain vehicles.

ut on the quad bikes.

The magnificent emperor pengui

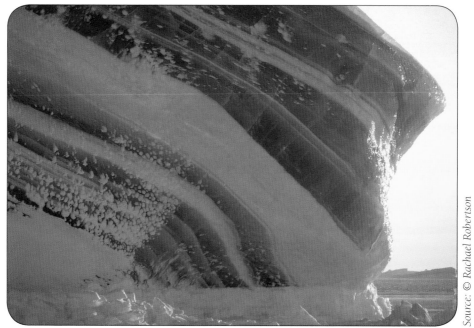

Some of the ice formations were truly wonderful.

Deep Lake—so saline it never freezes.

This Weddell seal pup is only
a few hours old.

Proof! Mid-winter swim in −13 °C.

We were glad to finally get up close and personal with the icebergs at the end of summer.

Chapter 22

When you're spending all your time managing, don't forget to lead

We had been on the ice for nigh on eight weeks and summer was quickly drawing to a close. We hadn't yet had a sunset, but already the air was chill with expectation of winter. We pushed on at a rapid pace for the rest of summer.

Driving under the influence

It was very important to stay on top of the technical management of the station but also to keep an eye out for simmering tensions. We had been lucky so far. Despite the availability of alcohol we hadn't had any alcohol-related incidents, until one of the summerers rolled a quad bike at 3 am.

Tuesday 25th January

Busy day. We had our station leadership team meeting at 9 am and all we could talk about was how to deal with the quad bike incident. One bad egg, and so on and so on.

I'm really annoyed with this expeditioner. After this and the plane crash our safety record has tanked. I was so hopeful that we would have a clean slate.

Wearing my deputised 'special constable' hat I threatened him a lot, but didn't arrest, imprison or formally write up the illegal aspects. Of course, I did all the workplace stuff like the asset assessment and the OH&S incident report. I'm so glad he's headed back to Australia in just a couple of weeks.

The end of science

We pushed on with our work with a greater sense of urgency than ever before. Days were long and the work was complex. The science programs were all nearing completion and we had just three groups yet to return to the field and collect their final samples and data.

Then the weather closed in with a bang. Unannounced. Unforecast. One minute it was sunny and 3 °C, the next minute a howling wind was ripping through, threatening to tear the skin from our flesh as we fought our way to shelter. The sky turned black with heavy cloud and small particles of ice swept across the station almost horizontally.

I was caught outside between two buildings when the wind hit. Wearing jeans, a tee shirt and polar fleece jacket I was chilled to the bone in the 15 seconds it took me to get to shelter. One by one we turned our home/away fire tags as we re-entered the station, bedraggled and numb with cold. To keep people safe it was a policy that any person travelling off station, for any distance at all, was required to carry a survival pack. The pack contained food, water, a radio, clothing, sleeping bag, compass, sleeping mat and bivvy bag. From the outset I was absolutely firm that we follow this policy and openly chastised anyone who did not. The result was full compliance. The result was that we were all safe.

Three expeditioners were out hiking when the weather struck. Within minutes they were on the radio and pinpointed their position. I sent out a small team in a Hagglunds and they brought them in quickly and safely. But this weather event was a harbinger of things to come. As Melbourne announced autumn with a cold snap, Antarctica sent a warning shot across our bows. In 15 minutes the temperature had plummeted to −15 °C with a wind chill factor of −20 °C. Being caught out in that was equivalent to standing outside in −35 °C weather.

People often ask me how cold it got in Antarctica. To most of us who live in temperate climates +5 °C is cold, −5 °C is really cold, and so is −35 °C. There's no real distinction for most people once you start getting into the minus numbers. But I explain it this way. Imagine you're on a tropical island holiday and it's +35 °C. Then you step off the plane at home and it's 5 °C. It's hot to cold straight away. It's the same thing for −5 °C and −35 °C. One is very cold and the other is a cold so extreme that you will die within minutes of exposure. It's hard to describe just how cold −35 °C is, but no matter what you are wearing you will still feel cold. One day I ducked outside after dinner to grab something from my office 50 metres away. I forgot I'd just had a shower and my hair was still wet. By the time I reached the office my hair was frozen! In just seconds I had created a very flattering, and totally unique, frozen dreadlock icicle hairstyle. Frozen solid. Gorgeous. No wonder I was single!

With the weather now highly variable and extreme I knew it was time to make a call about the science programs. The icebreaker would steam into the bay within three days. If everything went well we might just be able to finish our sample collections, but two things bothered me. Firstly, what if the planes did indeed have a design fault and we ended up with expeditioners stuck out on the ice during resupply? And secondly, what if the weather turned very bad, as it had just done, but stayed bad. At $80 000 of Australian taxpayers' money per day, keeping the icebreaker in port for four days longer than required would be an expensive, and public, mistake.

Wednesday 2nd February

A disappointing day for several on the station as the decision was made to stop all flights except repatriation. No more science. So Anya, Mike, Sam and Richie will now go home with unfinished projects. It was a tough decision but the right one. The weather is all over the shop like a mad woman's breakfast.

Most guys handled it really well. They knew it might be touch and go towards the end, particularly after we lost so many days to the VHB crash. But Anya was heartbroken and I really felt for her. She stands to lose five years' work. I can't even look at her without getting upset, the poor bugger. She is such a sweet and gentle person with such grace and dignity, it just doesn't seem right. All I could do was give her a big hug and let her know I was thinking of her. She's experienced enough to understand the 'A' factor and she gets it, but it still hurts.

(continued)

> ## Wednesday 2nd February (cont'd)
>
> The troops had a massive farewell dinner tonight and Kirsten pulled out ALL STOPS!!!! Roast suckling pig, shrimp, fish, roast beef, all with amazing flavours and sauces. It was a fitting night for an extraordinary team of individuals.
>
> Tonight at 11.52 a small portion of the sun dipped behind the horizon. Our first sunset since stepping onto Antarctica. I know it won't be long before I'm longing to have the sun shine on my face, but for now I'm looking forward to the month or so when there is both day and night, before we plunge into total darkness.

The end of summer

> ## Thursday 3rd February
>
> We did it! We retrieved all field parties and now have 120 people safely back on station. I can't believe how well it worked. Clockwork! And I'm very proud of my organising abilities!!! (Pat me on the back, 'Logistics 'R' Us').
>
> Back in Hobart they told me stories about chaos and mayhem and leaving the ship sitting there for three days while Station Leaders tried to drag back scientists stuck where they were. I wanted to prove that with good organisation skills, strong time-management and appropriate delegation you can achieve the impossible. Backed up by a gun team of professionals—we did it!

I woke up at 5.30 am and looked out my window. There was the *Aurora Australis* in all its bright-red splendour anchored in the bay. Resupply this time was not over the ice—the ice was gone. Instead the helicopters shuttled over much smaller parcels all day. Fresh fruit, the mail and some much-needed spare parts for our water makers. It was an exhilarating time to be on station—the air was full of the excitement and triumph of the returning summerers, and the anticipation of the winterers.

Friday 4th February

The *AA* is finally here, and what a frantic day of activity ferrying bits and pieces back and forth. The communications operator from the Russian ship sent over a present that brought tears to my eyes. They are so, so poor. He didn't have wrapping paper so it was wrapped in newspaper. He used barograph paper for the card. Inside were some old postcards from Leningrad. They hadn't been used but were so old the corners were bent and they were covered in dust. There was a pair of sunglasses that looked like they were government issue, a hand-painted wooden spoon and a medallion of sorts. The whole lot would be lucky to fetch $5 at a flea market. He obviously looked around for something of value to him that he thought we would like. It was such a sweet and sincere gesture. The more I get to know the Russians the more I love them. They are really gorgeous.

Resupply went well. Howie and I went out on the barge to meet the new people and then operations started.

Mum sent down a heap of ladybird knick-knacks to brighten up my room and Jane sent some homemade sauces from Tim's dad's garden. Note to self: hide the homemade tomato sauce!

Saturday 5th February

Day 2 of resupply. It's exciting to see some new faces, if only for a few days before they head back with the ship.

The station is chock-a-block with people. It's a pain in the arse that I can't get a seat at meals, and we ran out of lemon meringue pie!! *Quelle horreur!* After seeing the Russian quarters it's certainly a first-world issue!

The resupply has brought, with its presents, thoughts of home for the first time in a while. I called Mum to say thanks for the presents. She told me Sam had her ultrasound and all is OK. I'm so happy for her but sad I'm going to miss the birth of the first of the new generation of Robertsons.

The problem with Texas

The resupply wasn't without its unexpected challenges. The ship had brought down three new scientists to oversee the program transition and ensure an orderly handover. One of these people was a man everyone called 'Texas', and he drove me insane!

Texas seemed to carry a big chip on his shoulder. It felt like Antarctica, the expedition, the expeditioners all owed him some kind of favour and he didn't waste time letting us know. The first I heard about it was when Rob came to me to say that he was concerned we weren't going to meet our timeline for the resupply. 'Why not?' I asked. 'What's changed?'

'Well,' he replied, 'Texas apparently *has* to get out in the Zodiac boat to see the penguins. Apparently they had a hard time at Mawson.'

'Who had a hard time? The penguins? The expeditioners?'

Our boats were not yet even unpacked, and it would take two people half a day to get them ready. The outboards were full of anti-freeze and had to be flushed and the hulls had to be moved into a warmer building before they were inflated. It was a lot of extra work for two people who were already working to an extremely tight deadline.

I got hold of Texas. 'No way—we're not doing it. The boats are still packed and the ship leaves in 24 hours. I'm not putting the boats in.'

I felt that Texas reacted as many self-entitled people do—full of self-aggrandisement, and what I thought were veiled warnings of negative reports on our activities and political interference for the rest of the year. I stood firm. This was my expedition, my rules. We had a deadline and we were going to keep to it, and no amount of pressure from him would change this. I let my winterers know that should Texas approach any of them with requests they were to refer them straight back to me.

But he didn't let it go. Right up to the moment the ship left I think he attempted to destabilise the winterers by cajoling and spreading gossip. But by now we were a strong group, made stronger by the presence of a common enemy. And my people held the line.

Goodbye summerers

Sunday 6th February

They are finally gone! What an amazing three months. It feels like the summerers were here for years instead of just 12 weeks.

The station is eerily quiet, no noise from the bar tonight, no footsteps up and down the hall. The phone hasn't rung for three hours. It's a really strange sensation.

I'm sad that Cara has gone. She was due to stay with us for winter but when the reality hit her she started to have doubts. She sought my advice and I didn't know what to say. I just told her I thought Antarctica would be the last place you'd want to get stuck for nine months if you had any doubts or were homesick. It really isn't the place to be if you don't want to be there, it's way too extreme. I'm normally pretty good at offering support and advice to my staff but this time ... geez ... it's just too much of a personal decision. I can't influence it one bit; it would be wrong.

The transition from the driving, urgent pace of summer activity to the slow pace of winter takes just 24 hours. That's how long it took to load my summerers into the helicopters for the quick flight out to the ship, get everyone settled and wave them goodbye. The helicopters were dismantled and lashed to the deck. The summerers bubbled and chatted, handing around CDs full of photos and looking forward to the short trip back to Hobart to meet family and friends.

With a long blast of the ship's horn and a few flares lighting up the sky, the *Aurora Australis* weighed anchor and quietly slipped from the bay, taking with it 80 scientists, our air transport and all the left-over Southern Comfort. The scientists were mainly very happy. With the exception of the VHB plane crash, the summer had gone off without a major hitch. As I watched the icebreaker depart I felt proud that the first big milestone of my year in Antarctica had been reached.

Part of my heart went with them. As I looked around at my 17 winterers I saw in them a mixture of happiness and trepidation. For the next nine months there would be no more opportunities to get off Antarctica. I would not see another face and I would get to know each of my 17 very well. In fact, I had a hunch that by the end of our time in Antarctica I would know what everyone was thinking before they did, as they would me.

For nine months there would be nowhere to run, nowhere to hide. We would eat, sleep, work and relax together. It would be just like *Big Brother*, but no one would be evicted. And if we all wanted to hate one person we would have to deal with it. If any internal us-and-them developed I would have to bring us back together. If someone required performance management I had no carrot to entice them, and no stick to punish with.

Nothing can really prepare you for this kind of experience. No amount of leadership training could ever teach you all the things you need to know. I would be alone as the leader, isolated and under intense scrutiny, with no peers and no support network other than a patchy phone line back to Hobart.

And it really scared me.

Prime Aussie beef and potato gems for the Russians

With a long-remembered Pavlovian instinct the Russians arrived the day the summerers left. I could never get my head around exactly what they were doing in Antarctica. Not a lot of science appeared to be going on. The Russians didn't have an influx during summer and their expeditioners were sent down for a two-year stint. With no resupply!

Many people think countries like Romania, Russia and India are there simply to lay a territorial claim. Antarctica is the only landmass with no sovereign rights, and everything hinges on the Antarctica Treaty. If we lay a claim to an area or sector, perhaps when the technology arrives and we have run out of resources elsewhere, we'll start to dig up Antarctica as we've dug up every other country in the world. I preferred not to contemplate the *why*, but I was fascinated with the *what*.

I had visited the Russians over summer. Sadly, it was everything I expected a Russian station to be: dirty, smelly, cramped and ugly. It had the feel of a particularly seedy trailer-park in a run-down midwestern American town. A discarded pool table lay on its side rotting in the mud. Discarded oil drums bobbed in the water. Inside it was greasy walls and very poor food. And they had brought a *cat*! But in this squalor were men of incredible warmth and competence. In the middle of all this they had entertained us wonderfully and in no time made us feel like part of their family.

By incredible contrast, the Russians had a new Mil-8 helicopter. It was probably the best helicopter then in Antarctica. The Mil-8 can carry 4 tonnes of cargo at a time — it's a massive beast. And the day after the summerers departed the Mil-8 arrived. With an empty hold.

It didn't take long to twig to what was going on. They were after supplies left behind by the summerers. Supplies we wouldn't need, or possibly weren't allowed to serve given the food date issue. Hey, if we gave it to the Russians at least we wouldn't have to burn it or send it home. We all went exploring for goodies to hand over. In the freezer we found all manner of frozen meat that had been earmarked for summer and not used.

The Russians left Davis extremely happy. They had scored a tonne of prime Australian beef, half a tonne of lamb, numerous barrels of cooking oil and a host of odds and ends we would not require. But what they loved the most? When they saw an entire pallet of frozen potato gems, their eyes glazed over and I swear I could hear them salivating. By hook or by crook those Russians were going to squeeze them into their Mil-8, even if they had to leave some crew behind, which I'm sure they contemplated when it became apparent that not all their booty would fit!

Monday 7th February

It was so, so funny watching the Russians today. What is it about potato gems!! I hate them.

Helping them cram every nook and cranny with goodies was hilarious. But I was a bit concerned when at 2 pm they called a break and all drank vodka, even the pilot! Anyway, they got home safely, which is a relief. They are really just so appreciative of us and our little luxuries like meat. It's quite surreal and puts a new spin on the neighbour popping over to borrow a cup of sugar.

PS After today's unexpected activities it's all gone very quiet again. Spooky!

What I learned

- *Managing well can be extremely rewarding.* It is a great feeling to look back on a tough situation and know that you handled it well. When you're in the middle of these times keep your plates spinning, and remind yourself that at the end you'll have time to take a breath.

Part V

Antarctic winter

Keep your troops motivated during your own antarctic winter.

Like it or not, every workplace has its own antarctic winter. It could be the six months in between major milestones for a significant project, it could be being asked to do more with less. Sometimes work is just a hard slog. Your role as a leader is critical in these times. You have to keep the energy up, the creative juices flowing and the team intact. How, and how well, you do this will determine the shape you'll be in at the beginning of spring.

Chapter 23

It's important to know your people, not just the work they do

Antarctica abounds with mystery and mythology. We know so little about the continent and so few people have seen it for themselves that many interesting, and at times downright hilarious, urban legends have emerged.

Some myths dispelled

Recently I was presenting at an international conference for the finance sector. I had answered many insightful questions from the floor and was mingling with the delegates for an hour or so after the keynote presentation. A rather shy, well-dressed gentleman approached me and hesitantly asked, 'You didn't talk about the polar bears. Is it because they are nearly extinct? I heard that the Japanese had hunted them all from Antarctica.' I stifled a laugh. He was so earnest and I didn't want to embarrass him. I gently explained, for the umpteenth time in my life, that there are no polar bears in Antarctica. Wrong pole. Then there's the one about the incredibly spectacular blue 'wave-shaped' ice formations at Dumont D'Urville. Apparently these are 'waves of the sea, frozen in time'. (Or the secret Nazi base to which the baddies escaped in their U-boats after World War II ...)

Now I want to dispel the most prevalent myth. Antarctica is *not an exciting place*. Particularly in winter.

It is extreme, yes, gruelling, challenging ... but in human terms nothing ever happens. There is nothing we would consider exciting—no sports, no elections, no Boxing Day sales, no anything. It is a cold, barren place without trees, plants or shrubs. In summer Antarctica presents a moonscape of dirt, mud, ice and the odd scrap of extremely hardy moss. In winter it's, well, white.

We've all seen the *Frozen Planet* documentaries and the terrifically interesting videos of penguins being playfully tossed about by juvenile fur seals and penguins huddling in the cold. And you've probably seen images or even videos of the incredibly beautiful auroras. But that's about it for entertainment. Nothing happens. Ever.

By and large, even the seasons go by unnoticed. Extreme as they are, we humans occupy only 17 small sites, most no larger than a couple of football grounds. This on a landmass much larger than Australia or continental USA. That's a lot of unseen continent! For a reason. There's really nothing to see, unless you really, really, really like ice.

For the heroic adventurers, the excitement is about survival. It's personal, and great stories are told of surviving against the odds and overcoming adversity. These explorers leverage their experiences into public-speaking tours and books, astonishing their audiences and readers with their bravery and courage.

Time on our hands

But the stations? It's very quiet over winter. The repetitive monotony of the day-to-day work and the same old faces at breakfast, lunch and dinner create a nine-month-long 'groundhog day' experience. Each day ever so slowly rolls into the next. So while we are usually aware of what day of the week it is, it's a rare bird that can immediately recall the date. So yes, in winter we had time on our hands. Lots of time.

Friday 11th February

The sense of isolation is really starting to kick in. Despite our location I never felt isolated in summer. There was always so much work to do. Now there is very little. Dinners are very quiet but the winterers are warming to spending the nine months together.

There is seating for 90 in the mess and we rattled around the room wondering how to organise ourselves. Some wag suggested

---

> we should each have a table to ourselves, but in the end we made one long table and put the others into storage.
>
> The conversation topic at dinner tonight was all the stupid things the summerers had done and everyone was in hysterics. Particularly the story about the new expeditioners putting lip-balm up their noses to stop their sinuses freezing…at 8°C! We laughed about finding the wallet left behind by one of the summerers—Lord knows why he brought it in the first place!
>
> But I'm sure I'll have a good long list of stupid winterer things to write about when this is finished.

One of the positives about having so much time on my hands was that it would give me a chance to get to know and really understand my team as individuals, not just as employees. I could learn all about them, and learn from them, every single day.

Like most of us, in my professional life I'd seen my staff only during working hours and the odd social event. So the staff member who presented for work each morning, with his or her own unique set of behaviours, attitudes and actions, may or may not resemble the private person at home. As a manager you try to get the best out of your people, but without fully understanding the 'whole' person, as opposed to the 'employee', this is sometimes difficult.

Daytime jollies

The weeks immediately after the departure of the summerers were a perfect time to get out and about in Antarctica. The weather was holding and the sun was out so we organised a range of outdoor activities to keep us occupied.

The inflatable boats still weren't inflated. We had made no use of them over summer as there was still too much sea ice around. One misstep and *rrriiiiiiip*…a piece of ice would carve a chunk out of the boat and leave us swimming in frigid water. But now all the ice was gone and our bay sparkled invitingly in the dazzling light. So we pumped up the boats, prepped the outboards and spent many magical days pottering around the bay and beyond.

Saturday 12th February

What an amazing day! I feel like I'm on holidays and can't believe I'm getting paid to do this.

We took the boats out deep into the bay and visited many icebergs. The colours and shapes were incredible. Craig, our IT guy, had been reading up on the different shapes, colours and forms they take and he educated us all as we got up close and personal to the most amazing structures I've ever seen.

One iceberg looked like it had been daubed with blue paint. It was striped. A layer of white, a layer of blue all along the edge, it was absolutely stunning. Craig informed us it was a 'striped berg' ... Hmm, thanks Craig! I wondered who the genius was who came up with that name!

When we got home I looked in the book and found it's a strata berg! At least he got the 'berg' bit right! We stirred him about it over dinner.

Oh, I found out today that penguin colonies smell. Really bad. Some of the boys thought the smell was familiar but couldn't place it until dinner, when one exclaimed, 'They smell like a sports locker room'. Aha!!! Everyone agreed—it missed only that hint of disinfectant.

Monday 14th February

The emperor penguins have been amazing since all the people left.

They have been wandering between the station buildings and generally just hanging around. Until you get up close you don't really consider how big they are. They are massive compared to the Adélies and other birds we've seen.

One of the rules of the Antarctic Treaty is that people are not allowed to go to within 5 metres of penguins. This is to protect them so they don't get accustomed to people and become a nuisance, scrounging for scraps of food as the skuas do at Zhongshan.

Obviously the penguins haven't read the manual. I took my morning coffee outside today and went to walk down the stairs to stand in the sun. But I couldn't. At the bottom of the stairs was the most beautiful penguin I had yet seen. His feathers were silken and shiny and his colours shone in the low sun.

I sat down on the step, gobsmacked at his beauty. He just stood there, looking at me. We sat for probably 10 minutes until my backside was numb. I did want to go for a walk on the ice, but I didn't want to lose this precious moment. I looked at him and said, 'Dude, you're in my way'. I'm sure I heard him say 'Dude, you're in my home. I was here first'.

Tuesday 15th February

The tradies have been working solidly since the summerers left and tomorrow they start five days off. Hopefully most of them will get off station, go hiking and stay at some of the huts out on the plateau.

My winterers are slowly getting up their experience in boating and overnight trips but we still have a long way to go, given our lack of experience. I think all in all I prefer to have a new, mostly inexperienced crew. They are positive, enthusiastic, curious and willing to try anything new.

Wednesday 16th February

Yay! I finally got out to see Beaver Lake—they should call it Majestic Lake. It's incredible. It's a big, mainly frozen lake with jade-blue water peeking through the ice in places, surrounded by huge mountains. They looked like a wedding cake, all dark brown with thick marzipan icing on top.

We walked through an incredible ice canyon. It was fully covered over on top but the walls shone with the refracted sunlight. At one point we walked around a corner and stepped into an orange room—one wall was glowing in the low light and it was

(continued)

Wednesday 16th February (cont'd)

an incredibly beautiful sight. It was almost like Antarctica was putting on a special show just for me.

As we walked back we talked about what you could eat if you were stranded here. There was nothing. No beetles, insects, worms, fish, seals or penguins. It's just too far inland.

Friday 18th February

We had another flying visit from the Chinese today. God they make me laugh!

Yesterday they came and 'borrowed' three drums of fuel. Today was their 'official' visit. That is, if you don't count the seven other times they have lobbed over the hills to borrow something.

They are almost part of the furniture now. So much so that when I short-changed them on the tour they noticed! We had toured the LIDAR and SAS buildings and spent almost an hour at the post office, seen the Reverse Osmosis unit, the Main Power House and the trades workshop.

We were running behind time for our 1.15 pm lunch so I skipped the green store. But then over lunch the interpreter says he wants to see the store! They are fascinated by it. When the daily food budget is $4 per person (as opposed to the $15 per person it is with us), I guess I understand it. I guess they eat a lot of rice.

It was amusing having lunch with them and watching them try to eat a piece of salami with a spoon. And the looks on their faces when they tried vegemite was priceless. The fact that one of them smeared vegemite on his banana cake made it even more entertaining. I thought I'd cry from trying to hold in my laughter. After he composed himself he said to his interpreter, 'Very good'. I know I did similar things when I visited them on station. I had no idea what I was eating sometimes but I'm tipping it was the Chinese equivalent of vegemite on banana cake.

As we walked them back to their helicopter two of them decided they needed to see a doctor. Doc took a look and the x-ray revealed a broken toe on one and a fractured wrist on the other. They didn't want to miss lunch so didn't say anything until the end.

I got another wall-hanging for good luck. At this rate I'll be the luckiest person in Antarctica.

Doc's stressed about the amount of x-ray film we've got left. Between the Russians, the Chinese and the summerers we've given the x-ray machine a good hammering.

PS The Chinese are completely head-over-heels for Kirsten. She's tall, friendly, blonde and just gorgeous. They want her and me to come and live in Beijing at the end of this. Nice offer!

Saturday 19th February

Counting the cost of the Homer Simpsons of Antarctica living so close by. Doc told me he caught one of them leaving the green store with a whole box of sunscreen. Just ask, fellas!

Kirsten told me they took some yeast. YEAST! Unbelievable. And they made off with some more fuel. All borrowed of course, and ever so likely to be returned ... Not.

Super Tuesday

One of the most important things we had to come to grips with quickly was the voluntary roles. These roles would help to keep us all busy, cover important skills gaps and add to the character of the place. There were two types of voluntary roles — those we had been trained for (our carpenter, for example, had received two weeks' training as a theatre nurse), and those we hadn't (like brewing beer). At dinner one day, we drafted up the various voluntary roles we would need to fill over winter.

We had a home-brew unit and needed skilled brewers. Of the 18 expeditioners, nine volunteered for home brewing. We had two Chief

Brewers, in case one of them was ever off station, three Deputy Chief Brewers and four Master Brewers!

Hydroponics was similarly well subscribed. There was something less than appealing about not seeing a fresh lettuce leaf or a juicy tomato for three months. I put the doctor in charge of this project. I didn't want any 'unauthorised' plants!

And then we needed a social club secretary, station photographer, yearbook editor, newsletter editor and activities coordinator, among others. Later in the year we would add roles as required, such as compulsory fun coordinator, darts coach, music teacher and projectionist. It was all in good fun and it gave people things to do. Some of the efforts they went to were extraordinary.

The toughest times in winter were the nights. Each evening, all around the world, people are drawn together around the television. It's social, often educational, and mostly entertaining. We had no television, so it was important to have a variety of fun things to do in the evenings. I didn't want people disappearing on their own every night after dinner, as I didn't think that would be good for their mental health. I wanted to build a sense of community by getting people involved and having fun. But I wanted to give people choices: you could be alone if you wanted to, or you could hang out with the team if you felt like company. Also, I wanted to manage the use of alcohol so a night of 'nothing to do' wouldn't turn into a quiet bender in the bar, with all its consequent issues.

So Friday night was James Bond night. The 22 movies would take us through to about July, when we'd switch to another series. But I wanted to break up the week, so 'Super Tuesday' was born.

Tuesday nights from 7.30 to 8.30 pm were set aside as the time when anyone who felt like it could stand up in front of the rest of the community and present a topic that was of interest to them. There were no rules, besides the unwritten ones around decency and taste, and anything was possible. I wasn't sure how this would go, knowing that for most people speaking in front of a group of people is about as enjoyable as root canal surgery, but I optimistically placed a sign-up sheet on the noticeboard and invited people to pick a date to present.

Within five days the roster was full.

It was filled with an incredible array of topics and talents. We had people teaching how to speak Italian, how to play the drums; an astronomy buff taught us about the solar system; one of the more tech-savvy among us gave a talk on using a digital camera; one person shared their memories of living in Europe for a year; we even had our resident Goth explain all about paganism, to our absolute delight!

Super Tuesday became a raging success, with almost a full house every week. The benefits were enormous. Not only did we all get the opportunity to learn a whole host of new things at no cost and with minimal effort, but we actually got to learn about each other. We learned what people liked and didn't like; what life experience they had, which might not have been apparent at work; and most importantly, what interested them and what made them tick.

The upshot of all this was often a new-found respect for someone and their knowledge. It's unrealistic to imagine that 18 strangers, from all walks of life, thrown together around the clock will all love each other. It's perfectly normal that individuals will warm to some people more than to others. But after the first few nights of Super Tuesday I noticed something important happening. People who had previously shown a disinclination to befriend someone (is that diplomatic enough for you?) were learning a new respect for each other.

We learned about each person—their passions, their skills, their life experiences—in a relaxed, informal way. The benefit of this was that we began to appreciate each other as individuals, not just as colleagues. So even people who believed they had nothing in common and therefore weren't particularly friendly could at least respect each other's comprehensive knowledge in a certain area.

Tuesday 8th March

I was woken up through the night by the shriek of Antarctic winds ripping past our buildings. I knew they were big but wasn't sure just how big until I got downstairs and saw that someone had posted up signs saying it was gusting 100 knots (185 kilometres per hour!). This would be classified a cyclone or hurricane back home, I'm sure.

(continued)

Tuesday 8th March (cont'd)

There was no outside work today. It hovered around 80 knots all day. It's hard to imagine what it must be like at Mawson Station, where this type of weather is the norm. A couple of guys wanted to walk outside in their freezer suits just to see what it was like!

A great Super Tuesday tonight and I'm starting to see real value come from these sessions. Gary did a great talk on digital photography. Afterwards, one of the others came over to me and said, 'I'm not a huge fan of Gary's as we're just different people, but geez he knows his stuff about technology. I take my hat off to him for that'.

We're developing respect for each other. And it is respect born of appreciating the full range of abilities and capabilities that every single person has, over and above their work competence.

The events were also illuminating for me as I got to know the whole person, not just the employee. Knowing how a person thinks, what they enjoy doing, what life experience they have and so on, provides essential information for a leader. It is much easier to provide the tools to motivate someone when you understand what makes them tick. Similarly, a well-considered reward, recognition of a job well done, works better when the leader takes the trouble to carefully match the gift to the person. It shows your sincerity and will be much appreciated.

The key point is everyone is different. Every person brings to work an array of experiences, attitudes and skills—some that are quite obvious, others that are not. The challenge for every leader is to learn, understand and value the qualities each employee has over and above their work capabilities, and to use this knowledge to build a stronger team.

What I learned

- *Understand the whole person.* People bring a multitude of skills, experiences and knowledge to work each day. Often we don't see these things. Knowing what your people are passionate about and what they enjoy doing gives you a greater sense of who they are and makes it easier to match people and tasks.

Chapter 24

As a leader you are being watched, always

One of the biggest lessons for me during our 12 months in Antarctica was the scrutiny you are under as leader. I should have been more aware of this. Before the expedition I had held leadership positions for over 16 years, but this aspect really only hit me when one day one of the men came to me and asked, 'How come you always sit next to Kirsten and Chris at mealtimes?'

Perpetual scrutiny

In training the AAD had recommended to me that we use one large, communal table for meals. Having separate, smaller tables, they advised, could lead to cliques forming and their experience showed this could cause problems in such a confined environment. It sounded like sensible advice me to me. I respected the knowledge and wisdom of the staff at the Division, so we had continued with our single, long dining table. But when this question was raised I was caught off guard.

My impulsive answer was, 'Well, because we talk about the footy and State of Origin. It's easy stuff to talk about over a meal.' But I was still puzzled so I asked, 'Why are you asking?'

'Well, because we think you like them more than you like the rest of us.'

I was stunned. Absolutely gobsmacked. I had tried very hard to treat all of my team equally and not play favourites. I had been totally transparent with rosters, had put the same effort and energy into celebrating each person's birthday, and made sure I greeted every single person each morning at breakfast. So the claim that I not only had 'favourites' but chose to sit with them, and only them, at mealtimes really knocked me sideways. I had incredible respect for the person raising the issue with me and I believe it took great courage for them to come forward and share their thoughts.

It was a huge awakening for me to realise that my behaviour was being interpreted in a way that I hadn't imagined. Yes, I really enjoyed the company of Kirsten and Chris, and I looked forward to sharing a meal and a laugh with them each day, absolutely. But I also enjoyed the company of the other members of the team. As in any community, I simply had more in common with some people than with others.

But my behaviour was being scrutinised constantly. It really brought home to me the lesson that when you are a leader: YOU ARE BEING WATCHED … ALWAYS. From that moment on I chose to sit next to a different person around the table every day or so. Of course, even this was noticed and commented on, but I told them, 'A change is as good as a holiday and, hey, there won't be a holiday any time soon …' Leaders are under intense scrutiny—you need to know this and manage it.

Wednesday 9th March

I had a great catch-up with Doc today. I'm disappointed I haven't lost any weight but I've only been back on the treadmill for a week and I haven't changed what I eat yet. We discussed each expeditioner and how we both felt the station was going.

The lack of privacy and the scrutiny we're all under is really apparent. Doc and I reeled off the things that people have 'noticed' and commented on in the last week. Small changes to our routines have a big impact.

- Doc shaved his beard. This became the key discussion topic among the expeditioners for most of a morning. Many were concerned!

- We couldn't download the newspaper for three days in a row, which really upset those who read it at smoko. They kicked around looking lost.

- I put a dozen cans of Diet Coke in the fridge and even that was newsworthy for about a day.

- Everyone has commented on the fact that I go to the gym every morning now. Discussions about weight loss, BMI and nutrition abound. Everyone has an opinion about what I should do and how I should do it.

Equally unsettling was the knowledge that my team knew where I was — all the time. I could be in any one of the dozen or so buildings on the station, just chatting to the guys and catching up on their news, and the phone would ring and it would be someone who wanted to speak to me. I would ask every time, 'How did you know I was in here?' to be told, 'Dunno, we just know where you are, I guess'.

I seriously thought at one stage that someone had covertly placed a GPS tracking device on me, as I just could not explain how the entire community knew my whereabouts at all times and could track me down in moments. I soon realised it was just another part of the scrutiny I was under. And I became very conscious of my behaviour.

Never off duty

Movie nights were particularly challenging. Here we were, 18 strangers, male and female, red blooded and with all the normal urges. And it seemed like every movie had a sex scene — a 'must have' for Hollywood. Normally, in the anonymity of a cinema or the comfort of my lounge room, I would just relax and enjoy it. But surrounded by people who had gone without sex for many months it was awkward.

Sunday 13th March

Beautiful day today—snow everywhere and nice temperature outside. Sharon and JR made a little ski-run and we played around in the snow for a bit.

Tonight we watched *Wall Street*. No matter how many movies I watch here I don't think I'll ever get used to watching sex scenes with the boys. When you're the only woman and you're watching a sex scene with 12 men who haven't had sex for at least six months, it ratchets up the tension no end!

Mum was funny today. I spoke to her on the phone for about 10 minutes then she said, 'Honey I have to go, there's a show on Antarctica starting!' Unbelievable! I was telling her about life on station first-hand and she felt she had to watch it on TV.

Monday 14th March

Gosh I laugh a lot down here. Especially whenever Howie is around. He manages to come out with these classic one-liners that just encapsulate what everyone else is thinking. Tonight we did yoga after dinner and the DVD instructor spends so much time crapping on before she starts counting the six breaths that your muscles burn. So Howie yells out 'Just get on with it, will ya!' with not a hint of malice.

Then we watched *Run Lola Run*, which was a very odd movie. We all sat through it and when the credits rolled Howie pipes up with 'Well, THAT was different'. I laughed so much I cried.

It wasn't all laughs today though. I noticed that Craig was very quiet all day. I asked him if we was OK and he told me his wife was quite crook and his mum was back in hospital. It's an awful feeling being so far away, and unreachable should anything really bad happen.

I guess we all know this prior to coming down but the reality doesn't hit you until it hits you. I can't imagine what it would be like for the guys with kids.

About once a month or so we had a theme night, and that usually meant the obligatory costumes. Without the ability to drop by the local costume hire shop down the street our dress-ups were restricted to whatever items we could find on station. Trust me though, some people were incredibly creative and ingenious. They put in an amazing amount of effort, often spending weeks planning their outfit and sneaking around the corridors of the sleeping quarters with polystyrene, paint, coat hangers, cardboard and possible objets d'art. All in an effort to create some hilarious costume that would stun and amaze us all on the night.

Thursday 17th March

St Patricks Day!

What a great night! The quiz was a hoot and everyone loved my green satin dress! I found it in the dress-up box. I can't imagine who originally must have bought this from a shop. It's shocking to think that someone would have parted with cash for it. Great lamb stew with Guinness pie for dinner.

I spoke to Doc about how I noticed a few people were a bit flat during the day and weren't sleeping well. The changing seasons are having a real effect on our bodies. I am perpetually thirsty and my skin is dry. I asked Doc to run more info sessions on the effects on our bodies and minds of life on station.

There's a growing feeling of cabin fever so I need to make a concerted effort to get people off station now while we can. Some week-long traverses in the Hagglunds would be good for the team.

Friday 18th March

Woke up to a fire alarm at 6.50 am. It was bloody loud and frightening because it wasn't a drill. We all mustered in record time and worked out the problem. I was really annoyed when one of the guys complained about being woken up! At least it was just an alarm, not a fire.

(continued)

> ### Friday 18th March (cont'd)
>
> The funny thing was a few of them had only been in bed for a couple of hours after the St Patrick's Day event. Jason turned out with his pants on back to front and wearing one boot. Someone else ran straight to the driver's seat of the fire vehicle when his role was actually on the breathing apparatus team, and a third person left their glasses in their bedroom and couldn't see properly. But at least we all woke up! It's hard on the fire team, as someone always has to be on roster and so can't enjoy a drink the night before. And they're not paid for the privilege.

We had a 'B & S Ball', a 'Rocky Horror Picture Show', a 'D for Davis' night, a 'Punks & Goths' night—even a 'Fairies & Barbarians' dinner when the birthday boy couldn't decide on whether to go with a fantasy theme or brave the cold and go Viking, so went for both.

As leader I also needed to be part of the community, and to be seen to be part of the community, so I too rustled up a costume for each occasion. The difference for me, though, was the degree to which I was being watched, so my costume had to pass muster. Even if I thought it would be hilarious to attend the Rocky Horror night dressed up as Frank N. Furter, resplendent in a short skirt and suspenders, I knew that attire was not appropriate for a female leader in that environment—and once you cross that line of inappropriate behaviour as a leader, it's very difficult to get back.

What I learned

- *Leaders are under intense scrutiny.* People watch their leaders constantly, especially during times of change, looking for signals indicating what's really happening. The scrutiny is intense and constant. Where you sit for lunch, who you greet in the morning, what time you leave the office—all are noticed. Be aware of how your words, behaviour and actions can be interpreted by those around you.

Chapter 25

Find a reason, any reason, to celebrate

When you're away from home for a year you miss a lot of things. Christmas, Easter and birthdays without friends and family and without easy access to today's communication tools such as Skype and social media—we really felt it. That's why we made a special effort to celebrate among ourselves.

Families and friends missed

The traditional celebrations were usually quite difficult and our first major event for winter was our Easter Sunday dinner.

Sunday 27th March

Easter Sunday.

Spent most of the day in bed, feeling morose, sleeping and reading. Mum and Dad were away at Gary's house and Jane and Ben were also not around. I didn't have anyone to ring.

I was more homesick today than at Christmas. I don't know why. I was missing everyone, and dealing with the constant people issues is taking its toll on me.

I asked Howie to say a few words at dinner tonight. He started to say he'd opened the package from his kids and then he broke down and just complimented Kirsten on the amazing food. I imagine he's doing it tough like some of the others. I know Matt is wishing he was anywhere but here at the moment. He applied for

(continued)

> ### Sunday 27th March (cont'd)
>
> a six-month term but was persuaded into taking on 12 months. He'd figured 12 months wasn't that different from six. How wrong, as we can all now understand. I can't really do much to help him but I'll keep an eye on him. I guess I just need to convince him that since he's here now, and he can't go home, why not just make the most of it and try to enjoy his time here.
>
> PS The feeling of isolation runs through the entire station.
>
> PPS I hadn't realised how critical the role of chef is — food really gives us something to look forward to.

If in doubt, make something up

Apart from the obvious days, we used every occasion as an excuse to celebrate, to take the edge off the isolation and boredom. Antarctica has some historic special days, such as Midwinter's Day when the tradition is to go for a swim in the ocean! When there was nothing on the calendar I made reasons up, such as the day when the sun was up exactly 12 hours, the day the sun finally disappeared and then the day it came back! Sometimes I had to dig deep: 50 days without the server going down or 30 days since the last power outage. These markers might not sound important, and in themselves they weren't, but in the absence of anything else going on, they spurred the troops and made a nice opportunity to break up the monotony.

> ### Monday 25th April
>
> Anzac Day. What a great day! I really enjoyed it. We slept in then had the dawn service at 10.30 as the sun peeped over the ridge. Our minute's silence was broken by the loud farting of an elephant seal who had come by to see what the activity was about. It was hard to keep a straight face! Apart from that particular noise, it was the quietest moment I had ever had in my life. There was no wind, no traffic noise, no background city hum. I could hear my own heart beating.

It was such an Antarctic moment standing there remembering our diggers in −21 °C, our breath freezing into little ice crystals.

We had a BBQ in the green store, then Sharon, Chris and I hiked out across the sea ice to Gardner Island, a cruisey 8-kilometre walk.

The blocked sewer is causing an enormous amount of interest. Not because it's blocked but because when the blockage was removed it contained used condoms. Everyone's scratching their heads tonight and looking slyly at each other ... I have no idea.

I've been involved in many long, long projects in my time and am constantly talking with people whose next project milestone is months or years away. In many ways this is not unlike the Antarctic winter. In these situations it's critical to maintain momentum by finding reasons to celebrate, then celebrating with abandon!

Saturday 7th May

Birthday!

Thirty-six. It used to sound older than it sounds now. I woke up tired from my up-and-down emotions. Jane was first to ring and she made me laugh a lot, which was a great start to the day. I went downstairs and the troops had gone to a huge effort decorating. Balloons, streamers, Happy Birthday signs. After breakfast the family rang and it felt really good to connect again. A special surprise was that Mark Stone from Parks Victoria rang from his car on the way to the footy.

Everyone dressed up for the party, '80s theme ... Just my style! Enjoyed the Nutbush and Bus Stop, the B52s and Brandy Alexanders! Chris insisted on a Fluffy Duck cocktail. Didn't think it was his style!

Had a hilarious conversation with Dad tonight. 'So, did you have a party?' 'Yes Dad.' 'How many people came?' Hmmm ... if there were fewer than 18 I would have been slightly worried; if there were more I would have been mightily shocked!

Time for a holiday

We were now six months into our year. Halfway through, and I realised that apart from sleeping I hadn't been off duty for more than four hours in that entire period. I was worn out, strung out and the consistent and escalating 'people issues' had drained my emotional tank. Half of the time when people came to me with a request or complaint I would first think, 'Why don't you just go away and leave me alone'. The strain of keeping my emotions steady over six long months had taken its toll.

I knew I needed a break. I had to get away from it all, get some peace and quiet and do some things I wanted to do. I dreamed of collecting the $158 000 it would take for the AAD to launch a rescue mission to take me away to a tropical island for a week! In another three weeks even that window would be closed as the continent became completely unreachable by land, sea or air, or any combination of the above.

I knew that despite my best efforts, I could never truly be alone. The conditions dictated this. Even walking 1 kilometre from the station on your own wasn't possible—there were too many hazards. So I organised a trip up to the plateau and chose just two people to come along. I figured a party of three might give me the break I needed. Fewer than three and I would need to engage in conversation. More than three and there would be two sets of conversations going, and that would do my head in.

Sunday 1st May

I'm just back from a week-long holiday and it was just wonderful. I wanted to go to Fiji but didn't have the budget (!!). Sharon was a great trip leader and I loved being out there. Riding along on my quad bike towards the plateau with a big smile on my face will be a lifelong memory.

I got a real sense of our vulnerability out there. We were a long way from help if anything went wrong, especially with my record on quad bikes! Seeing the snow petrels was amazing. They are simply gorgeous. Brookes Hut is big and we all slept well, but it took three hours to heat it up to be warm enough to get out of our

---

gear. I will never live down putting snow in Kirsten's tea thinking it was sugar! It was sitting there in a container??

We just sat around and talked. After an hour I tuned out and enjoyed the space. Being able to sit in one place without the phone ringing or someone putting their head in the door was pure bliss.

Out on the ice I found going to the toilet in −25 °C really tricky. But brushing my teeth was a whole new experience. The toothpaste was frozen and as I put water on the toothbrush it instantly froze as well! Sharon showed me a great method of keeping my toothpaste inside my coat and brushing my teeth inside a balaclava!

I reckon I've conquered the quad bikes now. Driving them through snow drifts I got bogged four times on the first day but by the third I was sliding through like a pro. I also worked out pretty quickly that if you relax your arms and legs when you go over a bump it's a smooth ride. Just like riding a horse, Sharon reckons.

On the way back we spotted some emperor penguins getting ready for winter. We stopped about 800 metres away and dropped to our knees. Sure enough, they spotted us and came bustling over as fast as their legs could carry them. It was a funny sight, they were as excited as we were! They squawked and squeaked, came up very close and had a good sticky beak at us.

My feet were freezing the whole time. At one point my fingers were aching so much from the cold I quickly whipped them out to clap my hands together. In all they were out of my glove for three seconds. And I got frostbite! Very minor, but I have no sense of feeling in my fingertips, even now I'm back home and fully warmed up. I wonder how long before I can feel properly again?? Will go see Doc tomorrow to see what he says.

I have never felt so free and lucky and happy to be alive. This place is spectacular, special, unique and invigorating.

It didn't take long for people to notice I'm back and it seems like they've saved up all their questions! But I met them with good humour, I'm relaxed and refreshed. It's done me good, this holiday.

Caring for our physical selves

I can't begin to imagine what it would have been like if something had happened to Doc. He was the only one on station with any medical training. Our lives literally depended on him staying well, both physically and emotionally. Well, we did have two other doctors with us over winter, but I don't think a doctorate in optical physics would be much use in a surgery!

To support Doc if he ever needed to perform an operation, a couple of our people had done some basic training back in Hobart. Our carpenter had his two weeks' training as a 'theatre nurse'. Being at the ready with suction and scalpel while ensuring a sterile operating environment was a big call after just two weeks, nearly a year ago!

Also in the theatre was Ian, one of our IT guys. His day-to-day role was to keep the servers running, do our backups, troubleshoot and fix broken laptops, and maintain our phone system. His role in the theatre, again with just two weeks' training under his belt, was 'anaesthetic assistant'. We laughed at this one … who better to put you to sleep than the IT guy, hey?

So we really, desperately hoped that no one would need surgery, but inevitably the time came. And it wasn't a broken leg or something simple. It was a bad tooth. Despite the best medical checks and a thorough examination of our teeth before leaving Hobart, Simon had developed a very nasty problem with one of his molars. It was an extraction job. And our doctor wasn't a dentist.

Doc spent two days on the phone with various people who talked him through the extraction operation. He took x-rays, scanned them and emailed them off to our support team, who provided a diagnosis and outlined the operation.

At 7.15 am Simon went into surgery.

Saturday 4th June

Simon, oh the poor bugger!

Doc spent four hours working on him this morning trying to get his tooth out. JR and Ian came out looking shattered at lunchtime. I don't think they were expecting all the blood. It turns out the tooth broke off just below the surface just before lunch so Doc called a break so everyone could have a bit of a rest.

He tried again in the afternoon for several hours but to no avail. You realise just how vulnerable we are down here at times like this. Simon was crying, not from pain, but just from not wanting to be here when he was sick I think ... oh, and eight hours wide-awake surgery with his mouth clamped open and still no result!

I imagine he is also thinking about if Doc can't get the tooth out he will have to suffer for another five months before he can get to an oral surgeon. It must be a pretty depressing thought.

Doc was great and you realise what pressure he is under at times. He has a very quiet existence for most of the time but when he works he really works! It's tough on him as he hasn't got all of the specialist skills like dentistry, but he's all we've got and we back him 100%. If anyone can do it, Doc can.

Doc worked his magic on Simon's tooth the next day and we all breathed a big sigh of relief.

The impact of the cold and dryness we experienced in summer paled in comparison to what we experienced in winter. At the beginning of winter we were still making quick trips outside to do some cross-country skiing (not far from the station) or to ride the quad bikes to one of the outer buildings. By late autumn the air temperature routinely dipped to −30°C, with an apparent temperature of −55°C when the wind chill was taken into account.

Tuesday 24th May

We went out to Ellis Narrows today to check on some equipment. Halfway across the defogger on my helmet stopped working so I had to ride with my visor up. The cold wind was hitting me directly in the forehead and that, combined with the temperature, hit me hard. I got the worst ice-cream headache imaginable. I ended up so cold I had to stop the bike and vomit. I didn't realise the two were related until I spoke to Sharon and she said she was almost sick as well. It's now 9 pm, eight hours later, and I still have the headache. Another thing that wasn't in the brochure!!

Nor were the burst blood vessels in the eyes.

The things they don't tell us, or don't know themselves, back in training. My fingers are still sensitive and a bit numb from the cold. I spent 15 minutes with the shower on full-hot when I got back. My skin was absolutely white and my feet a funny shade of purple. It took that long to thaw out, but when blood came back to skin and extremities it hurt like hell.

Every time I feel sorry for myself I just remember how Shackleton spent two YEARS here, in tents without heating. Then I don't feel so bad.

Thursday 26th May

I still have an ice-cream headache! What have I done to my body!

I had a great run today, it's such a release to get on the treadmill with my headphones in and just zone out. It leaves me energised and refreshed to do something physical rather than emotional and interpersonal.

On the way back my hair froze and stuck to my head where it was wet from the sweat. That probably didn't help my headache! Howie came back in today with frostnip on his face after half an hour outside. It's getting too cold to go outside now.

I did an interview with Gold Coast FM for the beginning of winter and people just can't understand how cold it is. There is just nothing you can wear to get warm in this weather. There is a big difference between −10 °C and −30 °C!

On another note, the boys have been funny while the chef has been away. Many of them don't know how to cook and I've had every question from 'How many packets of pasta?' to 'How do I carve the turkey?'! And they keep putting shit back into the fridge! Stuff that no one will eat, like three slices of garlic bread!

I gave out double rations of chocolate tonight to perk people up.

Thankfully the common cold and flu were now a thing of the past. Bacteria and viruses do not survive outside and any nasties we had in our systems were now well gone. Doc gave us a presentation on the immune system one afternoon. He explained that as the immune system now had very little to do, it would lower its defences over the next few months. We could expect to be disease and infection free until November, when the resupply arrived. We were elated by this. It would be terrible to have a runny nose and have to go outside — our sinuses would instantly freeze and be very painful.

Then Doc gave us the bad news. The incoming expeditioners would bring with them all kinds of bacteria and viruses. They would have colds, flu, strange tummy bugs, and we would get them all. Our immune systems would be so supressed we would have no hope of maintaining our good health. In fact, it got worse. Not only would we get whatever the new summerers brought with them, but it could be months before we got back to normal. I tried to put it out of my mind. Like all of us, I hate being sick.

Friday 10th June

Thank God it's Friday. This has been a long week. The darkness is full-on and I find it hard to stay motivated in the afternoon. I feel like I've been at work for hours and hours at 4 pm but in fact I have two hours of work to go! It's hard yakka to keep going, staring into the computer all day.

I've been very sleepy at times today. I'm still waking up too early but at least it's not 3 am as it used to be.

Answered lots of questions from schoolkids today. Once again there is an abiding fascination about what we eat! I'll send them the menu for our upcoming midwinter's feast when Kirsten has finalised it. That'll dispel some myths. The interest from Australia is really wonderful, but it's largely misdirected. Because Antarctica is still such a foreign environment, people think we are heroes. We're not. We're comfortable, mostly middle-class, mostly middle-aged public servants, eating good food and staying warm!

The troops on station all appear to be steady emotionally and we're all healthy. I'm worried about the amount of processed food and preservatives we're eating and the lack of fresh fruit and vegetables. We're not taking any vitamins or supplements, which is a surprise. I'll chat to Doc about this tomorrow. Particularly about how we can get some vitamin D.

The highlight today was the sharing of another tomato from the hydroponics farm. This time there were no fights, each of us ate one-eighteenth of this gorgeous little vegetable (OK, OK, I know it's a fruit!). I distinctly recall the day the first tomato made its appearance in the Mess. It was a few weeks ago and as we came inside for lunch we stopped dead in our tracks. Because there in front of us was the most amazing sight we'd seen for some time — a big, fat, red, juicy and REAL tomato. We'd been eating frozen, dehydrated and packaged food for six months by this stage, so to see a real live tomato in our midst was just gobsmacking.

We were so excited, absolutely stoked. Until the penny dropped and we realised we'd have to share this single tomato amongst 18 people. Not so happy then.

What I learned

- *Find a reason to celebrate.* When a project has a long lead time, or budget constraints curtail new projects and it's all business as usual, it's important to find milestones to celebrate. Create them. Celebrating along the way gives a sense of movement and progress, and it builds momentum.

- *Take time out.* Schedule time away from work and, if needed, away from other people. Rest, reset and restore your energy.

Chapter 26

Check in on your people: ask R U OK?

Back in Hobart we had been briefed on the psychological effects of being cooped up indoors 24/7, under fluorescent lights and without the ability to go outside. We learned of a syndrome referred to as 'Big Eye—the 10-mile stare in a 10-foot room', which describes the situation exactly.

I get toasted

People zone out: something disconnects in their brain and they become zombie-like. The Americans refer to it as 'toasted'; in other places, it's called 'cabin fever'. But it all boils down to pretty much the same thing. If people get in to this state it's very difficult to get them out of it without a change of environment. It's also often a precursor to depression in its many different forms. Some people become aggressive, others despondent and still others anxious. There was no way for me to tell what would happen if someone got into this state and I saw it was my role as leader to pre-empt the problem.

Monday 6th June

Really tired tonight. Suffering from Big Eye—one of the expeditioners caught me in the Mess at lunchtime, just standing there mute, staring at the blackness of the outside world. It's completely dark now, all the time.

(continued)

Monday 6th June (cont'd)

I really thought that because I spent all my time indoors anyway it wouldn't matter to me if there was daylight or not. I sit under the indoor lights all day so I figured it would make no difference. I've spent the last three nights wide awake at 3 am. Last night I read until 5 am—I'm normally asleep by 9.30 pm! I feel like I've been hit by a bus. I need to check my people.

Tuesday 14th June

I got some bad news the other day and I just can't stop thinking about it. David, my best mate back home, was sacked from his senior government job by his Minister. They just told him, 'It's not working out, time to go'. I caught up with him on the phone and we had a good chat about it.

This place does your head in during winter as you have no other distractions. If something is on your mind it stays on your mind all day. It's the first thing you think about and because you don't have all the normal 'life' decisions to make, such as what to wear to work and what to have for dinner, you just dwell on things. I've been thinking about David nonstop now for three days, wondering how he's coping, thinking about how he'll live, where he'll work. While I'm doing this, something in the back of my mind tells me that things are starting to unravel on station. Time for a fresh focus.

Midwinter

Introduction page from Davis Station's Midwinter Festival program:

Midwinter is a traditional celebration that dates back to Shackleton's and Scott's parties. The winter months for these early expeditioners were a time of inactivity due to the extreme cold and absolute darkness. Therefore, when these Antarctic heroes made it to the halfway point, Winter Solstice, it was the cause of much rejoicing and celebration.

Midwinter festivities in Antarctica celebrate the shortest day and longest night of the Antarctica year and marks the turn of the season. 'Day' of course is a relative term, but from here on the long polar night begins to retreat and the light starts to return to this frozen continent. And then, after another eight weeks, the sun reappears.

Davis Station has seen 45 years of Midwinter Festivities dating back to 1957, when the first group of five expeditioners celebrated. Apart from the four years Davis was closed (1965–1968), we have celebrated Midwinter every year.

We now make up the next 18 of the 816 people ever to experience Midwinter here at Davis.

This is the single biggest event of our social calendar. You can expect an amazing amount of fun, distraction and a culinary event never to be repeated. This year's menu centres around this beautiful continent we call 'home', and the other countries who are occupying stations during the winter months: Argentina, Australia, China, France, Germany, India, Italy, Japan, New Zealand, Norway, Russia, South Africa, United Kingdom and the United States of America.

Saturday 18th June

Last rehearsal of the play.

I'd found a play online and bought the rights to perform it. The contract negotiations were hilarious, the royalties are based on the size of the audience. I told the playwright there would be three people in the audience, one on lighting, one on sound and a general gopher. She couldn't get it, until I explained our circumstance. She is stoked! This is the first time her play has been picked up and she can now call herself an 'intercontinental playwright'!!! We gave her a bit extra in royalties because we felt bad!

Things are all coming together for the four parties of Midwinter, and there's a great buzz around the place as we finally have something to do.

(continued)

Saturday 18th June (cont'd)

Two of the guys had been out at Bandits Hut and both came back in a bad mood. Simon went straight to his room as usual and Matt skipped rehearsal, which is unlike him. How do I explain to Simon that his bad moods affect the entire station? I think I'll relax and enjoy midwinter's and deal with it later.

More questions from kids in schools. If it wasn't in email I would tell them how bad it is to crap into a plastic bag when your bum is freezing off!

PS I've grown quite fond of the constant dark. Stockholm syndrome?

Sunday 19th June

Sharon and I snuck out to the spa today for an illicit soak. It was so relaxing and great to get away for a bit. When I came back it was obvious everyone knew where I'd been—furtive looks and a bit of body language.

The spa is open to anyone, any time, but I guess it's that scrutiny again. No one notices when anyone else has a spa but when I do it they notice who I'm with ... Sigh.

So now I'm holed up in my room writing myself to sleep and wondering if, when I get back, I'll appreciate the work–home distinction for long.

Monday 20th June

A warm night! We had positive temperatures (+1 °C) and that, along with the preparations, had everyone in a good mood. I'm looking forward to wearing the midwinter's dress I bought in Hobart so long ago. God, I hope I can fit into it! Tomorrow will be a day I remember for the rest of my life.

Tuesday 21st June

Midwinter's day! Let the festivities begin.

Today we put on our play. It wasn't videotaped so there will be no objective assessment of our performance. Which is excellent! The point is, we had a great time. The benefit wasn't just in the production, it was the planning, rehearsals and preparation. It has given us a much-needed lift.

Our meal was unbelievable. Kirsten had prepared a plate for each nation represented down here this winter.

Entrees: Oysters in Balsamic Vinegar (Australia), Sushi and Sashimi (Japan), Empanadas (Argentina), Egg Rolls (China), Crocodile Skewers (Australia), Native American Galettes (USA), Pretzels (Germany).

Mains: Grilled Indian Chicken (India), Dahl with Spinach (India), Lamb Sosalies (South Africa), Baked Whole Fish (South Africa), Mussels (New Zealand), Smoked Kangaroo Fillet (Australia), Vegetable Pie (Russia), Wurst Salad (Germany), Scallops in White Wine (UK), Black Beans with Tomato Salsa (Argentina), Cheese Pies (Norway), Potatoes and Cauliflower.

Oh. And a seafood buffet with freshly thawed oysters, prawns and crayfish!

As I was eating I worked back from the food on my plate to how on earth it all got here. Kirsten must have planned this nine months ago! Crayfish? Crocodile? Kangaroo? Amazing.

A couple of people got very drunk tonight but those of us more moderate kept a good eye on proceedings. No harm, no foul.

Well, not quite ...

Midwinter swim

A long tradition for winterers is the midwinter swim. Yes, that's right. We planned to strip down to our swimwear in sub-zero temperatures and plunge through a hole dug in the ice for a swim. I was petrified but absolutely determined. I spoke to Doc and he was well prepared. The spa, which had gone mostly unused up to now, was set to 40 °C. The defibrillator was on standby, and the ute would be running with the heater on full blast ready to ferry us straight to the spa. I could hear the sound of chainsaws outside as three of the guys cut a small swimming pool in the ice.

I reflected on our planned swim. Yes, there was an element of danger, and it wouldn't be something you would get away with in a normal workplace. By now I had reached a happy level of comfort with the ambiguity between what was acceptable at work and at home. My people had too. Up to now we had tiptoed along that line. We made sure we had good fun times, but did so safely and with great respect for each other. I prayed that it wouldn't backfire on us this time!

Friday 24th June

What an up-and-down day. I had a run-in with John in Hobart who wanted to 'raise some concerns' about the midwinter swim. I was busy and not interested in playing guessing games so was forthright in my response. 'Sure, tell me exactly what your concerns are.' I didn't have time today for riddles. I still don't know what John wanted me to do. But if he tries it again I will be clear. Come to me with issues to solve and solutions you have already thought of. Don't come to me with vague worries.

Then the day became great as we went for our swim. Luckily it was a balmy −13°C. After stripping off to my two-piece swimmers I jumped in and went right under. The water didn't seem that cold as I was only in for a few seconds. But when I got out!!! Holy crapoly!!!! They quickly wrapped me up in thermals, put me in the warm ute and whisked me up to the spa. It took me 30 minutes to stop shivering.

I feel a bit proud that I went all the way under. Some of the others didn't put their head in. The only reason I did it was that for me it'd be like going to Rome and NOT throwing a coin in the Trevi fountain. It's just what you do. I didn't know if I'd ever get back to Antarctica so, as always, I didn't want to regret missing the opportunity. I'd rather regret what I did than regret what I didn't do.

What I learned

- *Ask R U OK?* Look after the whole person by checking in on them personally. More times than you expect, the answer will be 'no'. Be prepared to back it up with a listening ear and empathy.

Chapter 27

Take care of the little things

Have you ever put the lid on a simmering pot of pasta only to have it boil up all over the stove? Our station was just like a pot of boiling water with the lid on. Without regular maintenance to check the state of affairs small niggles built and built, until they exploded. It can be the same in any workplace or family.

The bacon war

Friday 13th May

An interesting thing I'm finding out down here. We have much emphasis on tolerance and harmony because we simply HAVE to live together. But it can go too far. Things that bug us get ignored and we are under pressure to ignore them. But eventually it builds up to a point where you can't ignore it any longer. By then it's hard to raise the issue because it's been going on for so long it seems silly or trivial to talk about it now. It's difficult to know when a niggle will turn into a full-scale pain — until it happens.

We had a situation that I call 'the bacon war'. Trouble had been brewing and the station was under siege from a nasty but powerful blight that was pervading and undermining our happy little community. Like most insidious attacks, it was happening right under our noses and simmered for months before reaching its inescapable boiling point.

I was sitting in my office planning the resupply for November. There was a lot to think about. One question that was plaguing me was how to deal with people on station that head office and I were considering for NTR—Never to Return. Antarctica is not for everyone of course. It takes a certain flexibility to work and live together for months at a time. I had people over winter who were great 'on the tools' but lacked the self-awareness and self-confidence to make it a smooth journey for the rest of the expeditioners. By midwinter I was spending up to three hours a day dealing with personal issues, coaching, counselling and helping people deal with their daily, amplified struggles. One of these people was incredibly taxing on my time—one day it was tears, the next day tantrums, the next day a massive hangover. This person wanted to come back next year, but for the sake of the next Station Leader I would discuss this with head office and recommend against it.

As I pondered the issue and drafted and redrafted my assessment there was a knock at the door.

'Boss, we need to call a stop-work meeting.'

'Why?' I asked.

'It's about the bacon. The whole station is up in arms and it can't continue.'

'What's wrong with the bacon?' I was completely oblivious.

'Well, it's about how the bacon is cooked on Monday, when Kirsten has the morning off. Some of us want it crispy and crunchy, and others like it soft. It's out of control!'

I took a deep breath. Okay, I thought, you want me to stop a $20 million program to discuss how to cook the bacon on Monday mornings? Yes, I can see how that would look in my monthly report!

'Come again?' I asked. Surely there was something else occupying their minds.

'Well, the plumbers like it soft and the diesel mechanics like it crispy.'

'So?' I said, still unsure of the implications of this information.

'Well, the plumbers are cooking it soft, and the diesel mechanics are cooking it crispy, and I think we need to have a meeting to decide how to cook the bacon.'

Yep, this was a big one. I reacted instinctively. 'No. We will not stop work at taxpayer's expense to discuss this. The entire team is on a roster to cook on Monday mornings so when your time comes just cook it how you like it! Swings and roundabouts.'

So I didn't call the stop-work meeting for the bacon.

Tuesday 19th July

I'm still feeling sooky today. I can't work out if it's the lack of sunlight, lack of sleep, boredom or the niggling antics of some of my expeditioners.

Things are so quiet down here we nearly had a mutiny over soft or crispy bacon. I can't believe that in the absence of any drama or conflict some people feel the need to create it! I reckon the problem has now gone away. I'm in two minds whether to take it any further. Sometimes little things are just that. Other times they are the outworking of something else. I'll keep an eye on it.

But the bacon war wasn't about bacon

I thought that was it. Decision made. Job done. Move on. Only, the 'little thing' of the bacon was just a symptom. As word got around about my less than ground-breaking decision, other related issues began to emerge. This wasn't about bacon at all; it was the manifestation of a long-running dispute between the diesel mechanics and the plumbers about how to keep their utility vehicles clean. So, if it wasn't about bacon, what was it about? Respect.

The diesel mechanics had accountability for maintaining the fleet of station vehicles, while the plumbers had responsibility for looking after the ute, which had been allocated to them. Some of the mechanics believed the plumbers were not looking after their vehicle properly and were therefore creating more work for the mechanics when it came time to service the ute. They felt, rightly or wrongly, that the plumbers were deliberately being disrespectful.

Apparently both groups had discussed the issue several times but the situation hadn't improved. In fact, in the boredom and close confines of an Antarctic winter it had simply 'grown', until eventually it became a real sticking point.

Rather than the opposing groups trying to have the conversation *again*, the issue manifested itself through the bacon war. The person complaining about the bacon had drawn a link between the plumbers' disrespect of the vehicles and their deliberately cooking the bacon in a way they knew was disliked by other members of the team. The bacon war was a battle for respect. And disrespect is most often shown, not in the big bold moves, but in the little ways people treat each other. Once I'd worked this out, I stepped in quickly and dealt with the core issue.

Wednesday 20th July

Well, we might as well have had a stop-work meeting after all the time I spent hearing all views today. Everyone had an opinion about the bacon, including me—I must admit I do love crispy bacon!

It was good for the diesos to finally get the ute maintenance question out in the open and in the right forum. I think a lack of self-awareness meant that previous attempts to solve the problem were just finger-pointing exercises. But I got them to make their case clearly today without any emotion, and the plumbers got the message. It was an issue of respect.

I know exactly how I'm going to cook the bacon next week!

I had experienced a similar situation in my previous role as a Chief Ranger. Early in my tenure I had held a workshop to bring my people together and start to build some effective teamwork. Each person was given six Post-it notes and asked to write down the three things they enjoyed most about their work and the three things that they disliked most. I then collated and, where possible, grouped the responses. The answers were quite telling. The three most common responses to 'What I like most about my job' were:

1 I have a pretty good work–life balance.

2 I do a job I enjoy and the community respects.

3 I know what I'm supposed to do. (In business school this is called 'clarity of purpose'.)

All three responses were high-level, big-picture issues. The three most common answers to 'What I dislike most about my job' were:

1 People smoke in the work vehicles.

2 People traipse mud through the office with their dirty boots.

3 People bring back the fleet cars with no petrol left in them.

All three responses were detailed, small but significant issues that had an effect on our enjoyment at work. I had worked out back then that it's critical to take care of the little things so the big things, like teamwork, stand a chance.

Bacon wars are symptoms of deeper issues, usually about respect

As leaders our role is not to be the parent, and we're not there to sort out every little spat between team members. But we do have a responsibility to use our judgement and understand what are small, interpersonal differences that we all must tolerate, and what behaviours are in fact symptoms of a deeper issue.

In some offices people leaving dirty coffee cups in the sink can drive others to despair; in some investment banks I have worked with the issue is often night traders leaving their dinner dishes or pizza boxes lying around; in some primary schools it's the teacher who habitually starts their yard duty a few minutes late. In families it may be someone not putting away the clean washing and letting it fall on the floor and get walked on, leaving lights on or leaving wet towels on the floor. These are bacon wars. On the surface they all appear to be simple, insignificant things. But dig a little deeper and you'll find they could be signs of a bigger cultural issue around teamwork and respect.

Mr Scrapey

I had one team member who had an annoying little habit of scraping his cutlery along his plate. For me, listening to this noise was excruciating. It just drove me nuts. It happened at every meal, three times every day, and it was slowly driving me crazy. After several months I could tolerate it no longer so I developed a coping strategy of being the last person to arrive for meals. That way I could choose to sit as far away from this bloke as possible.

Yet my fiendish plan didn't work and somehow, some way, he managed to be seated near me every single time. Every time! I had already spent considerable time coaching my team about the importance of addressing issues that were affecting us and not letting them simmer away. Given our total isolation, with no way out, for nine whole months, I figured it was best to sort this out quickly!

The problem was he was also one of my best expeditioners, a great team player. He was the person who noticed we were running low on toilet paper and got the forklift out and took the toilet paper off the racks in the green store and restocked the bathrooms—without being asked. He cleaned windows and common areas that needed some love and attention—without being asked. He was kind, cheerful, intelligent, sensitive and loyal to my leadership. All the things you want in your people, apart from the plate scraping.

So it was a dilemma. I needed to do something to preserve my sanity, yet I felt this was one of those unconscious human foibles and I just needed to show tolerance and accept that people are different. What to do?

Friday 22nd July

Dinnertime has gone from being something I have hated to a pleasure. After eight months of eating together, the eating habits of one of my team had finally got to me.

But today Doc and I were chatting about things that got under our skin. He laughed in agreement when I mentioned the scraping plates! When it started tonight at dinner, we caught each other's eye and gave each other a wink. It's a personal foible, and having a comrade share the 'Mr Scrapey' joke has made it bearable.

These type of incidents came thick and fast over winter. We apparently needed a meeting to work out who was putting the milk jug back in the fridge without milk in it, who was leaving the weights on the barbells in the gym, who was making up the orange juice concentrate incorrectly, who put three pieces of leftover garlic bread in the fridge after dinner, and who was leaving the lint in the clothes dryer!

As the winter progressed and the sun slowly started to climb its way back to the frozen continent, I realised that true leadership comes from knowing when to intervene in these 'little' things and when to just suck it up. Knowing when to step back, step in, diffuse or escalate an issue is a key skill for leaders and will be covered in detail in my next book.

Monday 25th July

I was rostered on for morning tea today. Everyone was still talking about the bacon war and wondering how I'd cook the bacon.

I cooked it both ways—half crispy, half not. Everyone was amazed. I told JR that I had learned this technique at Station Leader School!

What I learned

- *Deal with causes and symptoms.* It's too simple to sort out the behaviours that are wrong or the things that are symptomatic of another issue. Look deeper and work out what's behind the symptoms. Deal with that as well.

- *Don't let it build up.* As soon as you're aware there is an issue, deal with it. Make a decision or build a consensus by discussing the issue and solutions together in more detail. Whether you decide on an emphatic decision or a discussion of options and alternatives, you need to act promptly.

- *Deal only with facts.* It's the behaviour, not the person, that you are trying to change. The behaviour, or habit, may be annoying, but (usually) the person is not.

- *Start informally.* Every workplace has a Bacon War, but identifying them can be tricky. Open up the discussion. Informal, regular, short meetings to discuss the progress of key projects and team outputs should include a quick opportunity to raise any bacon wars in a professional manner.

- *Ask around.* What proportion of the workplace is being affected and how? Leaders can't get involved in every workplace issue — that's not your role. But the judgement to know what is a behavioural issue that needs to be addressed and what is a simple human foible or idiosyncrasy and should be accepted — that is the real test of leadership.

Chapter 28

Judgement comes with experience

The voluntary activities such as brewing and hydroponics were keeping people engaged and entertained. Haircuts were another area requiring people to pitch in and help out. Back in Hobart six expeditioners attended two hours of pre-departure training at TAFE to become proficient in haircutting. (I'd like to say 'hairdressing' but that's drawing a long bow.) And hair became big news—very big news.

Who cut your hair?

Everyone noticed when someone had had a haircut. There wasn't a whole lot else happening. The only things that changed from day to day were hair and food, so everyone noticed both. One day one of the guys walked into the kitchen and someone asked:

'Who cut your hair, Greg?'

'JR did,' Greg responded. 'Why?'

'Well ... I cut your hair last time. Didn't you like the way I cut it?'

'Yeah, but JR already had the clippers out, so it was just easy ...'

'Well ... you could have asked me. I was right here.'

'Mate, just leave it, okay? It's just a haircut.'

Only there's no such thing as 'just a haircut' in the middle of an Antarctic winter. It's Very. Big. News.

> ### Friday 22nd July
>
> Tension in the air today over haircuts. I'm trying to stay positive and upbeat but it's hard when I feel like I'm caught in the middle all the time.
>
> Found a hairclip in my duffel bag. Didn't know I'd even packed it, a diamanté flower thing. I wore it down for breakfast and JR noticed. He said: 'I like your new hairclip Rach, it's very pretty. Is it so you can maintain some femininity in such a blokey environment?'
>
> Ah, no. It's because I haven't had a haircut for eight months and my fringe is hanging in my eyes! But hey, thanks for noticing.
>
> Still, the gym is going great and I've lost another kilo this month. On track to be looking sharp at the end of the year.

Some people believe the Station Leader role is the toughest on station, and believe me it's no walk in the park. But spare a thought for the chef. She had her work critiqued by 17 people, three times a day, every single day, for a year. In the constellation of conversation topics, food and haircuts were the brightest stars. The day-to-day minutiae of life provided my biggest challenges over winter and were also the catalyst for some of my greatest learning.

Footy killed the radio star

Football was at the core of one of the greatest changes in my leadership style. The slushy is one of those community roles that everyone takes on as part of their rostered duty. Each day someone is rostered on as kitchen assistant, the 'slushy', to help the chef in preparing the meals for the day.

Some people really look forward to their time as slushy as a welcome respite from the boredom of some of the critical but mundane winter tasks such as stocktakes. Other people grudgingly perform the role because it's compulsory, but they really don't enjoy being in the kitchen. As a sweetener for the person undertaking slushy duties, they have the choice of playing whatever music they like throughout the living quarters. The music is also transmitted around the station and picked up on the radio of each vehicle. So the entire community gets to enjoy whatever songs the slushy chooses to play.

One Saturday a couple of people on slushy decided they would prefer to listen to a live broadcast of the AFL rather than music. I didn't pay much attention to it until a small contingent came to me to complain: the policy was 'whoever is on slushy picks the music, *not* footy'. They simply didn't want to hear football being broadcast over the station's radio station.

The next day a separate group came and spoke to me to argue that the policy was 'slushy's choice'. Whether that choice was music or sport was irrelevant, in their opinion. The predicament for me was that, as with many small things, there was no policy. It was simply a cultural tradition that had evolved over time. There was never a clear, specific rationale for what should be played over the radio. I was at a loss on how to manage this one.

So I did what I do best. I consulted. I collaborated, I canvassed every single person on station and asked, 'What do you think?' Suddenly it became the biggest issue to hit Antarctica in 58 years of Australian expeditions. Everyone was talking about it, and I mean everyone. I struggled to understand what was happening and why this was such a critical issue. As I wrote in my journal each night, and I reflected on the day and my performance as leader, I just could not grasp what I was missing. Why was this so important? Why had it become such a big, hairy thing? What had happened?

Monday 1st August

A normal kind of day today. Found some interesting new websites on Antarctica and it's hilarious seeing how all the stations from all the nations have the same kinds of issues. I laughed out loud when I read about the 30-year-old salsa over at the American base. It topped our 28-year-old jam.

(continued)

> ## Monday 1st August (cont'd)
>
> Footy on the radio is my new bacon war. If it's not one thing ... But I'm not happy how it's playing out. No matter how much I consult on the issue it just seems to get bigger and bigger. Why? Why? Why?
>
> It's starting to get light and the colours are incredible. We're planning the first post-dark field trip and I can't wait to get off station.

Then the penny dropped. What had happened was *me*. By involving the entire community, by seeking their input on a decision, I had elevated and escalated the issue to the point where people who had previously been unaware it was even an issue suddenly had an opinion on it! By adopting my usual democratic style I had turned this straightforward problem into a complex monster. In hindsight I should have realised I would never get a consensus decision from the team. I already had one group totally opposed to listening to the footy and another group just as strongly supporting the slushy's freedom of choice. Common sense should have told me I'd have to make the call myself.

The incident reinforced for me the importance of changing and adapting my decision-making style according to the situation. Sometimes it's best to be consultative and democratic; sometimes I was being paid to make a decision and just needed to make it; and other times it was best to step back and let the team sort it out for themselves. The important skill for any leader is having the judgement and experience to know when to adopt which particular style.

In the end I did make the decision myself. I decided that anyone who didn't want to listen to the footy on the radio should just turn his or her radio off. A blindingly brilliant decision, even if I do say so myself! So do I regret the footy saga? No, because I learned an important leadership lesson from it. Would I do it that way again? Never in a million years. I hope!

Match the person to the task

To get good or great performance from individuals it is important that their skills and interests are matched to the work they are being asked to perform.

People choose to work in Antarctica for a variety of reasons. It's no different from any workplace in the world. Some people choose to work there for the money; after all, with no expenses it's easy to save your wages. Some choose to work there to get away or to get out of a situation back home. Some are attracted by the fun and excitement of working in Antarctica.

Even though summer is the time for science, there were still some science tasks to undertake over winter. One of these involved measuring the sea ice that froze around the landmass. The relative time it takes for the ice to melt and refreeze throughout the year is an indicator of climate change.

These sea ice measurements were taken once a week throughout winter and it was a tough job at times. Freezing temperatures, gusting winds, total darkness, cold hands—all the ingredients for a tough gig. I had to carefully consider who would be best suited to undertake this work. I figured that if I asked the people who were working there primarily for the money they would just hate it.

So instead I chose the people who were working in Antarctica for the excitement and the fun. While I can't say they loved every minute of it, I know they felt a huge sense of achievement when they had completed the measurements. They also saw it as a bit of fun ... well, sometimes!

Matching people to the task is an important skill for every leader to have. It's obvious that you should match people to the tasks they are good at, but if you can extend that and also match them to the tasks they enjoy, you will always get a better result.

It's the same with recognition. I made a point of celebrating the small victories along the way. I regularly acknowledged and thanked the team of people who braved the Antarctic elements to undertake the sea ice measurements. It was a simple 'thanks and well done', because I realised if I waited until the end of the expedition to say thanks and to acknowledge all the small victories, then it would be too late. Morale would drop and the expedition would seem to go on forever.

In Antarctica we didn't have the usual rewards available to a manager to recognise achievements. Instead I learned the power of a simple thank you. At 5.30 am one dark, windy morning with the temperature hovering at −30 °C, an alarm sounded on the plumbers' pagers. The main water pipes were blocked. We could not use any water throughout the station. This would mean no cooked breakfast, no toilets, no showers. Potentially dire straits! They woke me up to alert me, and so someone could raise the alarm if they didn't return on time.

Off went our intrepid plumbers. They fixed the situation and were back inside before the rest of the slumbering community was even awake. The next day at our regular monthly station meeting I simply said, 'I'd also just like to say a quick thanks to our gun plumbing team for going out and fixing the pipes in the middle of the night so we could have water in the morning. Thanks guys, and great work'.

The rest of the community gave them a round of applause, but the best part was the look on their faces. They were proud to receive the grateful thanks of their colleagues, but I also realised how important it was that they received the recognition of their boss.

A simple 'thanks' had worked wonders in making them feel appreciated and confirmed they had done great work. A very simple yet powerful tool for acknowledging achievement — and best of all, it was free.

What I learned

- *Adapt your style.* Make each decision taking into account the person, the issue and the situation at hand. Decide whether you need to be democratic and collaborate, to be decisive and autocratic, or to stay out of it. Make the right decision, and make it the right way.

- *Match people to the task.* Understand what tasks people enjoy doing and try to find a mix of work that needs to be done and work they enjoy doing. The work still needs to be distributed equitably, but of you can match skills and experience to the tasks people enjoy doing you will keep them engaged.

Chapter 29

'No triangles' takes effort and persistence

As I've already shared, we did have moments of conflict and personality clashes. Conflict isn't necessarily a bad thing, however. It's how it's handled that can cause the damage or create the benefit. Conflict can be great for generating a really thorough analysis of an idea or proposal. After all, if not everyone agrees on something, it's valuable to listen to, and try to understand, the differing viewpoints. This can lead to an even better outcome that covers points perhaps not yet considered.

Different strokes for different folks

The conflict that was most challenging for me wasn't caused by the obvious diversity within this disparate group of individuals. There was very little conflict caused by differences between the men and women, say, or the baby boomers and the Gen Ys. These more overt differences (age and gender) rarely caused concerns. The bigger challenges related to the diversity of thinking styles and preferences and the varied types of work experience.

The 'big picture', creative, often extroverted types really irritated some of the more subdued, 'fine detail', often introverted people. And vice versa. Neither style was better or worse; they were just different, and these differences in style sometimes caused conflict. Throughout winter I committed time with individuals to continue the work we had started on the journey down—understanding each other, our differences, what makes us tick.

An interesting quirk of Antarctic expeditions is that there is a mix of people with widely varied work experience. People who have been self-employed their entire careers (and have never reported to a manager) work alongside those who have always worked in teams within larger organisations. It created an interesting opportunity for me to coach the 'sole operators' to share their knowledge and skills as part of a team while encouraging the 'team people' to have the confidence to show their initiative and not wait to be told what to do next.

To build mutual understanding we created a calendar of 'showcase' events. These were designed around a half-day session where each team would run through 'a day in their life'. They would outline what they did each day; what their critical tasks were; and what their major aims and projects were for the year. And of course, it wouldn't be an Antarctic expedition if we didn't make each event memorable by serving great food!

Monday 1st August

More fun with potato gems. We're out of potatoes so we spent lunchtime designing ways to make these things more palatable. Parmigiana? Wrapped in bacon? Gems in white wine sauce? It would be hilarious if it wasn't so serious! The guys have even resorted to requesting that horrid dehydrated potato mash. (Deb, I think it's called?) How can they eat that stuff? They also like those Fray Bentos 'classic' steak-and-kidney pies in a tin, and orange Tang drink. I reckon the cold is finally getting to them … odd, very odd.

We had a very good 'Day in the Life' session today from our two meteorologists. Because they are shut away in the Met building most of the time it was great to see everyone appreciate the amount of work they do. It was topped off by a brilliant French-themed dinner.

I spoke to Dad after dinner and he reckons all we do is have parties down here!

As you will have gathered, the topic of food was never far from people's lips and was a focal point of our community. To take advantage of this, I let each team select both the catering and the venue for their event.

On Plumbers' Day we spent a few hours in their shed learning about plumbing work and then sat back and enjoyed a delicious spit roast and roasted potatoes. For his day, Doc hosted us in his surgery and we had a high tea with cream cakes and a fantastic array of other cakes and slices. On Station Leader's Day we spent the session in my office and topped it off with canapés and bubbly.

As well as creating some great memories and sharing a few laughs, these 'day in the life' events were an important tool for building strong teamwork through shared understanding. Every person fully appreciated the role of every other member of the team. After these sessions I no longer heard that old refrain, 'Yes, but what do they do all day?'

No triangles, and difficult conversations

I was very clear from the start of the expedition that I expected people to sort out interpersonal spats with each other, and only if they couldn't resolve the issue should they come and involve me.

There were several reasons for this tactic. Firstly, it was to encourage mature conversations and acceptance that we will, from time to time, get on one another's nerves. But if the other person's behaviour truly affected us and our enjoyment of our time on station, then something needed to be done.

Secondly, I wanted to protect myself from the emotional burden that goes with trying to sort out personal disagreements and issues in a workplace. It is not the role of any leader to sort out every conflict between staff; they are old enough to sort it out themselves and you will exhaust yourself trying to smooth over every little spat. Of course, the big exception to this rule is behaviour that involves bullying or harassment — that's clearly an issue where a leader must step in and act decisively and immediately.

However, for those everyday, garden-variety niggles that are common to every workplace the leader's role is to coach people in how to address the issue themselves. It took several attempts for me to hone this skill. The first time I tried to coach my staff about 'no triangles' was a miserable failure. Phil came to see me and said, 'Matt really annoys me when he speaks to me in that tone of voice'. I asked him if he wanted me to speak to Matthew and he replied, 'No, I'm just telling you so you know.'

Hmm… I thought, does the word 'dobbing' spring to mind?

'Well Phil', I said. 'It's now the second week of August. You've been with Matthew for the past nine months and we've only got 12 weeks before we head home. If you want to enjoy the rest of your time in Antarctica, I suggest you go and have a chat about it directly with him.'

I gave him some tips such as 'pick the right time of day, don't grab him first thing in the morning as he comes downstairs for breakfast' and 'be empathetic and try to understand where he is coming from'. He went away and returned the next day and told me: 'I followed up that issue with Matthew.'

'Great!' I replied, 'how did you go?'

'Well,' he said, 'I sent him an email and …'

I honestly don't know what he said after that as my head was just full of a voice saying 'No, no, no,' with a couple of Homer Simpson 'Duh!' noises thrown in. I gently explained to Phil that you never, ever broach these topics over email. I explained that as email has no tone or context it is very easy to misinterpret someone's words and often they can appear harsher than the author intended.

So I went through my coaching tips with him again: pick the right time, stick to the facts, be empathetic and so on. But most important, *speak* to him! So he did, and the next day he found me and told me, 'Well, I spoke to Matthew.'

'Terrific', I said. 'How did it go?'

'Well,' he said, 'I waited until he'd had a few beers …'

AAARGGHH!!! Yes, there is a reason they are described as 'difficult' conversations. The conversation itself isn't easy, but nor is it easy to coach people on how to have the conversation. After this episode, I put down what I reckoned we needed to do for these difficult conversations and we implemented the rule of 'no triangles': you don't speak to her about him, or I don't speak to you about her. Go straight to the source. Show courtesy and respect and create 'no triangles'.

Most people do not set out deliberately to upset someone at work (or at home). They just don't. Usually we aren't even aware that we may have upset someone, and it's a horrible feeling when we find out we have. And it's worse when we find out the person went to a third party to discuss it rather than coming directly to us. The decent and respectful thing to do is to be brave and go directly to the person. It's not always easy but it creates open and honest communication, which in turn builds teamwork.

Return of the sun

Slowly and steadily the light returned to Antarctica. It was a blessing to look out my window and not just see myself reflected against the inky blackness. The plateau behind us emerged as a vague shape, then the outline of the hills surrounding the station, until there was a blue-grey light that got brighter and brighter each day.

The day the sun returned we threw a party. A well-planned party, a welcome back party, and there was a lot of celebration. We headed out onto the ice and it was an amazing feeling to stretch our legs and feel the rush of cold air on our faces again.

Friday 12th August

Back home after two nights at Watts Hutt with Baz and Pat. We had a ball; it was really relaxing and just wonderful to be outside. I'm slowly getting over my squeamishness about going to the toilet in a plastic bag. It's the only thing I don't like about being off station. Even the snoring didn't bother me!

I got to drive the Hagglunds and use the GPS, which was fun. We went out to Crooked Lake and walked to the Sorsdal Glacier. We'd been walking for about 20 minutes when my 'cold' hand just froze up again. It hurt so much and was really stinging, and I had tears in my eyes. Baz held my hand as we walked back to the Hagglunds. What a wonderful gesture. He just grabbed my injured hand and held it between his two hands to warm it up. How cool is he? Sore hands, a minor whinge, but otherwise an amazing time.

(continued)

Friday 12th August (cont'd)

I never get sick of looking at the incredible ice structures and the colours the sun is throwing are just magic. The light was reflecting off the snow as we drove along and there were twinkles everywhere, like someone had decked out Antarctica with fairy lights.

Spring approached us at a gallop and took me largely unawares. I was used to the slow change of seasons back home, but when the amount of daylight increases by around 20 minutes each day I found that at the beginning of the week we had one hour of sun per day and at the end of the week three! It was an incredible time and slowly the sun started to have an impact on the temperatures.

It was amazing to see just how quickly the niggly behaviour disappeared with the eternal night. As a unit we went from cabin fever, sluggish, quiet and irritable to high energy and excitement. With the sun came the opportunity to de-ice the equipment, dig out the massive snowdrifts around the station and get back on top of life.

But the morning of my performance review dawned cloudy and bleak. Despite my lack of superstition, it made me uneasy.

Monday 15th August

My review was overwhelmingly positive but I'm really hurt by someone from head office saying that my leadership style is like being hit in the head with a piece of four-by-two.

When I asked what that was based on he couldn't, or wouldn't, say … If you're going to say it, back it up! Use data, use facts. If that's his experience of me over the three weeks I worked with him in Hobart then so be it, but give me some tangible feedback. Something I can work on, FFS.

This is something I have always struggled with. I so want to be liked by all that if one person has a bad thing to say I usually will just want to crawl away into a hole. Can't get it out of my head for days. I wake up at 3 am and replay interactions over and over and over again.

But I'm different this time. I'm stronger, I know I have done and am doing a great job. This journal has helped immensely and even writing this down now I feel a real sense of affirmation. It's almost like this journal is talking back to me saying, 'Yes, feel hurt but don't take it personally. This review is HIS issue, not yours. You focus on being the best leader you can be'.

So I will!

PS Although I AM fighting the temptation to take my foot off the pedal now we're only nine or so weeks from the end.

What I learned

- *Understand every team member's contribution.* People need to know where their 'bit' fits into the 'whole'. Similarly, they need other people to recognise the contribution they make. Understand what part each person and team plays in the wider organisation. Promote this. Invite other people to sit in on your meetings and learn 'what you do all day'.

- *'No triangles' is tough when you're starting out!* It can take a lot of guts to address an issue, particularly with someone you're friends with. So talk about it with your mentor or coach and make sure you deal with the issue and the person directly. Be brave and show respect and courtesy.

- *Leaders are under intense scrutiny* (2). Every person will have an opinion on the success, or otherwise, of their leader. Listen to all feedback and ask for examples if you need clarification. Seek frank and fearless feedback on your performance from people you trust. Build your self-awareness and spend time every day reflecting on how you handled situations.

Chapter 30

Watch out for three-quarter time — keep your energy up

Our final weeks in Antarctica went by in a blur. The energy that returned to the station was unbelievable and we went from stagnant to staccato almost overnight. Everyone wanted to maximise their last few weeks so I spent a lot of time organising off-site excursions, filling rosters and keeping up with the demands of head office.

Where to next?

One of the biggest demands was the final report. I had been working on this on-and-off for a good six months already, filling in pieces as and when they happened, but the report needed an overriding narrative. I was very happy with our expedition and the report reflected that.

Thursday 18th August

A really productive day. I finally finished writing the Operations Report. It has taken so long but it's worth it. I hope it doesn't upset too many people, but hey, it's my report and I've written it to say what needs to be said. In my opinion.

I also wrote the monthly report and the latest version of our newsletter for distribution to the families back home. I feel quite happy and relaxed now.

(continued)

Thursday 18th August (cont'd)

Flat Darcy arrived from the Balranald Primary School. They faxed down a drawing of a person based on the children's book *Flat Stanley*. We cut him out and stuck him on cardboard to be photographed around station for their school project. We set him up and took pictures of him drilling ice, driving a Hagglunds and doing some cross-country skiing. Our team had such fun putting Flat Darcy in funny, and often ludicrous, Antarctic situations that the school asked if they could send down more Flat People! So now we have a whole family of Flat People. It's hilarious. The schoolkids even added a little bio about what their particular Flat Person was like, and we did laugh about Flat Rosa who liked 'cooking, cleaning and walking the dog'. Get a life, Flat Rosa!

Minor issue with Flat Barney—we tied him to a Met weather balloon for a photo. Unfortunately we forgot to tie the balloon down and powered by a full load of hydrogen the weather balloon, and subsequently Flat Barney, took to the skies. Oops. Have to explain to that child that Flat Barney is off on a traverse...for a long time.

It's a nice break in the day-to-day rhythm to have the Flat People and it also makes us feel proud of what we're doing here and reminds us we are somewhere special.

I started thinking seriously about what I would do on my return to Australia. I knew that my leadership skills had increased massively over the past year and that I was ready to take on an executive role within Parks Victoria. But another big part of me wanted to lie down and rest for a very long time. Mark Stone offered me a great role as Chief Ranger of Port Phillip Bay on my return. I was in two minds but I accepted. They had shown me great loyalty and it was time to repay it.

Monday 22nd August

A busy day, even if it was spent working on my CV. At least it's current now and I won't have to update it for an executive application. I hadn't realised how much I have done until I started writing it down for this.

What is not appearing on the CV is my judgement and intuition. I reckon it's now really good. This experience has been incredible. I've gone from second-guessing my every move to acting with confidence in a wide variety of situations.

I'm also toying with the idea of doing an MBA—putting some theoretical flesh around my experience and intuition.

I wasn't convinced the role I would return to would provide the constant challenge I need so I researched the postgraduate management education scene from my desk in Antarctica. The MBA from Melbourne Business School stood out as a world-class postgraduate degree and I made some enquiries. I quickly found out I would need to sit an exam to gain entry! And not just any exam—it was the same exam that is run for all world-class MBA programs, from Harvard to Oxford.

A sample test showed me that despite my ability to 'do numbers' I was nowhere near the level required for entry into Melbourne. I asked a friend in Melbourne to buy the textbook and scan the chapters for me. I grabbed Doc and our fantastic engineer Peter and 'seconded' them to deliver maths coaching.

Wednesday 28th September

I'm tired again and can't work it out. Maybe I'm eating too much sugar. As soon as I woke up I couldn't wait to get back to bed tonight.

I went out with Sharon and did the sea-ice observations. It's so nice just to say, bugger it, I'm going out for a while. It was cold out on the sea ice and we laughed as we packed our survival pack. Nothing spontaneous here. Five layers of clothing and a backpack, just to go for a walk!

The sea ice is still getting thicker, which surprised me, as we're having long days now. I guess it's because it's still very, very cold here. Apparently it will start thinning out very soon. It's fascinating to see the seasons changing so quickly. Well... relatively quickly.

There are only eight people on station at the moment. My most 'challenging' people are off on traverses and in huts and I can't believe how quiet it is here today. No doubt when they all come back I'll have another round of hell to deal with. But for now Kirsten has prepared an awesome Spanish dinner. It's a special treat to have a formal dinner midweek. Bring it on!

Three-quarter time syndrome

The final weeks continued to amaze me for a couple of reasons. Firstly, there was all the planning and preparation and 'mechanical' things that had to be attended to. This was expected and we took it all in our stride. It was hard work with long hours but we managed it. Secondly, and what stopped me in my tracks, was that we all dropped our guard and many of our social niceties disappeared altogether.

Thursday 29th September

Had a run-in with Phil today. He rang up all cranky because he'd heard a team was heading out to O'Gormans Rocks tomorrow and they hadn't booked the Hagglunds and the quad bikes. He insisted they couldn't go out. I told him he had no right to decide who can and can't take out the Haggs and quads.

He admitted it was a reaction to them not booking the quads, but I wonder where our teamwork and grace has gone. I'm sure it was an oversight and six months ago there would have been a conversation and then it would have been over and done with.

I figure that as there's only five weeks left they are saying, 'Well I've put up with it for so long and I don't want to put up with it any longer'.

I feel this myself. These last few weeks will require me to dig deep and find the patience and tolerance to continue to be a strong leader. I'm almost over it all and would be really happy to spend the rest of my time here doing maths (!). But if I close up now, so close to the finish line, we might have problems at the changeover. Plus I don't want the last memory of our time here to be all about conflict.

Geelong FC wrote today to say that I (once on the cheer squad in my teens) had my photo printed in their annual report! Dad will be stoked. Probably his proudest moment of me so far!

Saturday 1st October

Well, it's turning to shit. JR and Phil had a run-in this morning, which brought to a head all the bullshit a few people have been carrying on with over the last two days. By 11 am today I'd received complaints about:

- someone who rebooted the servers by turning them off and on again at the wall (a big no-no apparently)

(continued)

Saturday 1st October (cont'd)

- another person who borrowed steel from the diesos without asking

- someone who cleared the snow from the beach when he wasn't asked to do it

- another person who put wet mugs on a newly cleaned kitchen bench.

I just look at this list and want to cry. We've done so well this year and it's really unravelling quickly. I don't want us to leave the ship in Hobart hating each other.

Rang Richard in Hobart to chat about the changing mood of the station. Told me it happens EVERY YEAR! The psychologists call it three-quarter time payback. Reassuring to know it's common, but a heads-up would have been bloody helpful. Still, at least I know what I'm dealing with now ... Onwards.

Monday 3rd October

STAND-UP FIGHT!

Well, sort of. It's the first time our conversation has ever degenerated into shouting. And it was at the dinner table of all places.

Over the year our conversations have covered everything. We've discussed anything from highly controversial and personal topics, such as abortion laws, capital punishment and gay marriage, to Paris Hilton, Shane Warne and whether *The Wombles* was better than *Fraggle Rock*. (*The Wombles* of course.)

It's a strange existence. Usually you wouldn't discuss any of these topics with your workmates. But we can't discuss the latest movies, or who we think should have been voted off *Survivor* last night ... so our dinner-table conversations are varied, broad and often unusual.

Yet we have always managed to discuss these topics amicably, showing great respect for differing opinions. It's been fascinating to hear from people with views vastly different from mine and I'm thrilled we've been able to do that. No one has yelled, no one has walked out, no one has been hurt or upset... until today.

And the topic today was 'Which Australian state has the worst roads?'!!

One person was so vehement the spittle was flying and the cutlery banged on the table. People weren't agreeing with him so he spoke louder and louder until he was yelling! If it wasn't a symptom of three-quarter time payback and the fact we are all now getting tired, it would be hilarious! The worst roads in Australia? Who cares enough to shout at someone else about it... Anywhere??

I sat on the sidelines and just watched. And it made me realise I don't have a position on many political issues. I have spent my life being a peacemaker and diplomat, so I don't actually take sides and can't articulate what I 'stand for'. Now I'm more determined than ever to get into Melbourne Business School.

In the meantime I'm going to have to do something to break this mood.

Thursday 6th October

Finally we had some good news. Well, not good news exactly, but a good outcome. The traverse team out on the ice took two Hagglunds and one of them broke a torsion spring in the suspension and is undrivable. So they were stuck out on the ice a good two days' travel from station. The weather's not great, but passable at −21 °C and no wind.

They tried to weld it back together but had no luck, so they wanted to bring all eight people back in the yellow Hagglunds.

(continued)

Thursday 6th October (cont'd)

I don't want them travelling in the back of the Hagg on the sea ice so I arranged a rescue team to meet them and bring them back. These vehicles have a hatch in the roof of the front cabin so if it falls through the ice the passengers can climb out. Riding in the second cabin, without a hatch in the roof, is not on. Someone could get killed.

All station is involved and we are back to working well together! The adversity is pulling us together and my inbox is empty of new grizzles.

Friday 7th October

Finally got to bed at 7 am, rescue complete. The guys rang in to say they were two hours from the rendezvous. I woke up Ian to get the waypoints, then Sharon and JR got the spare Hagg warmed up. They left at 1.30 am and arrived at Schnezy 1 at 3 am. They met the stuck crew and evened out the load between the two vehicles. Thirty minutes later the headlights on the lead Hagg packed in! Andrew took over the driving and they played follow-the-leader home. Matt and I made pancakes and hot coffee and he was great company, except for the smell of burnt pancakes. He's not such a great cook, but he's a terrific expeditioner!

I couldn't have planned a better team-building exercise if I'd tried! It was just the gee-up we needed.

Saturday 8th October

The events of the week have made me realise that we really need a set of clear, achievable goals to get the most out of people in the next few weeks. I made a conscious decision to start talking about our return today at lunch and subtly promote the work that still needs to be done. Hopefully we will be able to focus on that instead of each other.

International Darts Competition!!!

We played darts against Casey Station, the US base at South Pole and New Zealand's Scott Base. We communicated using our HF radio sets—oh joy! South Pole could hear Davis and Scott but not Casey. We at Davis could hear Casey but not Scott. We fiddled with the frequencies but that didn't help, so we used intermediaries and the South Pole kept the overall scoreboard.

I'm not implying there was any unscrupulous activity going on but I did laugh when I heard a collective shout of 'bullseye' and looked over to see the dart still in Howie's hand! Ian's next throw was very close to double 20, so we yelled out 'Double 20!' They came back with a Triple 19.

And so it went on. Thankfully the Americans were just as playful as we were. I don't know how you can physically fit six darts into a single bullseye but hey, if Americans can fly to the moon, anything is possible!

What I learned

- *Watch out for three-quarter time.* Most of the work is done, you're close to the milestone but there is a final flurry of activity required. At these times we all just want to get to the end and a natural response is to just push the work through and forget everything else. But it's precisely these times that require the greatest teamwork. Keep your leadership hat on, stay on the balcony and motivate the team to be true to their agreed values and behaviours.

Part VI

The return

Good leaders know themselves inside and out. Self-reflection is a critical skill that delivers great benefits.

After a year on the ice I had three fully completed personal journals. Each night as I wound down I reflected on my day. This enforced time alone, just my journal and me, was the most powerful of all my time in Antarctica. It taught me much about myself, my attitudes and behaviours. And it taught me a lot about the people around me.

Chapter 31

Go the distance

By mid October our thoughts really started to turn towards home. Now that winter had passed and we were halfway through spring it was a challenge to stay interested and involved in day-to-day interpersonal issues on station. I kept reminding myself that it was just three-quarter time. My beloved football club, the Geelong Cats, had lost many a game by taking their foot off the accelerator at this point.

For goodness' sake, go outside!

But there were pressing things to do, and if we weren't busy doing these then I expected everyone to be busy enjoying themselves on the ice, perhaps for the last time.

Monday 10th October

Really grumpy today. I was on slushy and skipped smoko because I just felt crap. Matt walked in and complained about (a) Ian cutting him off on the radio and (b) JR eating a pancake with his hands. I almost turned around and walked out. Why am I over it? I hope it's just fleeting, because I was really happy on Saturday, but today I'm a pain in the arse. I don't want to be here but I don't want to go home either. I expect the next few weeks will be a roller-coaster ride for all of us.

Tuesday 11th October

Feeling better today and not so out of sorts. Maybe Mum was right and it's just all the mixed emotions that are affecting me.

(continued)

Tuesday 11th October (cont'd)

Focused hard on the to-do list for going home and changeover. Made a huge list and started breaking it up into chunks and people who would be responsible for doing the work. It was great fun and I started to feel the heading-home excitement building.

Wednesday 12th October

First penguins arrived! Pat won the 'predict the date of the first penguin arrival' competition. Very excited to see some wildlife about the place now. It was a stunning blue day, still cold at −17°C but just beautiful. I walked out to Gardner Island with one of the guys, and sure enough, the little fellas were out and they made me smile. I took my coat off and sat on it and just watched and watched them. One little bloke got on his tummy and started sliding up to me at a million miles an hour. Then when he got about 4 metres away he chucked the brakes on, stood up and just stared at me! We held each other's gaze for a few minutes before he plopped back on his tummy and scooted back to where he came from. It was a priceless moment.

As I sat on the ice and looked up at the plateau and the station lights, with the fading pink light all around, I realised how much I love this place and how important it is to me. They say it gets in your blood and I now agree. I could happily live (by myself?) in a hut just watching this place. It's different every day and so overwhelming at times.

Preparing the station

Friday 14th October

Busy day. Got a few little jobs done. Took the humidifier to the tip, put the party costumes back in the dungeon, drilled up the timber box, took the yoga mats back and cleaned JJ's cocktail bar. It's good to be able to tick some things off the list. It was snowing this morning and beautiful.

I was slushy today (AGAIN!). Tomorrow is my last slushy and I'll be sad when that one's over. It's a nice break from management tasks and I doubt I'll ever have a job again where I'm paid to cook.

Sunday 23rd October

The *Aurora Australis* is just over a week away!

I went out with Kirsten and Pat on the quad bikes to look at the newly born and still-being-born Weddell seal pups! They are absolutely adorable, all covered in a soft, fluffy fur and with the most exquisite big brown eyes. They are still weak so spend most of their time snuggled up to their mummy and suckling.

One pup had died and it was heartbreaking to see the mum pushing it with her head and licking it all over trying to revive it. I was really sad on the way back, not about the pup so much but because it was likely the last time I would ever be out on a quad bike enjoying this beautiful continent, free from tour guides and tourist traps. But the Adélie penguins cheered me up no end on the way back and made me laugh out loud. They just look so ridiculous and ungainly on land.

It's so fresh and clean here I doubt I will ever experience anything like it again. I know I will miss the sound of silence.

Monday 24th October

Weekly station meeting today to update on the status of the to-do list. We seem to have everything under control, with most of it to be completed before week's end. I'm only getting stressed about the planes, which were supposed to arrive today. I hope they don't come at dinnertime because I'm really looking forward to roast lamb!

The ship is at Casey now and I'm trying to get my head around the fact that in just a few days our cosy little community will be upended by the arrival of 80 strangers. I can feel the winterers already closing ranks. They really want to go home but they are extremely protective of their Antarctic home. Hopefully we will all look back with extremely well-tinted rose-coloured glasses.

As the *Aurora Australis* neared Davis the preparation for docking, unloading and the influx of new people reached dizzying heights. We were back to working 16 to 20 hours a day. What made things worse was that I was no longer 'in charge' of everything. Head office took the lead role in scheduling the inbound flights for the returning planes and the logistics of the resupply. I'm thankful they did, as I would not have had the capacity to manage it myself, but it grated. Despite how I felt, I knew that my people were still watching me, probably even more closely than ever, and taking their lead from me.

Tuesday 25th October

I can feel myself reacting to the changes going on around me. With all the new activity I'm starting to feel like I'm losing control of my station. I need to be careful of my emotions and keep asking the question: 'Does it really matter?' Who cares if we do or don't have a hot breakfast during resupply? So what if the planes are arriving early and no one advised us? I should take it as a compliment that they think we have everything so under control that we don't need heaps of notice.

But I can feel myself getting angry and I want to fire off angry emails. The others will follow my lead so I need to call on all my leadership qualities. If I piss and moan they will too, but if I relax into it they probably will as well. Three-quarter time, Rachael. Hang in there.

I took this job to learn how to lead in difficult situations so I'll keep reminding myself that the idea is to be comfortable with ambiguity.

Thursday 27th October

There's a real sense of excitement and anticipation in the air tonight. Everyone is happy enough but there is an odd mix of relief and getting on with business. The reality is we've done nearly everything we need to do. I must enjoy this time so will head out to Gardner Island on my own tomorrow to say goodbye to Antarctica.

Friday 28th October

End-of-year dinner! What a great night! We had a flight theme with the room set up like a plane. Flat Darcy, the cardboard cutout, was our flight attendant and the boys made cardboard cutouts of a very voluptuous 'Mercedes' and 'Amber' as the pilots.

Pre-flight champagne was served before we 'flew' off to Japan, where we had miso and udon noodles. Back on board, then off to Hawaii for mai tais. Then the next stop was Italy for ravioli and bruschetta before arriving in Australia for prawn and emu sausage, crocodile, crayfish and baked potato. It was an important night, our last night alone.

I gave a speech to thank them all for their hard work over the year. I didn't single anyone out but thanked 'the team'. I also asked them to take the time over the next few days to say goodbye to good friends and to Antarctica. I wanted a formal chance to thank 'my' people and I'm glad I've had that.

An extraordinary moment. After I'd said 'thanks', Howie stood up and thanked me and proposed a toast to me and my leadership. As he sat down Pat stood up and offered thanks to me and the team. Then one by one, totally spontaneously, every single person stood and offered a heartfelt and sincere 'thanks'. It was amazing and I was speechless. I must have done something right throughout the year to build a culture of such humble and sincere people. I've never experienced anything like it before, and I doubt I ever will again.

The ship is just over the horizon now and the planes arrive tomorrow.

New faces and the newspaper

The aircraft arrived on time and landed on a newly graded and swept ice-way. We were desperate for news and fresh food so it was all hands on deck to secure the planes and help unload. We gathered excitedly in the mess as the parcels were opened. What really surprised us were the smells the delivery brought. There had been no new smells on station for the past nine months, and we seemed to know what was cooking before the chef did.

When the newspapers were opened we crowded around to devour all the little titbits of news we had missed. But it wasn't the news itself that was fascinating. It was the smell. One by one we handed the newspapers to each other, and reverently lifted them to our noses to relish the smell of fresh ink. It was our first new smell in nine months.

The air crews looked at us with disbelief and asked me, 'But you have internet access, so don't you get the news?'

'Yes,' I replied, 'but we don't get newspapers. We want to smell the print, read the ads, get ink on our fingers.'

We were so used to one another that not only did we know everyone's personality back to front but we knew their entire wardrobe, inside out. I was sitting in the lounge when Mark walked in wearing a nondescript but newly delivered shirt.

'New t-shirt, Mark? Sweet,' Pat remarked.

'Yes, I got it in the mail from home,' Mark replied.

A few moments later Phil walked in, saw Mark and said, 'Hey, is that a new t-shirt, Mark?'

Minutes later Dave walked in and said, 'Looking sharp, Mark. Is that new?'

I looked over at the pilots, who were staring at us as if we were some weird cult.

'We know each other by now', I said. 'We notice when someone is wearing something new.'

I didn't tell them I could even work out who was walking past my bedroom door just by the sound of their footsteps! I'd often test myself and think, 'Hmm, that's Sharon', and stick my head out to see if I was right. Hey, I was bored — there's not a lot to do in winter. The pilots would really think we'd lost if it I told them that!

Saturday 29th October

What a different station we live in now!

Eight new faces and the whole station turned out to greet them. We stood at the cold porch door with a glass of 'champagne on arrival' for our new guests. After nine months of seeing the same 17 faces, and hearing the same 17 voices, I think we are all very excited, and have gone a bit silly, at the prospect of new friends.

Wednesday 2nd November

The ship is stuck in pack ice and is waiting for a big breeze and a swell to break free, so we're sitting here on tenterhooks. After waiting so long the uncertainty of our departure time has affected the troops.

In other ways it's been a real eye-opener having the air crew here without the summerers. As usual, at 6 pm the kitchen was full of people eating dinner, but I noticed it was only the winterers. Not one of the eight new arrivals was there and I started wondering if I had made it clear that dinner was from 6 pm to 7 pm?

Gradually they all trickled in around 6.15 pm, 6.30 pm.

Matt asked me, 'I wonder if they know dinner is at 6 pm?' I thought to myself, 'I wonder if they know how thoroughly institutionalised we are!'

It makes me wonder about our reassimilation to normal life. I think I will spend a lot of time on the ship with my people helping them anticipate our return to the 'real world'...

120 new souls arrive

Sunday 6th November

The ship is here and I can hardly believe it. Now I no longer have to answer the same questions again and again. It reminded me of the old 'Are we there yet?' questions from the back seat.

(continued)

Sunday 6th November (cont'd)

We spotted the ship just before 4 pm as it rounded the headland and it quickly ploughed through the sea ice and came to rest a couple of kilometres out. The mail came ashore first and it was SO SO SO much fun!!! There were presents all round, news and knick-knacks from home. It was just like Christmas Day. It was great looking up from the ice to the eager and excited new faces, knowing that my home would now be theirs.

Monday 7th November

First day of resupply and already I have a sore throat! Arrgh!

I met with Jacquie, the Army psychologist who will debrief me on the journey home, and she is just amazing. I really like her and think I will be able to be 100% up-front about anything with her. Already she has explained a lot of the things about some of my expeditioners that I have struggled to understand.

Two people have already had their first debrief and both of them came out in tears and went straight to their rooms. Obviously some heavy-duty unloading is going to take place. Good thing it's getting done here, not on long-suffering families back home.

Tuesday 8th November

Had a great time helping unpack the pallets and put them away in the green store.

We all had an enormous laugh when I opened one box to find more shower-curtain rings! I KNOW they got the memo, and the email and phone call. Maybe they are locked into a 100-year deal with the supplier? Who knows? I should be concerned but I'm not. I'm just too excited to let anything faze me.

It's so fantastic tasting fresh fruit again. A couple of the boys and I skipped the cooked lunch and had yummy tomato sandwiches instead. Kirsten finally has her mangoes!

Letting go of the reins

Thursday 10th November

Last day as incumbent Station Leader.

I was excited all day and managed to hold it together until people started moving into our rooms, in some cases before we'd moved out! The handover ceremony was great and full of emotion. Many people were crying and I'll remember that moment forever.

Now the winterers are with me on the ship. We'll be here another couple of days waiting for a weather window, and then it's off to Australia!

Sunday 13th November

Last day in Antarctica. It was strange going back to the station after being on the ship the last few days. They have done some things with decorations and already it doesn't seem like home at all. The Minties and Snakes have been put away; apparently there is a new policy about Minties because of tooth fillings!

We are getting on each other's nerves—both the winterers on the ship and with the summerers. They can't wait for us to leave so they can get on with their expedition, their way. I walked past my old office and noticed the new Station Leader, John, had rubbed out my to-do list and started his own. I felt like an intruder and I think they feel the same way. Awkward.

Goodbye Antarctica, it's been real

The ship left at 5 pm the next day. I stood at the stern, alone, and watched as the station disappeared from view, until Antarctica was gone. Gone from sight, but not from memory. I could hardly breathe and tears came to my eyes as I watched my beloved home for the past year fade into the distance.

'Goodbye, Antarctica,' I whispered. 'Thanks for having me.' As if on cue a little Adélie penguin popped its head out of the water. I will miss this place. So much.

I was completely exhausted, physically, emotionally and socially. I can be a bit of a loner at times. I have a few close friends but most of the time I enjoy my own company more than I enjoy the company of crowds. My emotional bank was severely overdrawn and I knew it would take a long time to get back even to break-even point.

Monday 14th November

As I sit here watching the bergs go by again, it's not exhilaration or excitement I feel this time. It's a deep sense of gratitude and a peace in knowing I have led a team in the toughest, most gruelling, most intense workplace on the planet. And I've done it well. We all more than just survived. While right now we're spent, in two weeks I think we'll be full of energy, stories and passion for this place.

It's the colours I'll miss most.

My job was still not finished, however, not by a long way. I was still responsible for my expeditioners until the boat docked and unloaded in Hobart, some two weeks away.

As I lay in my bunk that night feeling satisfied and happy, I planned out the next two weeks. I would keep a low profile during the day; after all, there should be nothing to 'lead'. I would come to all meals and engage in conversation, even though I was talked out. I would retire early and leave my people to their own devices at night.

The journey home

The only 'leadership' activity I planned was to spend time with each individual and help them with their thought processes as they prepared to greet their family and friends and get back into the swing of life at home.

Saturday 19th November

What a day. This ship can't arrive in Hobart soon enough. I finally got up after having spent the last four days in bed seasick and went down to the mess only to have Mark and Matt carry on with their 'Oh, it's about time you surfaced' routine, so I walked out.

Then Richard came and saw me at 3.30 pm to tell me that one of my summerers from last year, who had just gone back down, had committed suicide. It was surmised he had waited until we were past the point of no return — with low stocks of diesel fuel on board so we couldn't turn back to pick up his body — before he hanged himself.

It was a total shock. I always knew he was a little bit different in the 'real world' — aren't we all? — but no one expected this. No one saw it coming. It must be hell on station and I can't help but feel for Sharon and John, who knew him really well. Bloody horrible and heartbreaking.

Then tonight at dinner Richard told me Phil is upset with me for not talking to him throughout the year! I lost it. Seriously, what does an average of three hours one-on-one counselling and coaching a week comprise? Part of me wants to rip shreds off him. I feel really betrayed. I think I will just ignore him now and leave him in the hands of Richard from head office and Jacquie the Psych. Wash hands. Job done. I think his year was a lot tougher than he expected or was prepared for.

So, tough day, but I won't let it burst my bubble.

Tuesday 22nd November

Ship life continues unabated. I'm pretty sure Phil is avoiding me — which he should. I'm still furious.

The rest of the guys are great, happy and relaxed and looking forward to getting home. Jacquie actually has an excellent repatriation plan, so I've handed most of the planned coaching back to her.

(continued)

Tuesday 22nd November (cont'd)

There was a memorial service on station today and on the ship we held a minute's silence. It's still surreal and heartbreaking. I've been passing the days doing maths and reading. I don't feel like I'm going home and I'm worried about the amount of affection I'm going to be smothered with. More than 12 months without a hug or a cuddle. I love affection, but I'm concerned it will be too overwhelming and my family won't understand it if I need to be alone.

It was 11 °C today and we were swanning around in t-shirts!

Thursday 24th November

Last day on the ship and last day of the expedition. I can't believe it's over. What an adventure! It has been the most amazing experience and I've loved it. Antarctica has captured my heart. It truly is a special place. It gets in your system and from the first moment I laid eyes on it I have been in awe and in love. Tony Hansen from AAD asked me today what the highlight had been. If I could pick one thing it would have to be the colours. The sunsets and sunrises were simply breathtaking—when they happened!

Reflections

I had grown and changed. I no longer felt the pressure to be the 'good girl', and in fact I felt great when I told Phil a few home truths on the way home. It was hard to do but I was proud to stand up for myself. On my final night aboard the ship I looked back through our yearbook and remembered all the great nights and fun times. As I stepped off the ship and said my final goodbyes to my crew I knew I would miss some of them. I knew there would be times when I would see something funny and want to crack a joke with Kirsten or Peter or Patrick or Doc or Ian or Howie. We may or may not stay in touch, I thought, but I will have the photos and the memories forever, particularly the memories of being off station, in the wild, alone on that amazing continent.

I thought I might feel sad that the journey was over, but 12 months was about right. Any shorter and I would have felt short-changed. Any longer and I would have gone mad. I didn't handle everything 100 per cent right first time every time, yet I have no regrets. Antarctica is a tough teacher and if it weren't for my mistakes I would not have learned so much about people and about myself.

I'm particularly proud of my journal. It was a constant companion and confidante. I'm so glad I kept it, because the process of writing out my thoughts, deliberating over my actions and planning the next day was incredibly valuable. Only now, in writing this book, have I gone back to the journals to re-read what I wrote. Eight years on, the journals speak to me of an incredible journey. Of course, the physical journey was tough in many ways, but the big journey I made, and continue to make, is the one towards being the best leader I can be. The journals helped me learn from both success and failure. If I hadn't taken the time to agonise over situations and write down my thoughts, I doubt I would have grown the way I did. But because I did, and because I pushed through time and time again when I didn't want to, my time in Antarctica was life-changing for me, satisfying for my people and successful for the AAD.

The year defined me and will continue to do so for a long time, and seizing that opportunity was the best decision I ever made. It proved to me, yet again, that if I 'regret the things I did, rather than regret the things I didn't do' my life would continue to be exciting, rewarding and fulfilling.

I'm often asked if I'd ever go back to Antarctica. I miss the place, I really do, and I have to stop myself getting on the webcam and looking at the station. That place has a tight hold on my heart, but my life is here now. So would I go back? No. I would not. If I knew then what I know now, would I still have gone? Probably.

But, do I regret going? Not for a heartbeat.

Appendix A

What it takes to be an inspirational leader

I'm convinced the ability to inspire and motivate people is the single biggest attribute of a successful leader. The *Randstad World of Work Report 2011/12* found that more than half of all employers and employees surveyed confirmed the critical need for a leader who inspires and motivates, yet half of the respondents rated their own direct manager as poor or average in this area.

There is a significant gap between what is expected of our leaders and what they are delivering. Add the fact that productivity is directly related to employee motivation and it becomes not just a people issue but one that impacts on the bottom line. So how does a successful leader inspire and motivate? What's below the surface of this particular human capital iceberg?

The ability to inspire and motivate my team, particularly through the long, dark Antarctic winter (when we couldn't even step outside for four months), was critical. Upon our return to Australia, 95 per cent of my winterers rated their general level of satisfaction with the expedition as *moderately satisfied* to *highly satisfied*. Keeping this team happy, productive, motivated and resilient required strong and constant leadership.

This book is not intended to be theoretical or 'preachy', but here I want to share the six things that led my expeditioners to rank me as 'inspirational', as I think these things apply universally to every leader in every workplace.

Vision

The ability to tell and sell a compelling story is crucial. Inspiring leaders are those who can articulate the big strategic directions of the organisation while at the same time clearly explaining how each individual contributes to these larger goals.

Feeling valued and recognised for the work you do is the bedrock of employee morale. The Randstad report reveals: '38 per cent of respondents said being valued and recognised was their top motivator, followed by a strong understanding of how their role contributes to achieving organisational goals. Salary and remuneration were not as highly valued.'

Our 'Day in the Life' sessions gave people the opportunity to show us the tasks they completed in an average day. This simple social ceremony turned into something vastly more important as each person came to fully understand, and value, the contribution of his or her peers. The question 'What do they do all day?' was asked and answered.

Self-awareness

Inspiring leaders know themselves and their capabilities. They dedicate time each day to reflecting on their decisions and evaluating their own performance critically and honestly. This ability to reflect enables leaders to learn and develop; more importantly, it enables them to correct a decision that may have been incorrect, no matter how well intentioned or how well considered.

In the 'Footy killed the radio star' episode I made the correct decision, but I made it the wrong way. There were some strong opinions about the broadcast, but by not reflecting on the situation I allowed it to escalate out of control. If I had stopped and thought before addressing the problem with my same-old approach, the problem would have quickly been solved. Yet it was only by reflecting on this issue for several days that I realised my role in creating this mountain out of a molehill. The self-analysis improved my self-awareness and, without doubt, my leadership ability.

Consistency

Leaders must be consistent in both their decision making and their emotions. A leader who displays appropriate emotion is powerful and human and demonstrates a strength and confidence that is inspiring. Disappointment at missing out on an important job the team pitched for; delight over an unexpected success; sadness over the departure of a valuable member of the team; relief at the closure of an event—these are all appropriate emotions. Expressing them consistently ensures your team can predict with some clarity how you will react and respond.

It's even more critical during the tough times that leaders respond consistently. During the plane crash incident, leading the rescue effort was just one part of my role. To ensure the remaining 116 people felt confident that their peers would be brought home safely, and to keep the rest of the community focused on delivering their work while the leadership team focused on the rescue, it was critical that I was consistently seen to be leading. Choosing my words with care, being seen about the place often so people could ask me questions, providing regular updates on the situation and, most of all, carrying myself with poise and calmness, were all vital.

Whether it's a plane crash in Antarctica, a financial crisis, a merger or a restructure, while the context changes the principles remain the same. The leader needs to be seen to be leading in a calm and consistent manner.

Empathy

Knowing and understanding the individual differences of each of your team members will inspire and motivate them. Appreciating their skills and capabilities means you can match individuals to tasks, increasing productivity as staff undertake work they are good at or enjoy, or even both.

Similarly, understanding that different issues affect people differently, and empathising with that, will improve motivation. On the surface, the Bacon War was one of those trivial issues that arise in any workplace, irritations like dirty coffee mugs left lying around or people routinely arriving late for meetings. After I had listened and empathised with my people I realised there was a deeper problem that was distracting people from their work and therefore affecting our productivity and teamwork. It requires empathy to address these little things that emerge in every workplace; ignore them at your peril.

Celebrate

An inspiring leader will find reasons to celebrate, regularly and at times spontaneously. During the long, dark Antarctic winter it was important that we celebrated along the way, not just birthdays and midwinter's day, but also the smaller successes such as a month without a power blackout, significant scientific data collection or uninterrupted internet access with a fully functioning server.

During long projects, or even in times when it's business as usual, an inspiring leader will find a reason to stop and salute even small accomplishments. Whether it's with an event, a reward or a simple thank you, the acknowledgement and recognition will inspire and motivate.

Responsibility

Inspiring leaders fully appreciate the responsibility that comes with the leadership role. They realise they are accountable for developing their team members and growing capacity.

Randstad reports: 'traditionally managers have risen through the ranks purely based on logical progression from one level to the next as opposed to their qualities and skills as a leader'. Developing leadership skills for the next phase of growth is the key productivity challenge for 51 per cent of Australian businesses.

Emerging leaders should understand that along with promotion comes greater responsibility. Leaders are under intense scrutiny, their behaviour interpreted often in ways they could never imagine. In Antarctica, where I sat at mealtimes, what time I left social events, how often I took my turn doing the community duties of cooking and cleaning were all closely noted.

Managing performance is also a key responsibility. Rewarding great work and counselling after poor performance are both core parts of leadership. Yes, it's tricky stuff that requires mental robustness and lots of energy, but try doing it in Antarctica where there are no sanctions or rewards and the HR team is based 4000 kilometres away.

Mapping out a development plan for individual staff is also a critical role of every leader. Inspiring and motivating staff by showing them future possibilities and the route to get there is more important than ever. The *World of Work Report* found, 'half of all respondents intend to leave their current role citing lack of opportunity for growth and development, [which is] more than double the number that will leave due to uncompetitive salary and remuneration'.

Appendix B

Build teamwork with 'no triangles'

The best way to deal with an issue is directly with the other person.

We all face difficult or troublesome situations from time to time. Your own experiences will tell you that when you make the effort to deal directly with the other person the chances of a good outcome increase tremendously.

We know this, yet we often find it much easier to 'rope in' others.

Sometimes the idea of confronting an issue head-on can be just too difficult. What if they react badly? What if I don't have the 'killer response' to their objection? We are worried about the response we might get, so instead we will often shop an issue around. It might be to see if other people have the same issue or to bolster support. It might be so the person concerned hears it from someone else. Or it might be simply to make it go away.

When we create a 'triangle', we create a new set of problems

The problems with the 'triangle' approach are numerous. Firstly, we are telling the other person that we don't have the courage to face them, which is bad for us. Secondly, we are telling the other person that we don't trust them to have an honest and open conversation.

And thirdly, we involve other people who may not really want to be involved in the first place. There is also the chance our words can be repeated, out of context, which can compound the issue.

A conscious practice of 'no triangles' is required.

'No triangles' means simply: 'You don't talk to me about her, and I don't talk to you about him'. Go straight to the source. It will create conversations that are direct and address the issue in a timely manner. When delivered with grace and humility it affirms both you and the other person, and leads to a successful resolution. It increases the speed at which issues are uncovered and ensures everyone is treated with integrity and respect. We don't deliberately set out to upset other people — we simply don't. Most of us feel terrible if we have unwittingly upset a friend, family member or colleague. Now imagine how much worse we would feel if we found out the person didn't come and speak directly to us to discuss how they felt, but instead went to a third party. 'No triangles' is about common decency and respect. It's about having the goodwill and courage to speak up and address the person directly.

How to spot a triangle

- When someone wants to tell you something about someone else, that's a triangle.

- When you are hurt or miffed at another person and tell someone else at work, that's a triangle.

- When you hear that so-and-so thinks or says such-and-such about you, there's a triangle.

How to make 'no-triangles' work for you

Unfortunately, you can't make a policy, wave a magic wand and all of a sudden have an organisation that practises 'no triangles'. There are three things you need to do first.

1 Provide the **why** and build awareness of the importance of acting with integrity and respect. Make it clear your team values direct feedback, both affirming and challenging, delivered in a professional and respectful manner. Ask for everyone to commit to 'no triangles' then do it!

2 Provide the **what** and equip people with the tools to have difficult conversations. People often do more harm than good when they give feedback or conduct a challenging conversation without practising what they will say. I developed a 10-point checklist for my Antarctic expeditioners and coached them through how to have a difficult conversation.

3 Provide the **how** by supporting and celebrating your people's efforts. Change takes time and effort, particularly when it involves behaviour. If someone tries to engage you in a 'triangle' conversation, calmly and firmly remind them of the team's pledge of 'no triangles' and suggest they speak to the other person directly. Leaders also need to make themselves available to coach and mentor people as they start to try this for themselves. It takes time, patience and lots of practice, but it will build open and professional communication and the result will absolutely be worth the effort.

Difficult conversations — a 10-point checklist

'No triangles' only works if you have both the processes and the culture to support it. The following process was developed to support my people when they knew they had to have a difficult conversation with someone. It's not exhaustive or comprehensive, but it's a useful guide that can signpost the way to prepare, conduct and conclude a difficult conversation.

Before: plan what to say and when to say it	
Timing and timeliness	Choose the right time and place. Don't hold the conversation when the other party is upset or angry. Respect the other person's privacy by minimising the chance that you may be overheard. Whenever possible, have these conversations face to face. As soon as you realise you need to have a conversation, do it! Don't dwell on it; leaving it too long only makes it more difficult. Never use email.

(continued)

Before: plan what to say and when to say it (*cont'd*)	
Anticipate that you may not be on the same page	Different perceptions of intent, interpretations of the facts, and judgements about what is right or best are usually at the root of all difficult conversations. When you begin with this in mind, you will not be surprised when these root issues arise. Try to understand the point of view as well the emotional state of the other person. Understanding the other party's position helps you make better decisions about how to address the situation. When you show genuine interest in understanding the other person's side of the story, you are more effective in resolving the matter.
Rehearse	If time permits, it helps to put the details of the situation in writing. Include what you wish both parties to achieve. Doing so gives you an opportunity to consider all views and nuances of the situation. Taking the time to prepare properly for any important conversation yields better results. Rehearsing in your mind and trying to anticipate how the conversation will go is often helpful.
During: keep the conversation on track	
What and why? Ask questions	Ask questions. Use specific examples: What is at stake? Why does this matter? Ask questions to establish what is going on in their view. We demonstrate respect for the other person when we acknowledge that we may not understand the full complexity of their situation. For example: 'I'd really like to understand what is important to you in this situation and what has occurred before.'
Identify your role in the situation	How have you contributed to the situation? Show some vulnerability, but be selective. For example: 'My part in creating a growing rift between you and the others is that I didn't bring this to your attention earlier.'

Maintain eye contact and stay in control	As in any constructive face-to-face communication, maintaining eye contact helps you gauge the receptiveness of the other person throughout the conversation and demonstrates your honesty and desire to listen to the other person. If you express anger, it is natural for the other person to respond accordingly to match your emotional state. Do whatever it takes to remain calm.
Clarify	Confirm you understand what is being communicated and paraphrase it to acknowledge their. This behaviour helps them to see that you are listening and also clarifies your understanding of the situation. For example: 'Okay, so what I am hearing is that you are disappointed with X because of Y. Is that a fair description of the situation?' Clarify your expectations and work together to identify options to meet those expectations.
Don't interrupt	When the other person is speaking, never interrupt. Show the other person the respect you want to be shown when you are talking. In addition, don't appear as though you are anxious to respond. People who can't wait to speak generally aren't listening, because they are so focused on what they want to say.
LADAR	Turn on your LADAR (language radar) and listen for 'ping' words such as *always, never, everyone, no one, can't* and *won't*. Avoid saying things like, 'Everyone in the department feels the same way' or 'I have heard about this from countless people'. Often when we hear these kinds of statements, we immediately discount what is being said because in most cases they are exaggerations. If the issue is so serious that you need to bring others into the discussion, make sure they are present. Listen to both yourself and the other person. If you exaggerate, quickly clarify. If they do, ask for specifics. Use facts.
After: consolidate and move forward	
Follow up	Try to speak to the person again within a day or two, even on an entirely unrelated matter. It keeps the conversation in perspective and shows you 'said what you had to say' and are now prepared to move on.

Index

ABOUT RACHAEL

Rachael is passionate about helping people unlock their hidden potential by uncovering, seizing and making the most of their opportunities.

Rachael speaks and writes from first-hand knowledge. She has experienced extremes of both opportunity and challenge. She led an Antarctic expedition, was one of Victoria's youngest Chief Rangers and was a key part of the response team during Victoria's Black Saturday bushfire tragedy. Her leadership credentials are unassailable.

Rachael combines her practical insights with contemporary leadership theory. She holds an MBA from Melbourne Business School, one of only two globally acknowledged post-graduate business schools in Australia.

But despite her accomplishments, the thing that people love about Rachael is the fact that she is normal. She is down-to-earth and engaging. She doesn't pretend that she 'held a lifelong dream' to achieve what she did. Rachael honestly and candidly acknowledges the importance of:

• doing the right thing
• being in the right place at the right time
• taking calculated risks
• making the most of the opportunities that come your way.

These elements, her self-belief and her approachable manner are the key sources of her success.

Rachael is now a full-time professional speaker, author and mentor, and is an internationally recognised leadership expert.

RACHAEL ROBERTSON INTERNATIONAL SPEAKER & AUTHOR

AUTHENTIC, INSPIRATIONAL, REAL LEADERSHIP

Rachael's speaking, writing and mentoring work is in response to a massively growing demand in the business world for real, practical leadership tools backed up by solid theory by someone who has actually led, and led successfully.

The intensity of the Antarctica leadership role, where the leader is on duty all day, every day, for 12 months with no respite, gave her the chance to roadtest her ideas the hard way! It was a 'leadership laboratory' in the most extreme, hostile environment on Earth.

LACONIC, DOWN-TO-EARTH, ENGAGING

Rachael speaks from first-hand experience and relates her own challenges to the challenges of every workplace. She needs no props, no 'rah-rah' moments and no forced audience participation to reach people at a deep level. This is a seasoned leader telling it how it is in her own approachable style.

Your people will leave inspired, equipped and motivated to make their own lives and teams extraordinary.

Interested in hearing more about Rachael's popular speaking and corporate programs?

Please visit her website or contact ric@rachaelrobertson.com

www.rachaelrobertson.com

Learn more with practical advice from our experts

The People Manager's Toolkit
Karen Gately

The Ultimate Book of Influence
Chris Helder

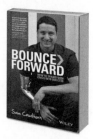

Bounce Forward
Sam Cawthorn

Hooked
Gabrielle Dolan and Yamini Naidu

Stop Playing Safe
Margie Warrell

Think One Team
Graham Winter

First Be Nimble
Graham Winter

Dealing with the Tough Stuff
Darren Hill, Alison Hill and Dr Sean Richardson

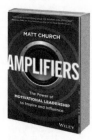

Amplifiers
Matt Church

Available in print and e-book formats WILEY